Wiccan Meditations
ༀ

ॐ

Wiccan Meditations

THE WITCH'S WAY TO
PERSONAL TRANSFORMATION

ॐ

Laura A. Wildman, HPs

CITADEL PRESS
Kensington Publishing Corp.
www.kensingtonbooks.com

CITADEL PRESS BOOKS are published by

Kensington Publishing Corp.
850 Third Avenue
New York, NY 10022

All Kensington titles, imprints, and distributed lines are available at special quantity discounts for bulk purchases for sales promotions, premiums, fund-raising, educational, or institutional use. Special book excerpts or customized printings can also be created to fit specific needs. For details, write or phone the office of the Kensington special sales manager: Kensington Publishing Corp., 850 Third Avenue, New York, NY 10022, attn: Special Sales Department, phone 1-800-221-2647.

First printing: September 2002

10 9 8 7 6 5 4 3 2 1

Printed in the United States of America

Library of Congress Control Number: 2002104316

ISBN 0-8065-2346-8

To my teachers

*To my parents, my first teachers, who taught me
about life, love, and the beauty of the world*

and

*To Judy Harrow, my priestess, my mentor, my friend
My deepest thanks, gratitude, and love*

CONTENTS

ᘒᘝᘒ

ACKNOWLEDGMENTS

ℭℛℰℴ

I wish to thank all my loving friends and family who helped to make this book possible.

I would like to especially thank Judy Harrow. The first two chapters of this book were derived largely from materials created by, and from long conversations with Judy about trance facilitation. She then graciously read and edited the manuscript, making sure I kept myself out of trouble.

To my husband, Tom, whose insights and patience were invaluable. Your love is always a source of inspiration and wonder.

To the members of Apple and Oak Coven, Geoff, Joan, Tim, Karyn, Ijod, for their love, support, and for understanding why their priestess was not always available.

Thank you to my dear friends who never asked me to change the subject, and always expressed happiness at seeing me, even when I used them to process my thoughts by talking nonstop for hours on trance facilitation and pathworkings.

To the individuals who offered their help and their favorite guided meditations to be used in this book: Anluan, Ashta'ar Arthura, Black Lotus, Cat, Hare, Rev. Joanna L. Malinoski and Sacred Space, Penny Novak, Ted Tarr, and Kirk White.

To Jennie Dunham and Bob Shuman for their support, and patience, and for cheering me on to completion.

And to my parents and family, who may not always understand what I do, but who have always loved and supported me.

Wiccan Meditations

INTRODUCTION

ᘓᘏ

And you who think to find me, know your seeking and yearning shall avail you not, unless you know the mystery, that if that which you seek you find not within you, you will never find it without.
From "The Charge of the Goddess" by Doreen Valiente

A pathworking is a form of guided meditation—a script crafted to induce various trance states and to take participants on journeys and adventures on the inner planes. The role of a guided meditation is to help the seekers open themselves to self-discovery and personal transformation. Inner change is often reflected in changes in the outer world of behavior and physical reality.

These adventures bring us to places where the natural restrictions of our bodies do not bind our spirits; where our inner senses are strengthened, our psychic and spiritual awareness increases, and we gain the ability to interact with the Gods and Goddesses.

This book contains a variety of pathworkings for use by groups or individual explorers of the world within.

Before you start working with this book, buy a notebook and begin a journal. Record your physical, emotional, and psychic states each day. Is anything happening in your family or work life that might make an impression on your mind or heart? If there is, note it in your journal. Keep track of your experiences in meditation. Include the exercises you try, and the results you

1

get, both immediately and in your dreams during the nights that follow. Look out for patterns and especially for connections between your inner and outer worlds. If you're practicing alone, you won't have someone guiding you on your journeys. I recommend that you either tape record each adventure and play them back while you relax or memorize the trip before you begin. Follow the guidelines in chapter 1 on how to facilitate trance. People who are working in a committed group will find exercises in the second chapter to aid in strengthening the psychic connections between its members and building a group mind. Just switch the *you* to *we* during the direction parts of any pathworking to allow for group participation and shared experiences. Please do also add suggestions and opportunities for group interaction.

Please note that this book is *not* going to explore the psychological or theological aspects of trance states. There are many good books on the market that focus on the theory of trance. I encourage you to read one of these books to help you become familiar with the vocabulary and principles of the subject before working the exercises in *Wiccan Meditations.* This book is a practical, hands-on guide for facilitating and recognizing trance states and for working with trance, either individually or in groups.

How to Use *Wiccan Meditations*

Each chapter of this book builds upon the previous. Occasionally tools or supplies will be needed or suggested in order to fully experience an exercise. This will be indicated with a ⌘.

You may flip through the book and use whichever journeys appeal to you, but for the best results, work all the exercises in the sequence given. When you've done them all once, you can return to those sections or journeys that worked best for you and do them again.

The first chapter is a guide for facilitators. Trance faciliation is difficult and demanding work, requiring that we stay aware of inner and outer planes at the same time.

The second chapter consists of simple exercises for stretching, grounding, and relaxation. It also includes techniques for strengthening visualization skills and methods for entering and leaving trance states.

Chapter 3 is devoted to journeys into trance for the purpose gaining insights: about trance, yourself, your environment, your beliefs, your Gods and Goddesses. The exercises are meant to reveal, without being confrontational. You will be creating a safe environment from which to journey, both within your physical reality and within your spiritual home. You will also begin exploring group exercises allowing you to meet your coven or group members and begin traveling together.

In chapter 4, we enter trance with the intention of transforming ourselves and our lives. When we make an inner change, we often induce related changes in the outer realms.

Pathworkings that incorporate active imagination with myth and sabbat celebrations will be offered in chapter 5 as a means of strengthening our understanding of our religion and its symbols.

The final chapter of *Wiccan Meditations,* "Coven Work/Coven Play," offers trance journeys and exercises speficically for covens or other committed groups. These workings or techniques are designed with the purpose of helping to develop or strengthen the psychic and emotional connections between group members.

Explore and enjoy. May this book and your use of it help you grow within yourself to find understanding, balance, and skill. May the journeys in this book help open doors and create connections to the ancient Gods, so that you may better serve them and Their people.

CHAPTER ONE

ᘉᘓᘔᘖ

Facilitating Trance—
Exploring the Inner Realms

What Is Trance?

Have you ever woken up in the morning—or think you have, but for a moment you're not sure? Perhaps you even swung your feet out over the bed and stood up, ready to begin the day. But then you paused because something just didn't feel right or familiar. Just as the question, *Is this real or a dream?* began to take form in your mind, you suddenly found yourself lying in your bed actually waking.

Have you ever been so absorbed in a favorite book or movie that the world disappeared and you *became* part of the story? As the credits rolled or you closed the pages, it may even have taken you a few minutes to realize where, and sometimes who, you really were.

Have you ever wandered into a daydream during a business meeting, class, or in the checkout line at a grocery store—the kind where you became so engrossed that it took someone repeating your name or even tapping your shoulder before you realized that a response was being requested of you?

Each of these examples is a form of trance or altered state of consciousness. These changes of consciousness take you from the ordinary to, well, somewhere else.

How We Enter Trance States

Some trance states begin spontaneously, without deliberate effort. Dreams are perhaps the most commonly recognized altered state. Almost every night, I take a trip out on the astral plane. I've flown around the world, spoken to interesting entities, participated in some beautiful experiences, and traveled through some not-so-nice, sometimes even frightening, adventures—all without leaving my bed.

Daydreams, the bane of every schoolteacher, are a conscious form of dreaming. When boredom strikes, the mind wanders off into a portable TV of imaginative possibilities. Many creative insights and scientific breakthroughs have found their start in thoughts that were allowed to wander unhampered. I'm sure that a daydream on how it must feel to fly was at the heart of the Wright brothers' creation of the airplane.

Other trances, created through artificial means such as drugs or alcohol, are familiar to many. Many cultures use poisonous plants to stimulate visions. Notice I said "poisonous"! Those who travel out by the power of plants might not return.

Hypnosis is another—much safer—method for inducing trance. We are becoming familiar with the use of hypnosis for self-improvement. Hypnotists can implant posthypnotic suggestions that will help clients quit smoking, study or practice consistently, choose healthier foods, or change their behavior in many other positive ways. Trance, whether induced hypnotically or otherwise, can also be used for inner exploration and exploration of the astral realms.

Trance is a state of heightened focus and concentration. It takes us into the "zone," tuning out noise and outside distractions. We have all experienced some form of trance in our lifetime. Most of these states occurred without conscious choice or control.

A Witch can enter trance by choice, without the aid of sleep or medications. Altering of consciousness in accordance with will is one of the primary skills of magic—the art of creating change. For this reason many of us spend a great deal of time learning how to enter into, and return safely from, trance states.

Pathworking—An Important Use of Trance

We intentionally enter into trance for many reasons. One purpose is to look inward for answers, to learn something about our world or ourselves. A journey to meet the Gods and receive information is an example of exploration for learning. Another is to facilitate a form of symbolic change. Doing battle and overcoming a representational image of a personal fear holds within it this concept that change in inner self will be reflected in the outer persona. Groups of covens will enter trance to develop group bonding. Trance workings are designed around various aspects of life to accomplish any, or possibly all, of these goals.

A pathworking or guided meditation is one way of using trance. By telling stories to people in a relaxed and open state, we allow them to participate in the experience. They get to hunt with Diana, swim with the whales, try out Pan's flutes, or wrestle with the Minotaur. The aim of the adventure is to gain self-knowledge, open potentials, develop or strengthen natural psychic abilities, and expand understanding. It's also done because it's just plain fun.

When trance is used within the context of a collectively held set of beliefs and values, as is found within a coven or magical practice, pathworkings will also help strengthen the practitioners' understanding of their religion. Through pathworkings, covens and other groups can share experiences of myths, stories, and symbols. The tale is transformed into a vivid and active imaginative experience in which the images are fully experienced through the senses (tactile feelings, colors, sounds, and smells) and the emotions. The participants become intimately involved with the voyage, merge with the words, and actually experience the story. The words are not just a myth, a metaphor, or some dry tale taken from a book, but a living and real adventure. Thus, the myth can be more deeply integrated into the hearts and minds of the explorers.

Ever notice that two people can witness the same car accident yet have two different versions of what happened? As with every occurrence in life, an event is seen slightly differently by each person experiencing it. The individual in the car has a different perspective than someone watching from the sidewalk. The same thing happens with shared trance experiences. When working within a group, these various individual pictures and emotional responses are then brought back to the conscious reality and shared with the coven to form a multidimensional view of the experience. This deepens and strengthens the personal connection among the participants.

Groups or covens enter into trance together to construct a collectively willed change in their collective unconscious. Shared trance experiences strengthen the psychic and emotional connections among members and help create an egregore or gestalt—a group mind. For a group spell to work really well, everyone present should focus on the same goal and hold the same vision. For example, we might use an apple as a symbol of good health. So visualize an apple. You might be seeing a red McIntosh apple, while I'm focusing on a green Granny Smith. When we all imagine the same variety, our group is more cohesive, and therefore more effective. If we are working toward forming a group mind and are adept enough, we will see the same shape and color. We may even all smell its fragrance and taste its sweetness.

Not all Witches choose to practice within a coven or group. If you're practicing alone, you won't have the perspectives of others and will need to rely solely on your own interpretations. It can still be done.

Make sure you have paper and a writing instrument or tape recorder ready to record what occurred during the journey.

While the memories are still clear, let them pour out onto the paper or tape. Don't worry about the grammar, the spelling, or even if it doesn't seem to make any sense. Note everything you can remember, from colors to smells, no matter how small or inconsequential you think it might be. You never know—that eight-legged horse you saw out munching hay in the field just might mean something to you later. Don't read or listen to what you recorded for at least twenty-four hours. This time will allow you to integrate the memories into your deep mind.

If you choose to explore with others, you will be working together in an intimate manner (and there is no greater intimacy than allowing someone to enter into your personal inner world). It's important that the members trust one another, and that all have a strong sense of understanding of their own core beliefs and ethics. If you haven't thought about it, or if this hasn't been previously discussed within your coven, you should take some time before exploring pathworkings to identify and create a statement of both your individual and group beliefs and values. It could address questions such as:

- What are my/our values, boundaries, and ethics?
- What are my/our core beliefs?
- What or who are the Gods? The Elements?
- What is my/our relationship to the Earth? To each other?
- What are our goals as a coven? How does the pathworking help achieve them?
- What are our shared myths? Stories? Symbols?

Pathworkings work best when all participants trust each other and are in agreement on the stories, symbols, values, ethics, and goals that are being worked with. One individual lacking the same visions and ethics can break that collective trust, creating a bad experience for the entire circle.

People relax into trance best when they feel safe. We need to be respectful of one another and sensitive to each other's feelings. Conflict, rudeness, and disagreements about values or ethics can erode this essential shared sense of safety. A coven to which I once belonged was fractured when one member laughed at another member's fears. Once broken, trust is difficult to restore.

Whether you're practicing alone or with a group, keep a journal as you begin to explore pathworkings. Write down all your daily experiences. Include your physical and emotional state as well as mundane or magical occurrences. This will help you recognize any patterns and their underlying connections.

I noticed, for instance, that whenever I experienced a stressful meeting at work on the same day I participated in a pathworking, I would end up meeting a bunch of nasty little creatures on the path during my trance journey. These entities were extremely annoying, distracting me from the focus of my trip. Understanding the connection allowed me to take steps to circumvent the situation. During stressful days, I now take a few extra measures to release the tension before I enter into magical space.

As you develop experience in trance states, you will also find your dreams becoming increasingly active. Keep a record of your dreams. Pathworkings are designed to teach you how to return to consciousness with the memories of your adventure still intact. This technique can also be used for visions revealed in a sleeping state. Keep a notebook or a tape recorder next to your bed and make a habit of recording your dreams as soon as you awaken.

What Is a Trance Guide or Facilitator?

There are many levels of trance, from a daydream to full anesthesia and amnesia. The deeper states are easier to reach with the help of a facilitator.

Pathworking is a form of guided meditation. Just the name

guided meditation indicates that there's someone who remains alert, directs the pathwork, and serves as an anchor holding you to the physical world. This is a role of great trust and responsibility, which requires both skill and care. The guide watches over the safety of those in trance while leading them through a journey of learning and growth. With perfect love and perfect trust, the facilitator is entrusted with the safety of the participants.

As director of the journey, the facilitator greatly affects, and therefore is responsible for, the experience itself. While carefully leading the group into and out of trance, the facilitator must also be unobtrusive so that each individual can have her own experience. You know you've had a great facilitator when, once the journey is over, no one remembers having been guided at all. Only the experience itself remains.

While we spend a lot of time between the worlds, few Witches receive formal training in how to lead trance for other people. Many of us learn by watching and trying to imitate our own elders or teachers. Such observation, however, can only teach basics. It does not provide a clear understanding of how or why something did or didn't work. Theoretical knowledge gives us the possibility of improving upon what we learned and making our own creative contributions. This is the ultimate goal of this book: to help you develop or fine-tune your own practice and presentation of trance.

I have been a participant in many guided pathworkings. Some journeys were excellent and rewarding, but unfortunately many were poorly done. The five most common reasons for a bumpy ride lie within the control or expertise of the facilitator:

1. Facilitator Lacks Knowledge of Trance States: The individual directing the pathworking is not familiar with the various stages of trance and methods for guiding the journeyers through these states and back again to full consciousness. The facilitator is unable or does not know how to monitor the members of the group who are in trance.

2. Facilitator Is Unprepared or Ungrounded: The guide is inexperienced in the role of anchor for the group, unfamiliar with the signs indicating there is a problem, or inadequately trained for handling problems.

3. Facilitator Is Unable to Use Voice as a Tool: The individual who is facilitating does not recognize how to use the power of the voice. This includes leaders who are too soft-spoken to be fully heard as well as those who speak gratingly loud.

4. Poor Environment: The external environment does not reflect the internal journey. This includes guides who insist on playing background music that is either incompatible with the working or too loud for people to hear the directions.

5. Poor Presentation:

- *Too much control.* The conductor gives too much detailed information prohibiting the journeyers from experiencing their own visions.
- *Lack of guidance.* The facilitator does not give enough information or guidance to sustain the trip. The facilitator is not emotionally or magically focused on the working. The pathworking, or the energy raised within it, has no clear goal or direction.
- *Poor pacing.* The journey is not well paced, meaning that the participants are not given enough time to fully experience the working, or they have too much time without direction.

When any of these things occur, the journey becomes so annoying that it is difficult for me to either enter into or remain in trance. I spend the time trying, often in vain, to remain awake so that my snoring will not offend the guide.

I wish I could say that all the pathworkings I've facilitated were wildly successful, but that would be a lie—or at least stretching the truth to a fine thread. It takes a lot of time and practice to learn how to be good at leading others into and out of trance and how to present a pathworking that resonates with all the participants. Reading a book, including this one, will give you only the theories and basic guidelines. While having an understanding of the concepts is very important, it's only through doing, through experience, that you'll become fluent and comfortable in leading pathworkings.

As is often the case, we learn not through our successes but through our failures. This means practice, practice, and more practice! If possible, work with someone who's experienced in facilitating guided pathworkings. Participate in as many journeys as you can so that you can learn the road map before trying to give directions. Immediately write down your experiences, noting what has worked for you and what hasn't, for later review. Ask to sit and watch as others go through the trip so that you can observe the physical language of trance.

Where Are We Going? Assessing Levels of Trance

Those who lead group trance have a difficult job in that they must walk within two different worlds simultaneously, monitoring both the trance and the physical realms. Guides lead the journeyers and are therefore along on the adventure, experiencing it with them, gently locating the pathways and opening the doors that will allow them to explore and grow. They must, however, also keep a conscious watch on the physical bodies of the journeyers, looking for outward signals of distress that might indicate that the journey should be quickly ended.

Guided visualizations that usually attain only a light trance state can be done with a group of any size. Facilitation of deep trance states, however, requires monitoring of the participants. This is nearly impossible and could be dangerous to do with groups of more than fifteen participants. Recently I was told of a large ritual that included a trance journey. One of the participants had an extremely bad reaction—yet her condition went unnoticed until after the event.

When we enter into a deep trance, we change physically as well as emotionally and psychically. Breathing alters, becoming deeper and more rhythmic; muscles twitch and relax; eyes water, flutter, or close. The senses may become sharpened or they may disappear entirely as focus narrows to the inner path immediately ahead. The body may feel heavier or lighter. Emotionally, there's often a feeling of euphoria or a sense of well-being. Vocal communication, from mumbles to laughter, is possible during all stages of trance, however, some find it easier to respond during deeper states. Since many of the group exercises will require vocal interaction, we'll work on developing this in later chapters.

There are a number of levels of trance. A light altered state aids in opening up the inner or intuitive senses. You'd use this level of trance in divination work. I always lead my Tarot clients through a grounding and centering exercise prior to beginning a reading. It allows both of us to shift our consciousness and open the psychic channels. Then there's the trance that generates outer energy. We find this at the heart of many magical workings when the circle is moving and speaking as one and the cone of power is raised, directed, and released. Finally, there are the deeper trance states where the outer world disappears and energy is radiated within.

When guiding trance, it's important that you know how to read the physical language communicated by your journeyers. You can determine how deep a trance they have entered and how their trip is progressing through their body language. The muscles of the arms, legs, and torso will show outward signs of relaxation before the facial muscles. Breathing will often start as fast and shallow, becoming slow, deep, and regular as deeper states of trance are entered.

Trance moves in a progression from light to deeper states.

Not everyone, however, will advance at the same rate. If you aren't monitoring the body language of each member, you can easily leave one of your journeyers behind. If someone has had an awful week at work, it may take him longer to release the stress and relax into a light trance state than someone who just came back from vacation. Unfortunately, I've found that some guides pay little attention, plowing ahead with their script without pausing to make sure everyone is walking with them.

While it's the job of the facilitator to keep the group together, you must also weigh the needs of the whole group versus those of a single individual. Relaxation and trance induction should be done for as long as is reasonable without becoming detrimental to the whole group's experience. What good is getting that one last person into trance to find that the rest of the party has fallen asleep? An understanding that there will be times when the journey must go forward without all attendees needs to be set among participants. If you're the one person unable to enter into trance, make yourself comfortable and try to be as quiet as possible until the exercise is over. For future reference, make sure you make a note in your trance journal of what occurred. Include what you did during the day, your physical and emotional state, the exercise used, and your reactions to it. Over time you might identify a pattern and be able to solve the problem.

A word of warning: Those who have a fragile mental state such as a poor sense of identity, or who are suffering from psychoses—especially those with paranoia or dissociative conditions—should avoid deep meditative pathworkings, particularly if they're working alone. It's crucial that those exploring these realms be very centered within themselves and grounded in the here-and-now. Pathworkings and advanced visualizations may trigger flashbacks. In addition, flickering lights, as found in candle flames, can trigger epileptic seizures. Make sure everyone present is mentally stable prior to striking a match and turning off the lights.

I've included a chart (see pages 18–19) that can help you assess the four basic stages of trance. Each is divided into five parts: (1) the state of trance; (2) what part of the journey corresponds with this state; (3) what the guide can typically expect to be observing; (4) what the journeyer will typically be experiencing; and (5) trouble spots and solutions. Because each individual is unique, the examples are strictly generalizations. The more you experience trance states, the greater familiarity you'll have in recognizing where you are in the process. Likewise, the more a coven works together, the more aware you will become of the unspoken signals of the individual members.

While the stages are presented here, the various forms of exercises associated with each will be offered in the next chapter.

STAGE ONE

Stage one is the warm-up or pretrance. It's split into two sections. The first half focuses completely on the body. People will be sitting, often in one position, for a long period of time. Making sure the body is stretched and relaxed will make waking up and moving a lot easier later. Various techniques to relax the muscles and help release their stored tension are employed. Clenching and releasing muscles, stretching, and shaking limbs are some of the methods used to help release nervous energy held within the body. Relaxed muscles will allow the traveler to sit more comfortably. Because there's often a heightened level of anticipation that needs to be liberated along with the physical tension, expect to hear groans, laughter, and light conversation.

When the body is relaxed and prepared, focus begins to turn inward. Breathing techniques and grounding and centering methods are used to help move the voyager's psyche and mind away from the mundane and toward the sacred, signaling to the subconscious that something special is about to occur.

Trouble Spots Look out for individuals who may not be physically or emotionally able to participate. Common signs of the latter are: inability to focus, excessive laughter, joking and tom-foolery, unwillingness to participate in stretching or breathing exercises, making fun of the exercises, making noises or inappropriate conversation.

People who are ill or who are showing signs of a cold or a headache may have difficulties being fully present for the working. Ask them whether participation at this time would be appropriate. There are no reasons those with physical or mobility limitations cannot participate. Breathing and stretching exercises can be done sitting or even lying down and can be limited to a comfortable level of intensity.

I was once asked to facilitate a workshop that included a trance journey. For the pretrance, I had all of the participants stretching and moving on the hotel carpeting. While some people shared groans and laughter as they made their bodies move and stretch, it also became obvious that one individual was not in the same head space as the others in the group. With each instruction, she would release loud, heavy sighs and roll her eyes in disgust. She later fell asleep during the light trance induction. Her subsequent snoring rattled the silence, breaking the group's concentration and almost ruining the exercise. It's hard to integrate a loud buzz-saw noise into a relaxation segment.

In retrospect, it would have been easier for all involved if I had spoken up as soon as I realized the potential problem. In many ways experience, with its successes and failures, does make the best teacher. A simple method to avoid this problem would be to remind the participants before moving beyond the pretrance relaxation that this is a group endeavor, asking if all are honestly prepared to begin. For those individuals who indicate that they aren't, ask if repeating stage one would help them join the group mind. If that doesn't work, or if they don't believe that repeating the exercise would do any good, then with the permission of the rest of the participants, invite them to

ASSESSING LEVELS OF TRANCE

Trance State	Point in the Trance Journey	Typical Physical Changes Observed	Typical Experiences of the Journeyer	Trouble Signs
Stage One—Pretrance	• Stretching. • Focus on breath. • Grounding. • Centering.	• Vocal expressions from nervousness (such as chatter, laughter, and groans) as muscles are stretched and tension released. • Physical movement (such as scratching and moving shoulders or neck) as participants get comfortable. • Breathing becomes regular.	• Sense of anticipation is heightened. • Focus shifts from outer activities to the physical self—e.g., to aches, pains, and comfort levels. • The body begins to relax.	• Lack of focus. • Physical or emotional problems with the exercise.
Stage Two—Light Trance	• Relaxation exercises. • Entering into a light trance state.	• Eyes flutter, roll, or close. • Extremities (hands, feet, legs) relax, followed by overall body relaxation. • Breathing slows and becomes deeper.	• If open, eyes smart and water. • Eyelids become heavy or close. • Body may feel very heavy or very light. • Sensations of pressure on or within the body. • Less conscious, or more conscious of body.	• Snoring or heavy breathing. • Facial muscles going slack. • Fidgeting and other movements not related to natural releasing of nervous energy. • Twitching or sharp movements.

Trance State	Point in the Trance Journey	Typical Physical Changes Observed	Typical Experiences of the Journeyer	Trouble Signs
Stage Three—Medium Trance	• Guiding into a deeper trance state. • The journeyers enter their safe space.	• Facial muscles relax. • Slight changes in skin color or tone may be seen. • Hands and feet may feel cold to the touch. • Exuding of heat from various points of the body. • Increased sweating.	• Tunnel vision as focus turns inward. • Less conscious of the physical body. • Less conscious of external temperatures and noise. • Alteration of sense of time.	• Signs of sleep, not trance (see above). • Shallow breathing. • Facial changes expressing fear or confusion. • Sharp changes in skin tone or color. • Excessive sweating. • Shaking.
Stage Four—Deep Trance	• The adventure, the situation is presented. • Exploration, play, and magic begin.	• Body is able to move and respond. • Eyes may open. • Vocal communication is possible. • Possible slurring of speech. • Breathing patterns may alter but generally remain deep and constant.	• Heightening of inner senses such as vibrancy of colors, smells, visions. • Increased range of motion. • General insensitivity to pain. • Lack of sense of time.	• Physical or verbal expressions of fear or confusion. • Nonresponsiveness. • Sharp changes in breathing patterns.

either remain and quietly observe or leave and participate another time.

What is true for those who are participating is equally true for the guides: If the guide is not emotionally or magically focused on the working, then the pathworking will not succeed.

STAGE TWO

With the body and mind prepared, stage two begins the relaxation techniques that will allow the participants to enter into a light trance. Don't be surprised if people continue to move around as they attempt to get comfortable during the beginning of the exercise. If excessive movement and shuffling continue, slow the exercise and, if necessary, repeat it until all have quieted down. As relaxation deepens, you'll begin to see arms, legs, and torsos slowly release the stresses of the day, and bodies will become still.

Some people prefer, and some techniques call for, journeyers to keep their eyes open and focused on a particular object or point, such as a candle flame, during this part of the trance induction. If this is the case, as they begin to enter trance, you will see their eyelids begin to flutter or their eyes to roll or water. If you're working with this style of induction, make sure you remember to give a cue to close the eyes at some point within the working. Continue the induction until you notice a change in everyone's breathing patterns. Breathing should become slower and more regular as they begin to enter into a light trance.

For those who are on the journey, the beginning of the induction moves the travelers' senses inward to focus on their bodies, not on any discomfort but on sensations: touch, smell, taste, sound. The scents on the air, the sensation of palms resting on skin, the last bit of kinks or soreness in a muscle, tastes remaining on the tongue, the sounds of memories and noises from events around them—all become heightened in an abstract collage of the senses. Then the outer sensations are let go and the voyager moves to the inward realms. Some participants turn completely inward, becoming acutely aware of every cell of their physical form, feeling their bones, connective tissues, and skin.

Trouble Spots The greatest problem in this stage is that some participants may fall asleep. In this busy day and age where people go to bed late and get up early, it isn't surprising that many doze off as soon as their bodies have relaxed enough for them to do so. Snoring is always a strong indication that you have a problem; however, there are other signs that warn of a potential sleeping traveler before the noise begins. Look for facial muscles going slack. The face is the last portion of the body to release its tension, and usually this doesn't occur until the next stage of trance. Twitching or sharp sudden movement is often a sign that someone is falling asleep. You may also see a head rolling to the side, forward, or backward as a participant begins to nod off.

You may be tempted to shake a sleeping person, but a light touch is a more appropriate way to rouse her. Chances are she will be embarrassed for disrupting your working. Suggest that she try a change of position. For example, if she has been lying down, have her sit up. If she was sitting cross-legged on the floor, have her try sitting in a chair with her feet resting flat on the ground. Repositioning the body is often enough to get the natural energies flowing, allowing participants to continue with the exercises.

Another problem is noise. At this point, the journeyers will not have entered into a deep enough trance to ignore outside sounds. Any unexpected noise that occurs, such as a barking dog, ringing telephone, or honking car horn, can break the moment and jar participants awake. You can certainly take some simple measures before beginning to eliminate distractions, such as unplugging the phone, putting a DO NOT DISTURB sign on the door, and making sure your alarm clock isn't set to go off at an inconvenient time. Still, you can't always eliminate sounds coming from the outside. There are, however, ways to work creatively with unavoidable ambient sound. One simple solution is to weave in references to noises that are occurring, acknowledging them and integrating them into the working.

During one relaxation segment, a low-flying plane passed overhead. This loud, irritating noise could have disrupted our journey, except that the facilitator creatively incorporated it into our vision. The plane, she explained, was flying by to pick up our stress and troubles. We were instructed to put them into small packages and, in our minds, toss them high into the air. Once in the sky, they were caught by the tailwinds of the jet. Captured and dragged behind the aircraft, our cares were carried far away. We found ourselves intently focusing on the noise of the plane, listening as it slowly moved away from us, the sound of its engines growing fainter and fainter until it was gone, along with our stresses, leaving us in a trance state. If a disruption occurs that cannot be creatively incorporated or that causes participants to fully awaken, repeat the relaxation exercise until all have returned to light trance. More examples of relaxation techniques will be presented later.

When all members of your group have entered into a light trance state, you can begin leading them into stage three.

STAGE THREE

Stage three moves the participants from light into medium trance states. With the journeyers now comfortable, relaxed, and open, the guide begins the actual trance journey induction. While various methods will be presented later, they almost all have one thing in common—they include some sort of visualization of motion. Most involve the voyagers picturing themselves in a form of downward travel, such as a riding in a descending elevator or walking down a flight of stairs. A few methods employ an upward motion, such as climbing a mountain or a tree. Up or down, the journeyer is traveling away from the conscious planes and into the subconscious realms.

You can expect journeyers to be experiencing a wide range of emotions and physical changes. The previous aches and pains of the body are forgotten, as is the body itself. Many travelers report the feeling of slowly becoming separated from their physical form. Some describe this as a sensation of being pulled or falling inward. Some express a sensation of heaviness or pressure all over their bodies, as if a heavy, warm blanket had been thrown over them.

In contrast, others feel lighter, relating it to a sensation of comfortably floating in a pool filled with water. People no longer feel heat or cold. They may lose awareness of passing time.

I usually have the feeling of being sucked down into a tunnel or birth canal as my focus narrows to one small point somewhere in front of me. My entire body tingles with small shivers, but I don't feel cold. As I enter into deeper states of trance, my body becomes numb—not the physical sensation of numbness but a dissociation of my body to the point that I forget I have a physical form.

At this stage, familiar outside noises do not usually distract. Voices, barking dogs, traffic noises . . . things that are a normal part of the background all disappear. Unusually loud or threatening noises, however, will still disrupt a trace state—fire alarms or slamming doors, for instance. Suggestions for what to do when you are or your group is pulled abruptly out of trance will be offered later.

While the majority of the body relaxed in stage two, in stage three, the facial muscles finally release and become slack as the mask of daily life is completely dropped. Yes, drool is a possibility. Hands and feet may feel cold to the touch, while heat will seem to exude from other areas of the body. Increased sweating is also not unusual. I have one friend whose ears turn very red and become hot to the touch when he is in a deep trance; another friend's hands and feet turn ice cold. Breathing patterns will be slow, deep, and even.

Those who are monitoring the journeyers may also notice subtle changes in the skin tone and color of those who are in trance. Some appear lighter in shade, while the skin tone of others takes on a darker hue. Sometimes the skin can look almost translucent. Other times, it displays hues of pink or red as oxygen is taken deep into the lungs and circulated. Observing skin tones that are blue or purple is not a good sign. This is an indication of poor blood circulation.

Trouble Spots The deeper into the trance, the more vulnerable and reliant upon their guide the travelers become. It becomes critical that those who are monitoring pay attention to the body language of their journeyers. They should be breathing deeply and slowly. Shallow breathing may be a sign that someone has not entered deeply enough into a trance state. People who've made it through the relaxation exercises can still nod off to sleep during this part of the trance induction. Watch for signs of sleep: twitching, snoring, and head rolling. Take a brief step back and gather your strays before continuing on.

For those who are experiencing it for the first time, the journey can be frightening or even threatening. Watch for changes in facial expressions indicating fear or confusion. Sharp changes in skin tone or color, as well as excessive sweating, could indicate shock and should be immediately addressed. A gentle touch or reassuring statement that all is safe may be enough to calm. Those who continue to express discomfort should be brought out of trance.

My first time in trance with a group was very difficult for me. The idea of traveling on the astral, walking with other people in areas that had been private and personal, was extremely intimidating and scary. I began the journey walking down a flight of stone stairs that led to deeper states of trance, where I was to meet my fellow journeyers. I stopped halfway and began to cry. I stood there on the cold stairs, leaning against a wet stone wall and shaking with fear, my feet unwilling to move. The facilitator noticed my discomfort, the fact that I had tears running down my cheeks, and came to my aid. Whispering words of encouragement and reminders that I was safe, he gently helped me down the steps and into deep trance. Because he paid attention and acted, I was able to get past my fear and have the first of many wonderful adventures.

For our purposes, the goal in stage three is to reach the platform from which the final stage of the adventure will begin. It is often called the "safe place," "inner home," "private garden," or "coven temple." It's a space of familiarity and comfort found within each individual. From this location, the paths leading to transformation and magic can be accessed. We'll talk about this in greater detail in chapter 3.

STAGE FOUR

Stage four is where exploration and play commence. From the voyagers' personal safe space, they are led into the realms and adventures. Breathing patterns usually remain deep and constant; still, they may change as various surprises present themselves or if something distressful occurs.

This is a unique point in trance, because movement and communication are possible. Eyes may open. The journeyers can often tell you what they're seeing. People may speak and interact with each other. Bursts of laughter or tears are also common. Sometimes bodies will move in response, or in reaction, to inner occurrences. For example, if part of the working includes seeing a ball being thrown toward him, the journeyer may physically, as well as on the astral plane, raise a hand to catch it or flinch as he moves to avoid it.

For those who are in this state, inner senses are heightened. Vision in the inner worlds needs no corrective lenses. Sight is clear and sharp. Like using a zoom-lens camera, fine details can be captured and brought forward for a closer view. Colors are often vibrant; smells and tastes, lush. The sense of touch and texture may be acute. Psychic and other natural intuitive abilities are more sensitive.

Trouble Spots Physically, at this level of trance, there is general insensitivity to pain. Anesthesia is one of the good uses of hypnotic trance when it is used intentionally for that purpose, such as in a childbirth without either pain or drugs. Did you know that one of the accusations made during the Burning Times was that Witches could take away the pain of childbirth, which was ordained by God as a punishment for eating the forbidden fruit of Eden? What the midwives were probably doing was hypnotizing the women by having them use the shining blade of a knife as a visual focus—"cutting" the labor pains.

Hypnotic anesthesia, then, isn't necessarily a "trouble spot." Still, the sense of pain is usually a useful warning system. When it's turned off, somebody needs to exercise compensatory vigilance—and this can't be the trancer. Most often the problem is excess heat or cold, which can lead to heat prostration or hypothermia. Or a person might accidentally bump into a candle. If you're doing a trance dance or walking meditation, there is a risk of falling, so the guide needs to be aware of the ground. What I am issuing is a word of caution: People in trance can hurt themselves and not realize it. Although the majority of participants remain in one position throughout the working, it's still a good precaution to "trance" proof your ritual space prior to the journey.

The Grounding Force—The Rope and Anchor

A rope and an anchor are what a friend of mine needed on his first time out exploring the astral realms. During the relaxation exercises, he began to feel himself shift in consciousness and slip into a comfortable state of euphoria. This would have been all well and good, but, as he was led into the deeper states of trance, he found that he had become separated from his group.

As he explained it, he felt himself lifting from his body and traveling to a location filled with a wonderful colors and bright light. Although the situation did not feel threatening, he intuitively knew that he had arrived at a place where he was not yet supposed to be. He attempted to bring himself back to consciousness but was unable to do so. As his concern grew, he heard the voice of the guide calling him, telling him to look for the cord that attached his spirit to his body. In his state of panic, he couldn't find it. So she crafted for him a rope made of her voice. My friend grabbed hold of this life preserver, and with her song, she slowly returned him to ordinary reality.

The most critical role for those who are acting as the guide is to be the anchor or lifeline for their group. Guides straddle the worlds of waking and trance realities. For this reason, they should have a solid sense of their own center and substantial experience exploring the inner paths. My friend was very lucky in that he had a guide who was able to discern that there was a problem, knew how to respond to the situation, and was familiar with different methods that could gently bring him back from a trance state. She remained calm. Her composure comforted him and helped keep him calm until he felt grounded and fully back in his body.

In the pathworking, the voyagers are the story, the myth, the adventure. They are meeting with the Gods and working magic while in a deep trance. With heightened awareness, their experiences are very real. I'll say it again: Monitoring those who are on the journey is imperative. On the physical plane, look out for physical or verbal expressions of fear or confusion, sharp changes in breathing patterns, shaking, physical thrashing, protective motions, or distraught vocal sounds. Indications on the inner realms are confusion, fear, inability to move forward, or a complete separation from the group.

If someone appears to be in distress, begin with a reassurance of his safety. Remind him that he is in control and that nothing can harm him. If he continues having difficulties, ask him if he would like to return to his safe place. Sometimes the journeyer may be outwardly expressing signs of fear or emotional pain, yet want to continue in order to face the issue and move forward in his personal development. If he does indicate he would like to leave, help him find his inner home or other place of safety, while continuing to reassure him of his safety. From there, he can make the choice to either come to full consciousness or to attempt a different adventure. If the traveler is nonresponsive, however, quickly move him out of trance and back to complete wakefulness.

When one person in a group is experiencing difficulties, depending upon the group's level of experience, it can be suggested to the other participants to come to the aid of their fellow traveler. They can offer reassurances or help guide the individual toward their coven or personal safe space. If an individual needs to end his journey, suggest to the others that this one person will be leaving but that they are to remain in a deep, relaxed state of trance. The trance return should be directed to the one individual in question, preferably whispered into his ear, with physical touch used instead of a loud noise to break the senses and help him awaken. Later, we will discuss ways to return from trance.

Solitaries, make sure to insert onto your tapes ropes and anchors that can be grasped if you run into trouble. The easiest method is to add reminders every three to five minutes that you are in control of your experience and can return to your safe space or return to consciousness at any point during the adventure.

If you're facilitating a pathworking, remember that you're responsible for those you guide in trance. Make sure at the end of the working that all have completely returned to normal consciousness. *Never* leave a person who is in trance state alone.

As my priestess, Judy Harrow has said, "When a person begins to explore their inner world, often the first thing they encounter is their own personal pain—bad, old memories, wounds, scars. Sometimes right there in your circle, the memories come up in the form of vivid and frightening flashback." While this is not uncommon, it can still be distressing for all concerned. Take some peace in the knowledge that this is the first step in the individual's healing process—the touching of the inner wounds. When the cyst ruptures, it may also release a gushing of unresolved emotions and pain. While the members of the circle can provide an open ear, it is not up to you, the coven, your priest or priestess, to fix or "cure" someone who is experiencing psychological trauma. Unless you are a professionally trained therapist, do not try to psychoanalyze or counsel. Normally, while the issue may return from time to time, it should quiet down as the emotions are processed and either integrated within the individual or released. If the matter doesn't resolve itself, or if the individual seems to have gotten stuck on the topic and is unable to more forward in her healing, suggest that she seek professional help.

No matter what occurs, from confusion to flashback, the facilitator must always remain calm and open. Remember, those who are in trance are also in a hyper-receptive state. If you are scared or tense, those you are guiding will pick it up. Keep your breathing slow, deep, and regular. This will provide a base for the group's breathing and, like a heartbeat drum, a continuous point to which they can always return. One trick using your breath to help calm and bring nervous journeyers back together is to pick up and exaggerate your breathing rate, then gently slow it back down. This will allow all to catch hold of your breath and, through breath synchronization, slow and calm themselves.

Those who are planning on acting as the guide should make sure they're able to be fully present. Those who are sick, tired, or under the influence of alcohol or drugs will not be in a position to offer their best to the coven or to their Gods, and therefore should not be leading a pathworking. (Although some traditions do incorporate drugs or alcohol into their rituals, it's my opinion that those guiding the pathworking are being entrusted with the well-being of their coven or group and need to be clearly focused and responsive. Drugs or alcohol can hinder judgment and cause attention to wander. I therefore believe the facilitator shouldn't "drink—or partake—and drive.") Having a fever or being overtired can hinder perception, and you run the risk of dozing off. Imagine being on a journey and in need of direction, but you can't find your guide because she's fallen asleep. Or maybe she has become distracted and has wandered off to go exploring her own inner worlds! The guide needs to be clearly focused and ready for anything. Take a good look at your physical and emotional state before taking on the task of taking care of others.

Listen to the Sound of My Voice . . . The Power of Speech

In guided meditation, the voice leads the voyagers into a trance state. The voice guides them while in that state. The voice provides the connection to the waking world, bringing comfort and security. And the voice will return them safely to waking consciousness. Your voice is your primary tool for leading a pathworking. Learn to use it to its fullest.

Remember when you were a child and a talented storyteller read to you? When the heroine or hero entered, the reader's voice grew strong and clear. The antagonist merited a sinister snarl. Speech patterns would slow or move faster in sync with the events being unveiled on the pages. Without even looking at the book, you could see the pictures fashioned by the tone and inflection of the reader's voice and be carried away, captivated by the tale.

Different sounds—tones, inflections, and speeds—resonate on different levels within the psyche. The voice becomes the tool, an instrument in a concert of sounds and symbols that transform the words into powerful notes capable of carrying listeners to other realms.

As in music, some tones are pleasing to the ear and will ease the listener into a state of relaxation, while others are energizing or even grating. Compare the musical sounds of the artist Enya, or any other New Age group, with the rhythm of tribal drumbeats. Each has a different effect upon the listener—one calming or tranquil, while the other can give a burst of energy, making people want to get up and dance.

Now think of the deep tones and the slow, careful inflection of the actor James Earl Jones, and compare his speech pattern to the higher squeaks and fast-paced voice of Mickey Mouse. Jones is a highly paid spokesperson because the tone of his voice is easy and pleasing to listen to; Mickey's shrill voice, on the other hand, can be very annoying over time.

Use your voice to its fullest. Speak slowly, with intent and inflection. Savor the words, allowing them to drip from your tongue. Allow pauses between thoughts. In some of the exercises, I've included notes indicating where you should add a pause. This is to help give you a sense of timing. For example, read this sentence, just as it stands, out loud:

> *Breathe deep and feel the energy rise within you.*

Now try it again with the pauses and inflection (/ = pause; dashes (-) = draw out the word):

> *Brea-the . . . deep / and feel the energy / ri-se within . . . you*
> (one breath)   (one breath)   (one breath)

Did you notice a difference? The second reading should have sounded more theatrical.

In the written word, different punctuation (which mimics inflection) changes the meaning of the sentence: "Oh, my Goddess!" "Oh, my Goddess?" "Oh my, Goddess." Such is also the case in speech. There are reasons why actors use pauses and inflection. These communicate emotion: empathy, or apathy, or even antipathy.

For trance induction, your voice should remain at a steady rhythm with a gentle rising and falling of pitch. It should be soothing, comforting, and clear. Mumbling, no matter how sweet or rich your voice may be, is annoying. Listeners must strain to understand what's being said, making it difficult to relax and enter into trance.

To help increase the energy raised during a cone of power for magical work, you speed up your chant or your dance. The same technique, increasing the speed or tone of your voice, is used to raise energy within your pathworking. Fluctuating the pace can set an emotional mood, one that intentionally creates suspense—for example, when watching a battle and not being sure of its outcome. Increasing of the tempo is also useful when your intent is to help bring people out of trance. But when used throughout the working, it can heighten anxiety, creating a very bumpy path. Slowing your speech, using pregnant pauses, and drawing out words to add inflection will allow the participants to maintain a state of relaxation.

In an orchestra, any instrument can play a musical score; however, some instruments sound better in certain pieces than others. The same applies to facilitating trances. For example, one Samhain ritual included a journey to the realm of the dead. The guide had a very strong Italian Brooklyn accent, reminiscent of the stereotype heard in some gangster movies. When he loudly called out, "I am Hades, *Lord* of the *Underworld!*" the entire group howled with laughter.

It wasn't that he couldn't facilitate trance; it was just that this particular piece was not the best use of his instrument, his voice. I have a strong, low-toned voice. It works best with pathworkings that require intense focus on the darker, mystery myths. My voice is not well suited for those dealing with the light, fairy realms. What types of pathworkings would best use your own voice?

Looking at the practical side, when you lead a pathworking, your voice should never overpower a room or be so soft that you can't be heard. Either can break the trance state for your charges.

Having to shout to be heard over the music greatly detracts from the experience as well. If music is playing, allow your voice to become one of the instruments, and to move with the tempo and flow with the volume so that your presentation becomes a part of the music. Think of any song that pulls at your emotions, and think about how it's sung. An artist uses inflection, volume, and tone that both work with and enhance the musical piece. Practice ahead of time with the piece so that you can get a good sense of timing.

Singers and actors will tell you to speak from your diaphragm. Place your left hand over your heart and your right on your diaphragm, which is located right above your belly button. Take a breath, allowing it to fill only the upper part of your chest so that your left hand raises and lowers yet your right hand remains still. This is how the majority of individuals breathe and speak, using only the air taken in through the upper portion of their lungs. Now breathe through your tummy, taking a deep breath into your lower lungs so that your diaphragm raises and lowers your right hand but *not* your left. This is breathing using your diaphragm. It may take some practice until you're able to separate the two muscles.

After you feel you're competent in being able to separate out the breath, repeat the exercise but add sound. Take a breath in, filling your chest, and say your name. Now take a deep breath in through your tummy and, while pushing the air out using your diaphragm muscles, say your name. When spoken through your diaphragm, the sound should be stronger and richer. Breathing through your upper chest is fine when you're in a small room and not using any background music. If you're in a large room, are outdoors, or are utilizing music as a backdrop for your path-working, try speaking through your diaphragm. This will help your voice fill the space, allowing it to project farther without losing speaking qualities due to shouting.

I officiate at a number of outdoor weddings and rituals each year. When speaking outdoors, the wind steals the sound of a voice. Yelling out the couple's vows so that those in the back can hear what I'm saying will destroy the solemn sacredness of the moment. Speaking though my diaphragm pushes my voice out to the last couple of seats, yet I maintain the flow and inflection of my normal speaking voice.

If possible, practice in the room where the working will be held before people arrive; however, remember to speak just a little bit louder or use your diaphragm when there are people filling the space, because the sound will be absorbed by their bodies.

Here's one helpful suggestion: Prior to directing a new path-working, tape record it and play it back to yourself. This will help you identify the bumps before taking others on the trip. Or try out the journey on a trusted friend who is experienced in trance states. Ask him to critique your working and give you suggestions for improvement.

Setting the Stage—Your Environment

If your voice represents the actors and the pathworking, the play—the space where the circle is orchestrated—is the stage itself. Your external environment should reflect the tone and the sacredness of the working.

Although you could if you wanted to, and I'm sure the Goddess would be very amused, you needn't transform your living room to look like a Grecian temple for a pathworking to visit Athena. What the process does entail is establishing an appropriate atmosphere that signals to the participants that something special is about to occur, helps them begin to shift their concentration from the ordinary to the sacred, and provides some sort of focus for the working.

Your pathworking will only be as good as your ability to make it understood and focused. The first thing is having a clear understanding of your intent and what you hope to accomplish in the working. What is its purpose? Where do you plan on going? How are you going to get there? Is there a particular deity whom you plan on meeting or a certain setting that you wish to explore?

Next, gather props that will help set the mood. Ritual pieces, colors, and symbols can add focus for the participants and give another dimension to their experience. For example, if you're traveling to meet Aphrodite, you might want to add to your altar fresh roses, seashells, seawater, pearls, and any colors or foods that are identified with Her. If doing a journey to confront a difficult situation, you may want to put objects on the altar that represent strength, such as a hammer or something made of iron.

To add a bit of extra pizzazz, the room can also be transformed with cloth throws, pillows, or cardboard cutouts that reflect the mood of the event. If you're doing a working that centers on an ocean theme, throw a few beach towels on the floor and add sunscreen, sunglasses, or even boxes filled with beach sand to strengthen the sensory connections to the seaside. A tape with ocean sounds playing in the background can round out the effect.

Collect any materials that are required and have them on hand before the working. If you're doing a circle in which each participant must have a particular prop, such as paper or pens, you may want to pick up a couple of extra pieces just in case something breaks, gets lost, or you have an unexpected guest. Also, finish your cooking, baking, or other food preparation before anyone knocks on the door. This will allow you to be completely focused on the circle and your participants instead of worrying about the flour sprinkled all over your counter or listening for the sound of an oven timer going off.

Next, begin preparing your space. For many of us, this means cleaning our living room. Instead of approaching it as you would your weekly housework, do it with clear intent so that it becomes, in essence, a part of the ritual. When we have ritual at my home, I have each of my coveners take a job in the cleaning and setup of the living room. It becomes a group project—the transforming of a mundane living space into the coven temple. Whether it's vacuuming the floor, removing old wax from the candleholders, or decorating the altar to reflect our upcoming working, each shared task aids in bonding the group together. It helps build up anticipation for the rite and begins the shift in consciousness to the sacred even before the circle is cast.

Incorporation of sensory stimuli also plays a major role in the transition of your environment. The primary ones are sight, smell, sound, and touch. Candlelight transforms even the simplest of rooms into a beautiful temple. Taking a ritual bath, allowing the warming waters infused with calming herbs to cleanse away stress, is a tactile sensory experience. Some individuals choose breathing techniques or listening to music; others narrow their sensory input through meditation.

The sense of smell is the most primal of all the senses. It has been shown that memory and smell are linked. For instance, the smell of cotton candy may trigger the remembrance of a particular day at the carnival. Scent and memory are also tied in with reproduction and survival. Studies have shown that we are attracted to people whose scent we find appealing. What this smell may be, of course, is very individualistic. It is, however, one reason why perfume is a major industry. The brain can distinguish thousands of distinct odors. Even when we're unaware consciously, unconsciously we are continually processing every scent that hits our nostrils.

As magic workers, we use candles, incense, and oils as means to induce or heighten trance states. Often the same scent is re-peatedly used to reinforce the memory cue to the subconscious mind to move from the mundane into sacred space, time, and trance. A regularly used incense or scented water signals to the participants that it's time to move from mundane thoughts to those found within ritual.

The presence of the coven is also a part of the environment. Just as the space is transformed and made ready, so should be those who are participating in the rite. No one is perfect. We all carry around emotional baggage. Life can be very difficult and stressful. Unless they're going to be the focal point for the work-ing, all mundane problems should be left at the door so that everyone will be able to focus completely on the energy of the circle.

Now realistically, if we waited until all the little things—the static and annoyances of life—were cleared before entering into ritual space, the rite would never begin. Grounding and centering, breathing, and other relaxation techniques can help us find a state of inner calm. Occasionally, the issues refuse to be ignored and these methods fail. If that occurs, postpone doing trance. You should always enter the inner realms with a clear head and heart.

My preferred method for the transition into ritual is having the celebrants gather in another room to sit quietly in the dark and breathe. This process allows them to shift their perception at their own pace. When an individual is ready to participate, she enters the candlelit room, where she is greeted with a warm bowl of salt water to wash her hands and a drop of scented oil on her third eye. Once all have gathered, the act of casting or creating sacred space, a protective environment within which the coven can experience the sacred in safety, strengthens the group mind. This completes the emotional, psychological, and psychic shift from the ordinary world to the sacred realms of circle.

I was recently told a story about a young man and his trance experiences. Every time he attended a workshop by his favorite teacher that included an astral journey, he would have a wonderful experience. His visions while in the workshop setting were always filled with vivid colors, textural sensations, and interesting adventures. But his attempts to re-create the experience at home always failed. No matter how hard he tried, when he was at home he couldn't enter into trance. Finally, frustrated and confused, he went to talk to the instructor of the workshops to ask what he was doing wrong.

"Tell me what you do when you are at home," the teacher provoked.

"I turn down the lights, get comfortable, put music on, and wait for something to happen," the young man replied.

"Do you smudge the space with sage like we do at the workshops?" the facilitator asked.

"No."

"Do you cast a circle?"

"No."

"Do you speak to the Elements and the Gods and ask them to help guide you?" asked the teacher, holding back a chuckle.

"No," the young man replied again.

"Well," exclaimed the teacher, "there's your answer! You weren't ready to go!"

The young man went home, smudged the space, cast a circle, asked the Gods for their help, and then joyfully traveled to the inner realms.

The creation of your environment plays a crucial role in your trance journey. It indicates to your "younger self," that part of your subconscious that speaks through symbols, colors, and magic: "We're going off on an adventure; would they like to come and play?" It fashions your physical, emotional, and mental state, allowing changes of perceptions and travel beyond the physical world.

Now some practical points. Despite all the setup, the props, and the whistles and bells, trance is still a fragile state of consciousness. As previously mentioned, inability to use the voice can shatter the experience. So can playing background music that's either contrary to the tone of the working or at a volume that makes it difficult to hear the facilitator. Imagine having someone lead a meditation that centers on a woodland forest while playing background music containing sounds of the ocean. Or doing a relaxation exercise to the beat of heavy-metal music.

Even New Age music, thought by many to be a good background accompaniment for trance, needs to be listened to carefully before someone hits the play button. You may discover what you thought was a working piece of music was actually not appropriate for the trance. In one of the circles I participated in, a guided meditation on connecting with animal spirits went very wrong when a haphazardly chosen New Age CD revealed itself to have music reminiscent of machinery and industry.

Make sure that no one in your groups has any preexisting associations with a particular piece of music that would be contrary to the working before introducing it in trance. When my first husband died, there was a New Age CD playing in the background. To this day I can't listen to any of the music on that album, especially the song that was playing the moment he crossed the veil, without remembering the trauma of that moment. It would be very upsetting to suddenly hear it while on a trance journey.

Music, when used properly, can add a wonderful dimension to a pathworking. I participated in a brilliant working that used as its focus a meadow rabbit. The facilitator incorporated the song "Fabled Hare"* by Maddy Prior within his guided visualization. He skillfully crafted the visions around each musical movement, allowing his voice to flow with the notes, adding depth to the experience without detracting from it. We ran and danced with the rabbits, carried by the music. It was lovely.

---

*Maddy Prior, "Fabled Hare," *Year* (Park Records, 1993).

Another note for those who wish to use music in the background: Having music start, stop, and start again is very jarring. If you want to use a particular song, then find the cut you want *before* you begin and have it ready to go. Don't go hunting for it during the working. If you're only using one piece of music, make sure it matches the length of your working. Or copy it onto a blank tape as many times as you need to make it long enough. Nothing is more annoying than having the facilitator clicking buttons on a tape deck trying to rewind a tape to play a song over again.

It you plan on using an entire CD or tape, make sure the music is consistent. We had one working where the tape repeated at least three times. I know, because the second song on the tape included a thunderstorm. Lovely in itself, it was contrary to the rest of the music on the tape and to the working itself. Every time it played, it was startling.

Another pet peeve of mine is the rustling of script pages. The best method for facilitating a guided meditation is to know the journey by heart. Unfortunately, this isn't often done. Instead, many guides rely on a printed script. To enhance the environmental experience, the ritual room is often illuminated only by candles. Reading is very difficult in this setting. The reader is then forced to do contortions in order to catch any reflected light. For those in trance experiencing heightened perception, every page that is turned or twisted can be heard. Even carefully placing one sheet on top of the other can be heard clearly.

Simple solutions:

- Print out your script in sixteen- or eighteen-point type. This will make it a lot clearer to read even in low lighting.
- Have a small book light or candle that can be used to illuminate just your pages.
- Put your script sheets into three-ringed plastic sheet protectors and put them into a notebook.

- Index cards rustle a lot less. Write on them with marker pens instead of ballpoint pen or pencil.

Privacy is another important factor in establishing environment. Those who are actively exploring the inner realms are also both physically and emotionally vulnerable. It's important that the participants feel safe. Unwanted visitors can break the moment. The knowledge that someone can barge into the room at any time does not create a feeling of safety and comfort. Without a sense of security, it can be very difficult to enter into a deep level of trance. Cast a protective circle prior to beginning and put a DO NOT DISTURB sign on the door.

Once you've begun, try not to stand up and move around. Remember, people in trance become hypersensitive. No matter how quiet you try to be, you will be heard. Knowing that someone is wandering around you while in this state can push the internal "am I safe?" button, bringing the traveler to wakefulness.

Creating the right environment—from being clear about your intent to choosing materials that support that vision—is an important part of the working. Careful planning is the key to crafting an experience that will allow the participants to feel comfortable enough to enter into sacred time and place, to transcend the moment, and to enter the realms of the Gods.

Where Are We Going?—Poor Presentation

TOO MUCH

There are two different kinds of group trance experiences. Within the first, the goal is the creation of a group mind in which each participant sees and experiences the same story. When a group wishes to work magic, it will be more effective if the members have gestalt. If the group is focusing on working magic to create change—for example, healing an ill friend—

holding the same vision will help strengthen the magical intent and its effect. This example was demonstrated earlier in the story of the shared apple.

The second is when a group participates in the same story but the purpose is for self-, not group, transformation. For example, group members can be led to a central point together with the purpose of meeting their own personal guardian. They may be brought down a similar path, but because each person has his own unique needs, each would then be encouraged to explore various side paths or go through different doors that would lead to his own personal experience. From my experience, this is the form of guided meditation used most often.

Imagine you're on a journey and your guides instructs: "You will now turn to your right. Before you is a green meadow filled with white daisies and surrounded by trees. In the middle of the waist-high field of hay stands a black-and-white cow with brown eyes, chewing on grass. The cow will now give you a message." How disconcerting it would be if you turned and saw a meadow—but instead of trees it's next to the ocean, and the flowers within it are not white but red. Your cow is purple and yellow with blue eyes. It's sitting at a table sipping cappuccino and doesn't seem to have anything to say to you. There's nothing wrong with your vision. This is a case of a guide controlling too many of the fine details of the story and not allowing the participants to form their own impressions.

A pathworking is a form of participational ritual storytelling. What makes the story unusual is that the facilitator presents the general environment and outline of the plot; the participants fill in the dialogue and action sequences. While a pathworking may be a guided story, it's still a personal adventure. The visions revealed are still seen through an individual's own life experiences. The facilitator needs to allow each person within the circle to see the visions through his own eyes.

This is not to say that exact details shouldn't be given at all. Use specifics if the symbolism is an important part of the work.

Certain colors, smells, tastes, symbols, animals, and so on are often associated with particular myths and deity forms. Integrating mention of them can help bring those energies forward to the traveler. They should, however, be a shared and previously agreed-upon set of symbols and ideas. Even if you're working with lots of pertinent imagery, still leave as much room as possible for participants' imaginations to flow.

If you're going to use a great deal of description, remember to remain consistent. Don't start off with generalizations, then move to specific imagery. If you begin by telling the participants that they're standing on a mountain edge, don't later describe a desert valley below. You will disorient those who have created an inner seaside cliff or snow-covered alpine valley.

In trance, we are working with the younger or child self. When you think of your younger self, think of a inner three-year-old. Avoid complex language and grammar. Younger self won't understand and will only get frustrated. Colors, symbols, and simple direction reach our child self. If the instructions and descriptions are too complex, the inner child is liable to pout, dig her heels in, and refuse to travel any farther.

While it can be useful for trance induction, avoid directions like "imagine" or "remember" once you're on the journey. Instead, apply direct experience, the present tense, as much as possible. You see, you hear, you do.

Depending upon the meditation, you will become either an active participant or an observer. Observation within a pathworking is less stressful than active participation. Before presenting a journey, consider the nature of the experience and the level of intensity you or your circle can handle. People who can happily join the Maiden in a May dance might still do better to simply watch the Wild Hunt go by rather than riding with it. Have a clear understanding of the purpose of your ritual and know your limits before you begin.

Pagans, in general, are polytheistic. Some individuals and covens work with specific deities, creating a personal relationship with them. Others may not feel as comfortable with your Gods and Goddesses. I may view Bast, the Egyptian cat goddess, as a strong protectress. You, on the other hand, may be a devoted vegetarian and feel very uncomfortable meeting this carnivore. A discussion with all participants prior to visiting a particular deity form is important.

Did you notice that in the example with the cow, you were ordered to turn to your right? Perhaps it's just our inherent dislike for being told what to do, or maybe it's because in most Wiccan practices, we don't command the energies but work with them . . . either way, you'll find your pathworking will be more effective if you use words of invitation instead of commands—for example, saying, "I invite you now to sit down and begin making yourself comfortable," instead of, "you will now sit down and get comfortable."

A good guided meditation allows the participants to formulate their own visions within a mutually agreed-upon set of symbols, beliefs, and values. Language used and instructions given are simple so they can be easily understood. The journey itself is set at the level of competency of the participants or intensity of experience desired. The reins of control are gently held, allowing freedom of movement within a prescribed setting.

TOO LITTLE

"You're on a path . . . you meet someone . . . they give you something . . ." Just as too much information can be disconcerting, so too can not receiving enough imagery or guidance. The story is the backbone off which the adventure, personal transformation, and contact with the Gods, occur. Without enough information to create the visions, the trip will lack substance, no energy will be raised or directed, and the journey will become too difficult to sustain. To avoid this situation, you need to have a clear intent of what you hope to accomplish, a vision of how you will achieve this goal, enough pertinent imagery that the adventure moves smoothly, and enough energy—both physical and psychic—to raise and move the magic forward and manifest the transformation.

If you don't know where you're going, neither will anyone else on the journey. Therefore, the question that must be answered is, *What do I hope to achieve?* Connection with the Gods? Healing? Balance with the cycles of life? I work with the Tarot. I often tell my clients, "If you ask a vague question, you'll get a vague response." Ambiguity will only create more fog. In order to receive clarity, you need to be clear on what you're seeking. To say that you want to "feel better" is too vague and leaves too many questions. Do you want to fight an illness? Strengthen your body? Your mind? Your emotions? Are you searching for guidance to decide which kind of professional would best treat your condition? Or are you asking the Gods for help or to grant you insights into your situation? Each of these questions will warrant a different approach in fashioning a working. Decide what you want to accomplish; then you can begin to build your journey around it.

Once you know what you want to attain, the next question is how you can achieve your goal. To say you want to "find your animal spirit guide" is a good start, but you need to fashion the steps to do it. Is this to be a observational or participatory experience? Will you walk down a wooded path noting which animals you see, or are you going to assume different animal forms? How are you getting to the path? Will you stay in the woods or wander to other types of environment? Will you be invoking a deity to help you with your search? If so, which one?

Do your homework; research your myths and stories before presenting them. Know what you're participating in before you begin. If you're working with God forms, what symbols are they associated with? What area of the world or environment do they reside in? What are their histories? What do they like as offerings? Who or what do they hate? The more information you have prior to embarking on the path, the more intense and multidimensional a vision can be experienced.

"We perceive the world through our senses," says Judy Harrow. "We understand it through our representational systems, the ways in which we code and store information, and build mental maps and models. We recognize five major representational systems: sound, sight, smell, and touch (the four sensory channels that most people favor and are most closely connected to consciousness), plus language, which is a more abstract representational system." What this means is that different people respond to, and therefore tend to favor, different stimuli. If you say the words *birthday cake*, one person may see the cake with its candles, another may call to mind the smell of the sugar icing, while another may hear the strands of "Happy Birthday" being sung.

We tend to structure our own worlds around our strongest sense. When facilitating trance for others, you must remember to address the different needs of those within your circle. Just as there's a high probability that we don't all eat the same breakfast cereal, so it's also very unlikely that every person in your group will favor the same sense. The vocabulary of the trance inductions needs to be adapted to include each individual's preferred stimuli. To neglect this means that someone will be unable to fully experience the trip.

Here are two examples using an invocation to water, one basic and one encompassing more of the sense-based stimuli:

> We call to the west, to the spirits of Water.
> Power of Water, deep oceans, flowing rivers, vast lakes
> Spirits of Water, be with us now.

or

> We send out our voices to the west, calling to the
>   spirits of Water

Vast oceans, crashing waves upon the shore, salty
    brine upon the air
Flowing rivers, fresh and clear, burbling over rocks
    and trees
Deep lakes, green cold water, frog calls of love
    breaking the stillness
Spirits of Water, be with us now.

Unless I totally blew it, you should have received a fuller vision with the second invocation because it touched upon more available stimuli. Here it is again, broken down to show the insertion of the memory triggers for various senses:

Vast oceans (visual), *crashing waves upon the*
    shore (auditory and visual), *salty brine* (taste)
    upon the air (smell)
Flowing rivers (visual), *fresh and clear* (smell and
    taste), *burbling over rocks and trees* (auditory
    and visual)
Deep lakes (visual), *dark green cold waters* (tactile
    and visual), *frog calls of love breaking*
    the stillness (auditory)

How people speak will often give you a clue as to their primary stimuli. Notice what descriptive words they use when describing others, particularly within relationships. Is she sweet like honey (taste)? Fast like a ferret (visual)? Comfortable as lamb's wool (texture)? Another hint can be seen by observing what people do for relaxation. Music? Cooking? Painting? Writing? Jumping out of an airplane?

If you can't figure it out, you can always ask. Inquire how they can tell when an object has been magically charged. Is it warm or cold to the touch? Does it hum, vibrate, or glow? This will give you a starting point.

Just as you would normally plan out a ritual from the moment of casting a circle to its conclusion, you need do the same with a guided meditation. Where are you going? How are you getting there? What are you doing once you reach it? In a circle, you wouldn't raise a cone of power without first deciding on what you wish to do with the energy. Neither do you approach inner transformative energies without focus or knowing how you wish to direct the changes. While leaving plenty of room for personal imagery and enough flexibility for change if situations warrant it, plan the outline of your journey step by step before you put your, or another's, feet upon the path. Throughout your planning, remember that when you're in trance you're working with child self. Keep the language uncomplicated and your directions easy to follow.

POOR PACING

You can plan out a beautiful experience, have a great voice for the presentation, and set up your environment so that it's easy to slide into trance. If your journey isn't well paced, however, then all your preparations will have been in vain. Pacing is all about timing. It means balancing—giving enough time to fully experience each aspect of the working without giving too much time without direction.

As in any ritual format, a guided meditation has a beginning, a middle, and an end. The beginning is the relaxation and trance induction. The middle has three points: (1) the descent to the traveler's safe inner space or home; (2) the subsequent journey from that space to where the action occurs; and (3) the return to the traveler's personal safe home. Just as they were guided down into trance, the voyagers are then led back up to complete consciousness. The pathworking should be completed with a check-in to ensure that all participants have fully returned and a discussion or writing down of the visions experienced.

Each step must be completed prior to moving on to the next. Those who move too quickly through a trance induction will leave some of the participants, or themselves, behind; those who take too much time risk losing people to boredom.

In general, the warm-up or stretching exercises need not run more than five to ten minutes. Do enough to get the kinks out, but not so much that muscles are overstretched and become sore.

The grounding and centering portion that follows the stretching helps bring consciousness to the present and create a sacred frame of mind. It's also fairly brief.

The pace is slowed with the introduction of the relaxation techniques. You want to allow the body enough time to work with the relaxation guide, but not so much that people fall asleep. The length of this segment is based upon the response of those participating, but plan on a minimum of eight to ten minutes. Remember, as people begin to enter trance, their perception of time shifts. An hour will feel like fifteen minutes. Taking ten minutes to do a portion may seem long in real time, but in the world of trance it's a blip.

The trance induction continues with a slow and steady pace. Because the journeyers will have entered into a light trance during the relaxation section, the induction should just continue the steady flow. An example of a typical bridge would be, "Now that you are completely relaxed, I invite you to see in your mind's eye a door begin to form before you . . ." There are, of course, numerous forms of trance induction. You should devise how to gently move from the relaxation to deeper trance. The amount of time until all have completed the induction and entered into a deep stage of trance again varies with the level of experience of those participating. Over time, this portion can be shortened as familiarity with trance is strengthened and group trust is developed. A long descent down a staircase may turn into a slide or walk through a doorway. Eventually, with time and practice, you may simply need to bring to mind what it feels like to be in trance, breathe deeply into it, and enter a trance state.

Once there, the length and pace are set by the story, myth, or adventure, and the occurrences that take place. Remember that although you and those participating may not feel discomfort while in trance, when you wake up your body will know that it's been sitting in one position for a long time. Use a suitable amount of time for the working, then return people to a waking state.

The pace is picked up to aid in the return from an entranced state. The voice and the tempo are slightly increased with each step that brings the journeyers closer to wakefulness. This reflects the movement and raising of consciousness. Once all have completely returned, time should be given to allow for discussion or journal writing.

Words of Caution

It may be tempting for some, whether intentionally or not, to misuse trance as a form of escaping reality, controlling others in their group, or avoiding personal responsibility.

Trance can provide information, but the signs and messages brought forward from the journeys need to be placed into context on the physical plane.

For example, there was a journeyer who was desperately in love with a woman, "Lucy," though she had no interest in him. He participated in a trance journey in which he sought out and encountered Aphrodite, the Goddess of love, to ask Her what he should do. She emerged from the foam of the sea and walked to meet him. When he gazed into the eyes of the Goddess, he saw the face of the woman whom he desired. She then turned away and walked back into the waters. As She disappeared, he heard the sound of a woman's playful laughter somewhere behind him and felt a sense of familiarity. The journeyer, when he returned from his trance, was convinced that this was a sign from the Goddess that Lucy was destined to be his. He intensified his amorous advances until, feeling harassed, she threatened to obtain a restraining order. With hurt feelings, he relinquished his quest, allowing his hopes for a relationship with her to dissolve. It was only then, as the cliché goes, that he finally noticed a longtime friend. She had been behind him all the time, so familiar that he hadn't recognized the possibilities of a relationship.

In this case, the journeyer refused to consider the reality that the woman whom he lusted after did not reciprocate his feelings. He chose to interpret his trance message only in the context that best suited his emotional state.

One possible way of avoiding this as a facilitator and as a coven is to discuss the events that occurred and information received immediately after returning from the journey, allowing others to present their various interpretations of the voyage. Perhaps someone may have suggested to him that Lucy was a symbol of love, as is Aphrodite, which may be why he saw her in the Goddess. Still, the Goddess/Lucy turned away from him and dissolved into the ocean. Like the waves, you can't catch her. There is someone, however—you already know who, based on the playful laugh—you enjoy spending time with. You just need to turn around and look.

If you aren't working with a group, then you don't have the benefit of other views. An alternative is to write down your visions in a notebook immediately after you return from trance. When done, put your notebook away for twenty-four hours and try not to obsess about what occurred in your journey. After the time has passed, read what you wrote. If it's still unclear, jot down whatever ideas come to mind, then put it away and try again later. Writing it down while it's still fresh in your mind, then allowing some time to pass before focusing on it, may help bring deeper clarity.

Another scenario is found with those who attempt to use trance, either consciously or unconsciously, as a means of controlling the group or individuals within it. One means goes like this: Either during the journey or immediately afterward, they inform the coven or individuals within it that, "The Goddess or God told me that you/we must _____ [fill in the blank]." The inference is that the power of the Gods is behind their statement, and it must be obeyed. Sometimes it is, but again, the message needs to be brought forward and looked at objectively before responding. If it's unclear, other journeys may bring more clarity.

Another means is to manipulate the imagery or story to reflect their personal opinions, insecurities, or needs. This is usually not done with malicious intent, but the results can be hurtful and sometimes harmful to themselves or others.

This is not to say that the visions seen are not the seeker's truths. Symbolic interpretation is completely subjective. Astral visions are a combination of creative imagination and real forms. While internal forms have basis in external realities, the danger is seeing all internal visions as being external truths.

Always remember that while you can read many books on trance and trance techniques, the real understanding of them comes only from personal exploration. You've got to go out and walk the paths and find out where they lead. Trance is an intricate piece of Witchcraft and magic, but it still is a place of mystery that we can understand only through experience.

ᘓ

Trance speaks in colors, symbols, and metaphors. Hopes and fears often rise up, demanding attention and resolution. Still, where else can you get insights into your own psyche from a purple cow sipping cappuccino? In this world, the magical threads sing when they're plucked, producing chords of energy. Here you can touch the face of the Goddess.

The rest of this book will focus on different exercises to enter and leave trance states and various adventures that you can explore, either alone or with a group. It's meant to be fun, so please, play, explore, and enjoy!

CHAPTER TWO

CRED

Walking In and Out of Trance

Think of the following chapter as a smorgasbord: It offers you a little of this and a little of that. Included is an assortment of different techniques for stretching, grounding, relaxation, and trance induction. Most of these exercises can be done either with a group or alone. Try them all out, then use what you like. The best methods are those that you create yourself, so adapt and change them to fit your personal practice.

The Key

The exercises assume that you have prepared yourself and your environment prior to beginning. This means your candles are lit, the phone is unplugged, and you're in a ritual state of mind.

Each section will offer three different levels of exercises or journeys. They are: Basic—☆; Intermediate—☆☆; and Skilled—☆☆☆. The 👪 symbol indicates a group exercise. Suggestions on adaptations for solitaries have been included where possible.

In some cases, tools or supplies will be needed or suggested in order to fully participate in the experience. This will be indicated with a ⌘ at the beginning of the exercise.

Before Beginning

Before attempting an exercise, read through it completely. Get the pace set in your mind before presenting it to others or tape recording it for your own use. If recording, remember to speak clearly and gently. You may want to include a safety feature in case of mechanical problems. Suggest that if the listener (meaning you) doesn't hear anything for five or more minutes, because the tape broke or the batteries ran down, you should awaken from trance, refreshed, and return fully to your body.

When an exercise is completed, if you're with a group, discuss and compare your experiences. This will help solidify the memory and perhaps give you insights into some aspects of your journey. Whether you're working with a group or alone, remember to record your experience and any reaction you may have in your trance journal.

Getting the Kinks Out—Stress and Stretching

Before setting off down the path, you must get ready for the trip. The first step is all about the body, the "warm-up exercises." Remember, your body will be sitting in one position for an extended period of time. If your muscles freeze up, you're in for a very unpleasant awakening. So get the kinks out before you set your buns down on the unforgiving floor. A few floor cushions would be helpful.

Stretching and moving will help increase the circulation of blood, which carries oxygen and energy to your muscles. Physical activity is also a great stress releaser. It's hard to relax and stay focused when your mind is stuck on rewind, constantly playing back the troubles of the day. Stretching and moving help break the tape, at least for a while, strengthening your ability to focus and increasing your perceptions. Don't skip this step.

The exercises listed below can be used on their own, combined with others, or seen as a beginning point for your own creativity. Please do adapt these exercises to suit your own needs.

This isn't an aerobics or physical education class. Gentle stretches and tension releasers are all you need to prepare for trance work. Please consider your own abilities or restrictions. Do only what's comfortable for you. If you have difficulty standing, then sit. If you're unable to move your lower extremities, then focus on the upper body. If the exercise suggests repeating movements three times but you're only able to do a single set, then congratulate yourself for having completed it once. Over time, you may build up stamina and reach three or more.

There's often a heightened level of anticipation that needs to be released along with the physical tension. Let both out with sighs, groans, noises, and laughter. All this is part of the process, so give yourself and your body permission to crack, pop, and giggle.

WORKING THE MUSCLE GROUPS ✩

This exercise can either be done standing or seated. Gently stretch your body in whatever ways feel most comfortable. This task is actually split into two sections.

Part I Start with some light, general stretching. Here are a few suggestions for movements to start with. The list is very far from complete. Try to move every portion of your body, from toes to nose, at least once.

Most people store their stress in their neck and shoulders. Rolling the neck and head may damage fragile vertebrae. Instead, try the alternative here.

Keeping your body straight and your head level, slowly turn your head until you're looking over your left shoulder and can feel the tension. Hold, then release. Repeat looking over your right shoulder.

Roll your shoulders, forward three times and then backward three times.

Keeping your knees slightly bent, lean over and, if possible, touch your toes. Hold your position for a count of three. Slowly return to a standing position and repeat.

Place your hands on your hips. Keeping your lower body as stationary as possible and your weight evenly distributed, carefully twist your upper body to the right as far as is comfortable. Hold for a count of three. Return to a normal position. Repeat on the left side, carefully twisting your upper body to the left as far as is comfortable. Hold for a count of three, then return to a normal position. Finish your stretch by shaking out your limbs and body.

Once you've finished with the light stretches, continue to stand or sit comfortably, breathing gently in and out.

Part II The second half of the exercise is based on the "deep muscle relaxation" techniques introduced by Edmond Jacobsen in the 1930s. Jacobsen's exercises are a form of self-massage in which we squeeze and release our own muscles to wring out toxins and tensions. Done mindfully, they also offer an effective metaphor for the release of emotional or mental stress, clearing the way for deeper self-exploration.

Begin with breathing slow deep breaths. Notice your body and how it feels at this moment. Bring awareness to your right foot. Scrunch your toes and the muscles of your foot as tightly as possible. Breathe in deeply with the tension and hold for a count of ten. Exhale, and at the same time, quickly release the muscles in your foot. Bring awareness to your left foot. Scrunch your toes and the muscles of your left foot as tightly as possible. Breathe in deeply with the tension and hold for a count of ten. Exhale rapidly, while suddenly letting the muscles in your foot go limp. Feel the tension drain out.

Bring awareness to your right thigh and leg. Inhale and raise your right leg up slightly, tensing the muscles as tightly as you can. Hold for a count of ten. As you exhale, quickly release the tension of the muscles in your right leg, allowing it to gently drop. If you're sitting or lying on the floor, roll your leg from side to side to help the muscles relax. If you're standing, gently shake out the muscles of your leg. Repeat the exercise with your left thigh and leg.

Now raise your arm. As you inhale, clench the muscles of your arm and hand, making a tight fist with your fingers. Hold for a count of ten. Then release the breath as you quickly release the tension in your right hand and arm, allowing it to gently drop. If you're lying on the floor, roll your right arm from side to side to help the muscles further relax. If you're standing or sitting, gently shake it for a moment. Repeat with the other arm.

Bring your awareness to your buttocks. Take a breath, clench the muscles of your right cheek, and hold for about ten seconds, then very suddenly relax them with your exhale. Take a breath and, with your intake of breath, clench the muscles of your left cheek. Hold for about ten seconds, then very suddenly release and relax the muscles of your left cheek with your exhale. End by taking a deep breath, clenching the muscles of both your right and left buttocks simultaneously for a count of ten, and releasing them together.

Turn to your tummy. Suck in your belly, tightening the muscles as much as you can. Hold the tension for a count of ten and quickly release as you exhale. Now take a deep breath and fill your belly with air. Feel it expand, becoming round, full, and taut. Hold for ten seconds and release.

Bring your shoulder blades together, as if they could touch in the middle of your back. Take a breath and hold for a count of ten. Release as you exhale.

Clench both of your shoulders, pushing them up toward your ears. Take a breath and hold for a count of ten. Quickly release with your exhale. Repeat, clenching your shoulders two more times.

Now push your shoulders down as far as they will go. Take a breath and hold for a count of ten. Quickly release with your exhale. Repeat two more times.

Scrunch up the muscles in your face so that your eyes close, your nose is crinkled, and your jaw is tight, looking like you just ate something very, very sour. Hold for a count of ten and release. Repeat two more times.

Now expand and stretch your facial muscles. Open your mouth up wide in a Cheshire cat grin and stick your tongue out as far as it will go. Roll your eyes upward as far as you can and *hold* for a count of ten (while you hope that no one has a camera), then quickly release the tension. Repeat two more times.

You can finish with massaging or shaking out any leftover kinks and residual tensions.

SHAKE AND SHOUT ✩✩

⌘ If you're standing, you can use a chair to help with balance. Remember to remain consistently slow and easy during this exercise. The shakes are meant to help release tension, not to add to it. It might help to imagine that you're gently flicking drops of water off the portion of the body you're focusing on.

We'll start with three rotations per body part, but you're welcome to increase the number of rotations as you or your group becomes more comfortable with the exercise. Still, remain consistent. Don't do three rotations for your knees and then ten for your hips. Your breathing should remain slow and even throughout the exercise; your spine straight.

Stand with your feet slightly apart, your weight evenly balanced. Allow your arms to drop and hang at your sides.

Putting your weight on your left foot, raise your right foot slightly off the floor. Shake your right foot a couple of times, then slowly rotate just your right ankle for a count of three. Place your right foot back on the floor.

Now put your weight on your right foot and raise your left slightly off the floor. Shake your left foot a couple of times, then slowly rotate just your left ankle for a count of three. Place your left foot back on the floor.

Putting your weight back on your left foot, raise your right leg slightly off the floor. Shake your right leg a couple of times. Place your foot back on the floor. Repeat with your left leg.

Keeping your lower body stationary, gently twist your upper body to the right as far as is comfortable so that you're looking over your right shoulder. Hold to the count of three and release. Twist your upper body to the left as far as is comfortable so that you're looking over your left shoulder. Hold to the count of three and release. If your hands were placed on your hips, allow them to gently hang again by your sides.

Stand comfortably once again, with your weight evenly distributed. Keeping your arms hanging loosely at your sides, pull the fingers of your right hand into your palm. In a motion that resembles flicking water off your hand, quickly flick your fingers outward so that your fingers are stretched wide and your palm is open. Shake your right hand from the wrist a couple of times. Slowly rotate your right wrist, three times counterclockwise and then three times clockwise. Repeat the finger-and-wrist exercise with your left hand.

Keeping your upper shoulder and body as still as possible, shake your right lower arm from the elbow down. Slowly rotate your lower right arm from the elbow three times in a counterclockwise motion, followed by three times in a clockwise direction. Repeat the lower-arm exercise with your left arm.

Shake your entire right arm. Slowly rotate your right shoulder and arm three times from your shoulder counterclockwise and then three times clockwise. Allow your right arm to once again hang at your side. Repeat the arm-and-shoulder exercise with your left side.

Keeping the rest of your body stationary, turn your head *slowly* to the right as far as is comfortable and hold for a count of three. Turn your head *slowly* to the left as far as is comfortable and hold for a count of three. *Do not shake* your head and neck.

Scrunch up the muscles in your face so that your eyes close, your nose is crinkled, and your jaw clenches. Hold for a count of three. Release. Repeat two more times.

Take your hands, place them on your head, and massage your head and scalp for a count of nine. It's also good to tap the scalp—striking it briskly with your fingertips in a motion something like typing, all over the scalp.

Take a deep breath and shake your *entire body*, especially any parts that still feel tense, for a count of three. Take another deep breath and shake your entire body again—but as you do so, let out a noise. Take another deep breath, shake your entire body, and let out a louder noise or a yell.

FROM CHINA WITH LOVE—TAI CHI EXERCISES FOR BALANCE AND STRENGTH ☆☆☆

Chinese Taoism fosters a reverence for nature, a belief in the flow of natural energy forces *(chi)* within the body. There is a focus on duality and balance, reflected in the concept of yin and yang. Yin is seen as the embodiment of the receptive, while yang is all that is active. Many Taoist beliefs are very compatible with contemporary Paganism.

Tai chi is a system of mind and body work based on Taoist concepts. These exercises, shared with me by Ken Zaborowski, a tai chi instructor, can help bring harmony to the body and mind. Since they require visualization as well as movement, they may be a bit more challenging for beginners than the previous exercises in this section.

Begin by standing with your feet slightly apart and your weight evenly distributed between them. Your spine should be straight, your arms slightly extended and away from the sides of your body.

Imagine that your body is being slowly filled with weight, as if someone opened up the top of your head and is pouring water into you. You can feel your feet become heavy with the weight of the water and begin to sink into the floor.

More water is poured. Your legs are filled with water and become heavier, followed by your thighs. Still more water, so now your hips and your tummy are filled. The weight pulls your body downward toward the ground. You feel your feet and calves slowly sink deep into the Earth, becoming one with the ground.

The undersides of your arms, which are still slightly extended and away from your body, take on the appearance of balloons filled with water, bottom-heavy pendulums pulled taut by gravity and internal weight. Feel the weight as it pulls you down and roots you solidly into the Earth.

But the weight doesn't topple you. At the same time, you notice that a wire coming from high above supports you. The wire is fastened securely to the top of your head. You can feel it as it holds your head and body upright, even as the weight within you pulls your body downward.

Notice that, like a puppet, there are other strings attached to your body. Wires are attached to your shoulders, arms, elbows, and wrists. These wires are pulling you upward, supporting and balancing the weight within your body. The puppeteer gently pulls on the strings and you feel your spine straighten, your shoulders drawn erect, your arms growing lighter.

It's a paradox in that you feel both the heaviness and the lightness simultaneously. The upper portions of your arms feel weightless while your underarms are as heavy as stone. The lower parts of your body are firmly rooted into the ground while your upper body is suspended in air. You may feel a gentle stretching in your body as the two halves find balance.

About three fingers down from your belly button, you will find what the Chinese call your *tantien*. This is where you find your center. Your spine, pulled straight by the wires from above, creates the vertical centerline connecting your body from sky to ground.

In Chinese philosophy, there are three separate things that can be worked individually: Heaven, Earth and human. Your *tantien* unites all three, bringing balance and harmony within. It's the horizontal center between up and down, heavy and light, above and below. Stay connected with this centerpoint as you continue with the tai chi exercises.

Maintaining the visualization set at the beginning of this process, stand with your feet slightly apart. They should be a little wider than your shoulder-width. Bend your knees slightly. Hold your arms up in front of you a little above waist-height and focus your eyes on your hands. The palms of your hands should be open and facing each other, as if you're holding a medium-sized ball.

Keeping your spine straight and your feet grounded, take a deep breath and slowly turn right. With your eyes and head following, allow your right arm to gracefully open and extend (think of a ballet dancer), continuing the stretch as far back to the right as is comfortable. Gently exhale as you slowly return to center, bringing your right arm and body forward and into place.

Now take another deep breath and, as you do, slowly turn left. With your eyes and head following, allow your left arm to gracefully open and extend, continuing the stretch as far back to the left as is comfortable. As you exhale, slowly return to center, with your hands once again holding the imaginary ball. Repeat twice on each side.

WITH A LITTLE HELP

The following exercises require two or more people. Along with stretching muscle groups, these exercises help create group bonding and trust. They can be done as a supplement to any of the other techniques included above.

Sit on the floor facing your partner. Both of you should have your legs apart in a V shape, with your knees slightly bent and your feet touching, so your legs make a diamond shape in the open space between you. Join hands across the space. With hands joined, your partner leans forward while you lean backward. This will cause tension in your inner thighs. Go only as far back and forward as is comfortable. Hold for a moment. Return to an upright position. Repeat with your partner leaning backward and you leaning forward. Repeat, alternating, two more times.

Lie on the ground with your legs together, knees slightly bent, arms by your sides. Your partner should be standing next to you by your feet. Slowly raise your right leg until your partner catches it. Relax the muscles of your right leg. Allow her to slowly raise your leg until she feels resistance or until you feel the tension and tell her to stop. Hold the position for a count of five. Allow her to lower your leg back to the floor. Repeat with your left leg. Repeat the exercise two more times, then switch places with your partner.

Sit in a very tight circle, so that your knees are touching the people sitting on either side of you. Everyone turn to the left, so that you are now facing the back of the person who was on your left. Place your hands on the back and shoulders of the person in front of you. Enjoy a group back massage. Don't stop there: Partner up and do each other's feet, legs, arms, head, and face.

Grounding and Centering

With the body stretched and relaxed, the focus now turns inward. In this section are various breathing and visualization techniques to help move the voyagers' attention away from the mundane and toward the sacred, signaling to the subconscious mind that something special is about to occur.

It's important that those who are exploring altered states of consciousness be very grounded in the here-and-now. Recognizing the connection to yourself and the world through your personal center will help make an easy transition among trance states. I know that no matter how far I roam in the inner realms, I can always find my way home. My connection to the world and my body is strong. Like an invisible thread that joins my center and my tranced self, this connection will guide me back. Although some individuals will begin to shift consciousness during these exercises, this is not the exercises' primary purpose; their goal is to center you, creating a point of inner balance.

These exercises also begin building up your visualization skills. The ability to work with visualization will be important in the sections to come. As in the previous section, the number of stars indicates the exercise's degree of difficulty based on the level of visualization skill required. In order to help you learn pacing, I've included indications for pauses.

When an exercise is completed, remember to discuss your experiences and record them in your trance journal.

FOUR-SQUARE BREATHING ☆

This is a very simple breathing exercise. It can be done anywhere, while sitting, standing, or lying down, for as long as you desire. Because it's a counted exercise, it works well for both solitaries and groups.

Make sure you keep your back straight to help allow the energy to flow. Keep your attention completely focused on your breath as you fill your lungs, hold, and exhale.

For those working with a group, this exercise is easily adaptable and can be used to prepare for deeper group work. All participants should sit together in a circle and join hands. If that's uncomfortable, simply allow a portion of your bodies to touch so that a circle is formed and closed. Throughout this exercise, you breathe together.

> *Relax . . . close your eyes . . . and listen for the sound of your heartbeat . . . breathing gently in . . . and out.*
> *Breathe in to a count of four.*
> *Hold for a count of four.*
> *Breathe out for a count of four.*
> *Hold for a count of four.*
> *Breathe in . . . 2, 3, 4 . . . Hold . . . 2, 3, 4 . . . Breathe out . . . 2, 3, 4 . . . Hold . . . 2, 3, 4 . . .*
> *Breathe in . . . 2, 3, 4 . . . Hold . . . 2, 3, 4 . . . Breathe out . . . 2, 3, 4 . . . Hold . . . 2, 3, 4 . . .*
> *Breathe in . . . 2, 3, 4 . . . Hold . . . 2, 3, 4 . . . Breathe out . . . 2, 3, 4 . . . Hold . . . 2, 3, 4 . . .*
> *Breathe in . . . 2, 3, 4 . . . Hold . . . 2, 3, 4 . . . Breathe out . . . 2, 3, 4 . . . Hold . . . 2, 3, 4 . . .*

CLEANSING YOUR AURA ☆

This exercise works best if you stand. Try to remember to keep your breathing deep and regular. The visualization should be as clear as possible in your mind.

Stand relaxed, with your feet about shoulder-width apart . . . your weight evenly distributed between them. *(pause)* Your eyes may be open or closed. Your breathing should be deep . . . and regular. *(pause)* As you breathe . . . feel, sense, or see the aura surrounding you . . . your personal energy field. *(pause)* While staying relaxed, move your hands up to your face . . . Your palms should be turned in toward your face . . . about two to four inches from your body. Each of your hands is like a cleansing brush. Keeping your hands slightly away from your body, and beginning with the top of your head, start moving your hands in a scrubbing or circular cleaning motion downward toward your feet. *(pause)* With each downward motion, you are clearing away any unwanted energy . . . any unwanted stress . . . releasing tension. *(pause)* Scoop and clear it off. When you reach your feet . . . shake your hands to clear them of the excess energy. *(pause)* Bring your hands back up to your head and begin again, moving down your sides . . . cleaning your aura of any unwanted energy . . . unwanted stress. *(pause)* When you reach your feet . . . shake your hands to clear them of the excess energy. *(pause)* Bring your hands back up to your head and begin again, this time clearing your back, as much as you are able. When you reach your feet . . . shake your hands to clear them of the excess energy. *(pause)* You should feel a tingling sensation as you remove all the grit and stress . . . leaving your aura fresh and clean . . . your focus clear and ready for the magical work to follow.

After you've finished this exercise, you may want to "clean your mop" by rinsing your hands in running water or a bowl of salt water to remove any leftover energy bits.

This exercise works even better if people do it for each other. You can either partner up or do this as a group exercise (assuming there aren't more than six people—for a larger group, you could try creating an assembly line, like a car wash). One at a time, each person has his aura washed and scrubbed. Remember to rinse your hands in salt water in between each participant.

BALANCED BETWEEN EARTH AND SKY ☆☆
Sit or stand in a comfortable position, with your back straight. Close your eyes and take a deep breath in . . . and let it out

slowly. Take another breath in ... and also let it out slowly. Keep breathing gently in ... and out ... with each breath ... becoming more relaxed ... with each breath ... becoming more at ease. *(pause)*

See, if you will, the very center of the Earth beneath you ... the heart of the Mother ... and she is gently beating. *(pause)* With each beat, a portion of that energy begins to make its way up toward you ... this warming energy ... from the Earth below ... with each beat ... it climbs higher ... moving through molten lava ... higher ... up through solid rock ... and higher ... this energy from the Earth below pushes through dirt ... and sand ... you can feel it getting warm beneath you as the energy continues to climb ... up and up ... moving through concrete ... steel ... and wood ... until you can feel it touch you ... this energy from the Earth enters into you ... moving through your body ... filling you with wonderful, warming energy from the heart of the Mother ... binding you to the Earth. Take a moment and feel this connection to the Earth. *(pause)*

Now you see another energy. This one is coming from high above ... moving quickly through space ... It passes through solar systems ... shooting past planets ... moving faster and faster in the darkness ... until it finds this solar system ... this small, blue planet ... and makes its way toward it. This energy from the heavens above ... penetrates the atmosphere ... moving quickly across the sky ... parting the clouds ... moving downward ... and downward ... you can see it as it makes its way toward you ... moving faster ... It touches the top of the building ... passing through the roof ... cement ... steel ... wood ... and empty space ... until you feel it right above you ... this energy from the skies above. When it touches the top of your head, it breaks into a million pieces ... cascading over you ... engulfing you ... connecting you to the sky above. Take a moment and feel this connection to the sky. *(pause)*

You are now filled with the energy of the Earth ... cradled by the energy of the sky . . . balanced between the two. Take a deep breath and feel this energy within and without.

WORKING WITH THE CHAKRAS ☆☆

There are many variations of working with the chakras, the energy centers found at points along the spine. You can bring energy up from the ground, filling each of the centers with Earth energy or relaxation. You can work from the crown chakra down, filling each with sky energy and grounding your stress into the Earth. The following is a basic example. While it can be done standing or lying down, it works best in a sitting position with your buttocks on the ground. If you like, you can place your hands on each chakra and feel it fill with the Earth's energy rising along your spine.

Get comfortable . . . Relax . . . Take a deep breath and allow your body to relax. Keep breathing gently in . . . and out. With each breath, you can feel the energy of the Earth beneath you . . . growing warmer beneath you . . . as you acknowledge the energy of the Earth and it reaches up to meet you. Feel the ground beneath your buttocks grow warmer as the energy rises from below. Feel it touch the base of your spine . . . enter into your body . . . filling your root chakra with warming energy until . . . filled . . . it glows red.

The energy from the Earth below continues to move up your spine to your womb . . . filling that space with warming energy . . . until it is filled . . . it glows orange.

The energy continues to move up your spine to your *hara,* your *tantien,* the solar plexus . . . Filling that center with warming energy . . . until it is filled . . . it glows yellow.

Continuing to move upward . . . the energy from the Earth below moves slowly up to your heart . . . Filling your heart with warming energy . . . until it is filled . . . it glows green.

Upward to your throat, the energy slowly climbs . . . Filling your throat center with warming energy . . . until it is filled . . . it glows blue.

The energy from the Earth below continues to move up your spine . . . flowing upward to your third eye on the center of your forehead . . . The area fills with warming energy . . . until it is filled . . . it glows indigo.

The energy moves up higher . . . to the top of your head, your crown. You feel the top of your head grow warm as the energy from the Earth is pulled up through your body, filling each of your centers . . . up to touch the top of your head . . . it fills and expands . . . glowing white.

The energy moves unhampered up from the Earth and through each of your centers. Feel the energy as it flows up your spine, filling your centers. *(pause)*

Once the energy is flowing among your chakras, there are a couple of possibilities for working with that energy. You can just sit and enjoy the connection, or you can use the energy to clear away stress and negativity. I offer two variations on this theme, but remember the best methods are those that you create yourself, so adapt and change these to fit your personal practice.

Version 1 Run your hand from the top of your head . . . down the front of your face . . . over your throat . . . your heart . . . down in front of your solar plexus . . . then push it outward . . . pushing out all imbalances . . . sending the energy to the universe to reuse in a positive manner.

Version 2 Run your hand from the top of your head . . . down the front of your face . . . over your throat . . . your heart . . . down in front of your solar plexus . . . over your womb . . . down past your root, and push it downward . . . pushing out all imbalances . . . sending the energy to the Earth to reuse in a positive manner.

THE ELEMENTS ☆☆☆

Sit or stand in a comfortable position. Close your eyes, take a deep breath in, and let it out slowly. Take another breath in and let it out slowly, too. Keep breathing gently in . . . and out . . . with each breath becoming more relaxed . . . with each breath becoming more at ease.

With the next breath, feel the air enter your lungs . . . expanding them with its mass . . . and then release the breath back out to the world. *(pause)* Although the air is transparent, in your mind's eye you can see it as you breathe it in . . . taking it deep within your lungs . . . expanding your chest with its life force . . . and then exhaling, returning it to the world. *(pause)* With each breath . . . you breathe in the element of Air . . . With each intake, Air brings to you its gift of clarity . . . and insight . . . blowing away the cobwebs of your mind . . . expelling the confusion and stress of the day. Air carries sounds to us so that we may hear and enjoy the vibrations of voice and music. *(pause)* We give thanks to the element of Air. *(pause)*

I invite you to feel your heartbeat, the fire within you. If you wish, place your hands on your chest and feel the movement beneath your fingers. *(pause)* Sometimes it's fast . . . sometimes slow . . . your heart is beating the dance of life. In your mind's eye, you can see the fire move within you with each pulse . . . traveling through every portion of your body . . . circulating and warming . . . passing through arteries and veins . . . until it returns to the beat beneath your hand. *(pause)* With each throb, you are experiencing the element of Fire, the spark of life . . . With each beat, it brings to you its gift of passion for life . . . the desire to create . . . the warmth of friendship shared. *(pause)* We give thanks to the element of Fire. *(pause)*

I invite you now to feel . . . To remember what it is like to be among friends and family . . . To be embraced by those who love and care for you . . . To reach out with your inner being and touch the deeper mysteries. *(pause)* Tears of joy . . . and tears of sadness. To fully know one . . . you must also embrace the other. With each tear, we are given the gift of Water. *(pause)* The blessings and the pain of birth as we emerged from the ocean of our mother's womb. *(pause)* The wisdom of the ages, the mysteries of life. We give thanks to the element of Water. *(pause)*

I invite you now to feel the weight of your body . . . Feel your feet and legs . . . knees and thighs . . . buttocks and hips . . . stomach and chest . . . shoulders . . . arms and hands . . . neck and face . . . your head. This is the shell that houses your spirit. *(pause)* This is your center, from which you can explore the inner worlds . . . This is your physical home. It is the gift that Earth gives to you, your body. It brings pleasure . . . sensuality . . . texture and movement . . . smells and tastes, sights and sounds. *(pause)* We give thanks to the element of Earth. *(pause)*

You are Air . . . you are Fire . . . you are Water . . . you are Earth. Feel the elements as they move within you and around you. Feel every aspect of your being alive and vibrant. *(pause)* You are a part of this world . . . and the world is a part of you. Whatever realms you may travel, you will remember this feeling of being alive . . . being present . . . being home. Take one more breath and be fully at this moment . . . and ready to begin.

YI CHI LI ☆☆☆

Tai chi combines movement with breathwork to help their students focus and become centered in the present. The Chinese have a saying: *yi chi li. Yi* is your willpower. *Chi* is your energy, generated by breath—it is the life force. *Li* is physical strength. In tai chi, you're using your mind to direct your intrinsic energy to create physical strength.

These exercises are a continuation of the tai chi stretching moves from the previous section. Please go back and reread the tai chi visualization portion of the exercise, so that it's clear in your mind before you continue.

These exercises are traditionally done in a standing position;

people with mobility issues, however, can sit or lie down. What is important is to keep your spine as straight as possible so that the energy can flow unhampered.

Upper Clearing Breath Stand in the basic stance, with your feet about shoulder-width apart, your weight evenly balanced between them, and your knees slightly bent. Allow your hands to rest in front of you at the level of your *tantien,* your centerpoint, with your palms turned up as if you were holding a basketball.

Take a deep breath . . . filling your belly with breath. As you breathe in, simultaneously, in one motion, move your hands and arms upward like wings unfolding, while straightening your body. By the time your lungs and belly are filled, your body should be fully extended, your hands over your head with your palms flat as if you were holding up the sky, your spine and knees straight, and your eyes looking up toward the heavens. This is called the Hotai Buddha or the laughing Buddha position; it's a symbol of good luck and health. The energy raised during this motion is considered to be very yang.

Breathe out. As you exhale, allow your knees to bend slightly and your hands to float back down to their original position as if they were feathers on the wind. Concentrate on letting your cares float down and out with your breath. This motion is considered very yin. The alternation of the two movements brings balance of yang and yin. Repeat both motions four to nine more times.

Sea Plants Take the same starting posture as the previous exercise, feet about shoulder-width apart, knees bent, and spine straight. Imagine you are a sea plant rooted in the bottom of the ocean, your leaves gently floating, carried on the waves. Breathe in and let just your left hand slowly float up, carried with your breath. Breathe out and allow your hand to float down, with your fingers trailing as if they were being moved through water. The motion should be smooth and soft. Repeat with your right hand. Watch your hand as it moves slowly upward . . . and back down. As it moves, it is bringing the *chi* up and out to your fingers and palms. Where *chi* goes, blood goes. This is a good exercise for those whose hands get cold easily.

Continue with the exercise, allowing your muscles to relax so your blood flows freely. While you focus on your hands, be sure to keep rooted in the ground so the currents don't carry you away. Keep your spine straight, your knees slightly bent, your breathing regular with the motion. Repeat this gentle exercise for as long as you are comfortable.

Do only what is comfortable. It shouldn't hurt. If you tighten up, you'll lose the flow of energy. When you're done, slowly lower your arms, loosen your ankles and knees, and stretch your body. Then shake out any remaining kinks.

Once you get more experienced in entering trance states, you may be able to shorten the grounding and relaxation segments. For very experienced folks, a simple cue like, "Remember what is feels like to be in trance," may be sufficient to open up the previously laid tracks to an altered state.

Relaxing Into Trance

With body and mind prepared, it's time to get comfortable and begin the relaxation segment. This portion will allow the participants to enter into a light trance. Facilitators, please remember to keep your breathing slow and regular, the tone of your voice calm and soothing, your muscles relaxed. Your calm voice and manner will help move people toward an altered state of consciousness.

Again, I am offering a number of different forms of relaxation techniques. If they seem incomplete to you, it's because these exercises are meant to flow into a deeper form of trance induction. Try them all and use the method that works best for you. The more frequently a particular set of imagery is used, the stronger the associations will become. The visions become more vivid and effective with each trip. For this reason, when you identify a technique that works well for you or your circle, stay with it. Over time, it will slowly adapt to your, or your group's, personality, becoming your own personal or group signal for entering trance.

When an exercise is completed, remember to discuss your experience and record it in your trance journal.

MASTERS AND HOUSTON'S MIND GAMES RELAXATION ☆

Robert Masters and Jean Houston wrote the book *Mind Games**
in 1972. The focus of this wonderful book is on different "games" that can be played while in trance. Their basic technique for entering trance is my personal favorite. It's simple, but it works well. What follows is my modification of the trance induction from *Mind Games*.

Make yourself comfortable now, so that your body is at ease and you are relaxing as fully as you can . . . Are you comfortable? . . . Good. Relax into your position, gently close your eyes, and listen closely to the sound of my voice. Through my voice you will discover that you can relax even further than you are now. Follow my voice and it will lead you into a warm state of deep relaxation. *(pause)*

We will begin . . . with your toes. Become aware of your toes. *(pause)* Feel relaxation enter into each toe . . . let them go limp . . . and relaxed. *(pause)* The relaxation moves up from your toes to your feet and ankles . . . allow them to release their stress . . . as they relax, let them go limp. *(pause)* Now your toes, feet, and ankles become completely relaxed. *(pause)*

The warmth moves up your body. Become aware of your calves . . . and knees as the relaxation makes its way up your

---

*Robert Masters, and Jean Houston, *Mind Games: The Guide to Inner Space* (New York: Dell Publishing, 1972, 1993).

legs. *(pause)* Allow them to relax . . . let go . . . and become limp. *(pause)* The relaxation continues to move up to your thighs as your legs become very, very relaxed . . . very, very limp . . . filled with deep relaxation. *(pause)*

Become aware of your pelvic area as warming relaxation fills it . . . relaxing . . . relaxing . . . becoming ever more relaxed. *(pause)*

And now the stomach . . . and on up to the chest . . . going loose and limp as it fills with relaxation. *(pause)*

Flowing down your arms now to your fingers and hands . . . Your fingers lose their tension . . . your hands go very limp and relaxed. *(pause)* Your forearms, elbows, upper arms, and shoulders all are filled with relaxation . . . going loose and limp . . . relaxing . . . relaxing . . . deep relaxation. Feel the tension slipping away . . . leaving your body relaxed and limp. *(pause)*

Bring your focus to your neck as it fills with warm relaxation . . . becomes loose . . . tension leaving . . . slipping away . . . filling with relaxation. *(pause)*

The relaxation flows up to your face . . . relaxing your jaw . . . your lips . . . your cheeks . . . and your eyes . . . Relaxation flowing up to your forehead . . . and over your entire head . . . all feeling relaxed . . . going loose and limp. *(pause)*

Your whole body is relaxing now . . . and relaxing even more . . . and more, so that you're just as limp and relaxed as a beanbag doll appears to be. *(pause)* Continue to relax . . . and while in your relaxed state listen closely to what I have to say to you . . . and you want to listen extremely closely . . . very, very closely . . . listen to my voice . . . very aware of just what is being said to you . . . and your response to what is being said to you. *(pause)*

And for a little while now, with closed eyes, remaining relaxed, breathing slowly and deeply, focus your awareness on your breath as you gently breathe in . . . and out . . . in . . . and out. *(pause)*

Let yourself feel this state of relaxation and deep comfort, all of your body at ease, and know that you can return to this state,

as often as you please, by simply working with your breath and
your muscles as you have just done. *(pause)*

COUNTING DOWN   ☆☆

There are many variations of counting down. The following is a
basic example. It should be done sitting or lying down. Some
people may fall asleep when they lie down and close their eyes.
If this is a problem, ask them to sit up, with their back supported, and gaze at some focal point, perhaps a candle flame.
Suggest that the numbers are superimposed on the visual focus.

The secret to an open-eye meditation is the "soft-eyed gaze."
Don't stare at your point. Allow your gaze to fall upon it in a
manner more like a caress than a penetration. Images may
arise, or your vision may blur as your body relaxes. Often your
eyes will gently close as you move into a deeper trance state.

Make yourself comfortable now, so that your body is at ease and
you are relaxing as fully as you can while still keeping complete
attention on the sound of my voice. Close your eyes and let
yourself relax. Relax as completely as you can. With your eyes
closed, breathe gently in . . . and out.

Behind your closed eyes, the insides of your eyelids, is your
personal mind screen. See a red number 7 on your mind
screen. *(pause)* Now let your image slowly fade away. It's replaced with a glowing orange 6 . . . it is. *(pause)* Let your image
slowly fade and replace it with a yellow 5. *(pause)*. It washes away,
and in its place is a green 4. *(pause)*. It slowly disappears. A blue
number 3 appears. *(pause)* Allow it to disappear. Deep purple 2.
(pause) Transforms into a violet number 1. *(pause)* You are in a
state of relaxation. *(pause)* I will now slowly count backward
from ten to one. With each number, you will find yourself relaxing deeper and deeper. 10 . . . 9 . . . 8 . . . 7 . . . 6 . . . 5 . . .
4 . . . 3 . . . 2 . . . 1. *(pause)* You are now completely relaxed.

POINT OF FASCINATION ☆☆☆

⌘ A candle or some other object that can be used as a focus.

This is an open-eye meditation using a point of focus. It can be done sitting or lying down. It works best if you don't cross your arms or legs. Remember to keep your spine straight.

Note of warning: You should never look straight into a candle flame, or any other flame source, for prolonged periods of time; it will cause retinal burning. Allow your gaze to rest lightly upon it, taking in the area in and around the flame.

Make yourself comfortable now, so that your body is at ease and you are relaxing as fully as you can. Let yourself relax. Relax as completely as you can and as you do, allow your gaze to fall upon an object. Let your eyes rest there, focused upon your object. Pay close attention to your point. Look at it steadily, but without straining. Don't take your attention away from it. Stay gently focused on your object, with your eyes open. It isn't difficult for you to keep your focus there. You do it easily, effortlessly. As you gaze at your point, you feel your body begin to relax. It will become very, very relaxed. You feel your feet relax. Your legs relax. Slowly you feel your body become more and more relaxed. Your hands relax. Your arms relax. You become unaware of your arms and legs, perceiving only your point as you continue to softly gaze at it. You feel your body relax. Your neck relaxes. Your head relaxes. Your eyelids are beginning to feel heavy, and your eyes are starting to feel tired as you continue to look at your object. Your head is getting heavy as you relax deeper and deeper . . . falling deeper into a state of sleep and relaxation. Your breathing is slowing and getting deeper and deeper. Your body and mind are completely relaxed, and soon you will fall deeply asleep. You're getting drowsy and sleepy. Your eyelids are now are very, very heavy. Your object is a blur; your eyes are very, very tired; they are heavy with sleep. They feel like closing. It's becoming harder to keep them open.

It would feel so good to allow them to close and go into a deep sleep. You are very, very sleepy. Your lids are drooping more and more. They are closing. Allow them to close and go into a deep and sound sleep.

Developing and Strengthening Visualization Skills

Before we begin the deeper trance inductions, we'll work on developing and strengthening visualization skills. Active imagination is the heart of magic. In order for the spell to work to its best capacity, you need to formulate your intent and "see" it—using whichever form your primary imagination takes— manifested within your mind's eye. When doing a healing spell for Aunt Betty, for instance, you want to focus on the idea of her being healthy and happy. This is the intent that is held within the minds of all those who are working for Aunt Betty's health.

This takes the development of active imagination skills. Some individuals have a very strong and creative fantasy experience. Others have difficulty remembering their dreams. One of our purposes for entering into trance is to learn how to guide and control our inner visions, to create through imagination a realm that can be explored and developed.

SPEAKING WHILE IN TRANCE

Speaking while in trance is usually a developed skill. After allowing your body to become completely relaxed and your mind guided into a lovely realm, it can seem contradictory to try to form words or to make your mouth and tongue work. It takes work to put the thought and the action together.

If creating a group mind is a part of your goal, then learning to speak while in trance is an important tool. Describing your visions to each other while they're occurring helps create shared symbolism and empathic links between members. It also helps keep people together in their experience, creating trust and familiarity.

A few exercises in this chapter will ask participants to speak out loud. Most of the responses at this level are simple, one-word answers. As the exercises continue through the other chapters, more dialogue will be requested. It takes practice to get the tongue and mouth to respond while in a deep trance state. Begin by consciously allowing air to move through your mouth. Then work on getting your tongue to move, followed by your mouth. Your first few attempts may produce only guttural noises. Each step takes you closer to reaching the speech center of your brain, which will allow the words to form while you remain in a state of deep trance. Keep at it, and soon you'll be chattering away.

Developing Visualization Skills ☆

Before beginning any of these visualization exercises, make sure you're physically and mentally prepared to begin. Use one of the relaxation techniques to enter into a light state of trance.

SHAPES AND COLORS

Close your eyes and begin to breathe gently in and out. Behind your eyes, on the back of your eyelids, see on your mind's screen the color red. And let it go. See now the color blue. And let it go. The color yellow. And let it go. The color purple. And let it go. The color green. And let it go. Continue with as many colors as you would like to project on your mind's screen. (pause)

Clear your screen, and continue to breathe gently in and out. See a square. And let it go. A triangle. And let it go. A circle. And let it go. An oval. And let it go. Continue with as many shapes as you would like to project on your mind's screen. (pause)

Clear your screen, and continue to breathe gently in and out. See again a square and fill it with the color red. Let it go. See now a triangle and fill it with the color blue. And let it go. See a circle and fill it with the color green. And let it go. Continue now with as many shapes and colors as you would like to project on your mind's screen. *(pause)*

THE HAMMER

Close your eyes and begin to breathe gently in and out. Feel in your hands a heavy hammer. Feel the roughness of the handle. The heaviness of the metal. Before you is a rock. Pick up your hammer and, with all your might, strike the rock. Feel the weight of the hammer as it hits the stone. Feel the stone give under your blow. Repeat until the stone is shattered.

THE MATCHBOX

⌘ A matchbox that contains wooden matches.

Find a matchbox that contains wooden matches. Pour out most of the matches, leaving just a few inside the box. Sit with the box, exploring it from every angle. Notice the structure of the box, how it opens and closes. Examine the matchbox, inside and out. When you feel you have absorbed as much as you can about your matchbox, put it aside and close your eyes.

Imagine your matchbox growing. It becomes so large that you can easily fit inside it. Explore every aspect of your box. Climb inside with the matches. Smell the sulfur of the match heads, the cardboard of the sides of the box itself. Crawl through every crevice, both inside and out. Climb on top of the box and notice how the sides are constructed. Find the rough strike strip and run your hands over its surface. Spend ten minutes completely focused on your matchbox.

THE PLANT

⌘ A green plant of some sort.

Place a large green plant in front of you, far enough away

that your vision can take in the entire plant. Focus your attention on the plant and begin to gently breathe in . . . and out . . . while keeping your attention focused on the plant. Notice the color of its leaves, the shape of its branches. Allow the image of the plant to sink into your consciousness . . . into your subconsciousness . . . soon it will be difficult for you to forget the plant. Nothing else matters to you right now except the plant. Your awareness is completely focused on the plant.

(Allow the meditation on the plant to continue for two or three minutes, then remove the plant but keep the focus on where the plant was.) Continue to see the plant in your mind, just as clearly as you saw its physical form. *(Meditate on the plant for an additional two or three minutes, then replace the plant in its original position.)* Continue to focus on the plant for a few more minutes.

Strengthening Visualization Skills ☆☆

THE APPLE AND THE ORANGE

⌘ An apple, orange, banana, or other fruit.

This is a standard. It keeps being used because it's very good for building visualization. Notice how it's filled with a wide variety of sensory stimuli.

Put an apple within arm's reach. Focus all of your attention on your apple. Absorb its color, its shape. Reach forward and take the apple. Hold it in your hands. Turn your apple around slowly. See the changes in the apple's skin as the light strikes it. Notice how the stem is attached. Turn your apple upside down and view where the flower kissed the fruit. Focus closely on your apple.

Bring it up to your face. Breathe in deeply and take in the scent of apple. Let its skin touch your skin. Caress your checks, your lips with its scent. Feel its smoothness, its hardness, its softness.

Bring your apple to your mouth and take a bite. Hear it crunch as your teeth bear down. Taste the juice of your apple on your tongue . . . on your lips. The mist of apple rising to fill your nostrils with its sweet scent. Slowly chew, savoring each bite, each taste. Feel it in your mouth, as you chew.

Look again upon your apple and the change a bite has caused. See its inner flesh. The groove cut by your teeth. The difference in color from the inside to the out. Take one more good look at your apple. Now put your apple to one side.

Close your eyes and see your apple as it was at the beginning when you first focused all of your attention on it. See its color, its shape. In your mind, reach forward and take the apple. Hold it in your hands. Turn your apple around slowly. See the changes in the apple's skin as the light strikes it. Notice how the stem is attached. Turn your apple upside down and view where the flower kissed the fruit.

In your mind, bring your apple to your face. Breathe in deeply and take in the scent of apple. Let its skin touch your skin. Caress your checks, your lips with its scent. Feel its smoothness, its hardness, its softness.

In your mind, bring your apple to your mouth and take a bite. Hear it crunch as your teeth bear down. Taste the juice of your apple on your tongue . . . on your lips. Smell the fragrance of apple rising to fill your nostrils with its sweetness. Slowly chew, savoring each bite, each taste. Feel it in your mouth, as you chew.

In your mind, look again upon your apple and the change the bite caused. See its inner flesh. The groove cut by your teeth. The difference in color and texture between the skin and the flesh. Take one more good look at your apple and open your eyes.

Repeat this exercise with other fruit. Because bright colors are easier to visualize, I suggest using an orange and a banana, but use whatever is available.

PAPER AIRPLANES

⌘ At least five standard pieces of paper.

Take a single sheet a paper. Focus all your attention onto this single sheet of paper. Feel the paper between your fingers. The weight of the paper. The color of the paper. Turn the paper over. Notice how the paper moves. The breeze caused by its movement. Focus completely on your paper.

We are now going to make a paper airplane. With your complete attention on your paper and your hands, fold over the left side, and then the right so that they form the point of your plane. *(figure 1)* Feel the paper between your fingers as you fold. Notice how the paper creases beneath your fingers.

Figure 1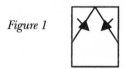

With complete focus, fold your paper in half, forming the full body of your airplane *(figure 2)* so that it looks like an elongated triangle. Continue, making your airplane without letting your concentration waver from your paper. Fold over the two edges, forming the "wings" of your plane. *(figure 3)* Pick up your plane and let it fly on the winds. Watch it as sails across the room. *(figure 4)*

Figure 2   *Figure 3*   *Figure 4*

Take another piece of paper and, with the same focus and intent, make another paper airplane. Make another. And another.

Make at least five paper airplanes. As you make each one, keep your focus completely on the paper, the motion that your hands are making, the feeling of the paper beneath your fingers, the vision of your plane flying.

Next, close your eyes and go through the physical motions without the physical paper! With complete focus, seeing and feeling the paper between your fingers, make your next plane. Feel the paper creasing and folding beneath your fingers. Feel the weight of it as you send it flying. Repeat. Make at least four more airplanes, physically going through the motions.

Make three more paper planes, each time working step by step with just your mind's hands. See the paper clearly as you pick up a sheet, fold it . . . fold it again.

Make one more plane. This time, instead of sending it flying, put it down on the floor. Like Alice in Wonderland, feel yourself begin to shrink smaller and smaller until you are small enough to ride your plane. Walk over to it. You can admire your well-crafted ship for a moment. It is a lovely plane. Climb on board and make yourself comfortable.

Feel a wind blow. It catches the underside of your glider, picking it up off the ground and sending it into the sky. You are not frightened; you know you are completely safe. Your plane circles the room. You can see your furniture, your floor. A window opens, and your plane soars outside. You can see the buildings and trees below. Feel the air rush past you as your plane glides upon the winds. Enjoy your flight for a few minutes. (pause)

Your plane heads back home. You can see the window open, and you glide back inside. One more pass around the room before it lightly lands again on the floor. Slide back out of your paper plane. It was a good flight. As you stand next to your plane, take a good stretch. Feel yourself begin to grow larger, and larger, and larger until you are your normal size. Take a deep breath and return. Welcome home!

Fine-Tuning Your Creative Visualization Skills ☆☆☆

THE SANDBOX

⌘ A box or pail three-quarters full of either sand, strips of newspaper, or Styrofoam packing peanuts. As an alternative to things that can make a mess on your rug, use a blind box—a closed box with a hole of the right size to allow a person to insert a hand and feel its contents. This should be within reach of every participant, so you'll need at least one such box or bucket for every three to four people. Various small objects of differing textures, weights, smells, and colors should be hidden in the sand or box. Here are some possibilities: a small rubber puppy chew toy, fuzzy cat toy, candle stub, hard-boiled egg (with shell), metal Matchbox car, a key, a dollar bill. Do *not* use anything that is sharp or has rough edges. Hide the objects before the group gathers. *This exercise works best if participants don't know what's hidden.*

This is a very simple exercise that helps build on creativity and visualization skills. Guide people into a light trance. Suggest that they close their eyes. Wait until all eyes are closed, then suggest that they stay closed throughout this exercise. Next, introduce the box or bucket of sand. *Note:* You may need to guide participants' hands to the box or bucket.

Place your hand on the sand. Feel its coarseness and texture. Fill your hand with sand and feel the grains slip away through the cracks and grooves of your fingers and palms. Caress the sand. Feel the grains as they part and make way for your probing fingers. Explore the feel of the sand for a moment. *(pause)* The sand holds a gift for you deep within it. Dig now, deep into the sand and find your gift. *(Pause until they find something and remove it.)*

This is your gift. Now, explore your gift. Touch it, smell it, notice its texture. *(pause)* See your gift clearly in your mind . . . its color and its shape. *(pause)* Your gift is a symbol. What does it represent? *(pause)* What message does it bring to you? *(pause)* Take a deep breath and open your eyes. Stretch and shake out your body.

Make sure you write down your experiences after the exercise. Were you able to "see" your gift clearly in your mind? How did your inner image compare with the physical object? What did it represent to you?

Building A Group Mind ☆☆☆ 🏼

Although these exercises are mostly for building group consciousness, I've included some suggestions for the solitary to adapt them.

ACROSS THE CIRCLE

All the participants should sit in a circle so that everyone is visible to everyone else. Follow the normal stretching, grounding, and centering exercises. Group breathing and relaxation techniques are a good way to prepare the circle for this exercise.

Half of this exercise is an open-eye meditation. You'll be asked to open your eyes and look around the room at each of the members of your circle. Allow your gaze to gently fall on one person . . . then the next. Don't try to burn their images into your retina. Allow them to float on to your unconscious.

During this exercise, the participants will be asked to speak while in trance. It may be difficult at first to get the words out. If your mouth refuses to work, start with making noises . . . grunts, groans, ahhs. Focus on your throat and mouth. Take a breath and allow the exhale to leave through your mouth. Practice moving your mouth and tongue. Eventually, you'll reach the speech center of your brain, which will allow the words to form while you remain in a state of deep trance, and you'll be able to express yourself while in trance.

Solitaries Follow the exercise, but allow friends or relatives to come fully to mind. When you can clearly see them standing in front of you, speak their names.

Take a deep breath, and let's all breathe together into the middle of the circle. As you continue to breathe, I invite you to open your eyes and look around at those who sit in this circle with you. Allow your gaze to fall softly for a moment on each person . . . taking in many aspects, the sweet and spicy essence of who they are. *(pause)*

When you're ready, close your eyes again . . . and let's all breathe together for a moment more. *(Pause—gently invite participants to deepen their trance a bit more. Once all are in a trance state, continue with the exercise.)*

Turn your attention to [name one person in the circle]. Allow him to come clearly into your mind. See him as he sits in this circle. Allow the sound of his voice, the scent of his skin, the touch of his hand, everything that you associate with him to fill your mind. When he becomes fully present for you, speak his name out loud. *(pause) (You can also suggest that they sing or intone each name for a while.)*

(Repeat the exercise, focusing on each member of the circle.)

When the exercise is over and all have returned to ordinary consciousness, discuss the experience and whether there were any differences between seeing someone across the circle, and seeing his form while in trance.

FRUIT SALAD

⌘ An apple, orange, banana, or other fruit. A bowl and a big spoon.

In this exercise, participants will continue to learn how to speak and respond during trance. Take your time. Although the requested responses are only one word or even grunts, it may still be difficult for some to verbalize at first. Keep practic-ing; eventually the connection to the speech center will be made, and words will flow naturally.

All participants sit in a circle so that everyone is visible to each other. The fruit is placed inside the bowl, passed to each participant, and then put in the middle of the circle. Bring the group into a light trance state. The circle should sit and focus on the fruit and the bowl for a few minutes.

Close your eyes. I invite you to clearly see the bowl of fruit in front of you. Now in your minds, you may lean forward, remove a piece of fruit from the bowl, and hold it in your hands. *(pause)*

Who has the apple? *(Allow time for someone to verbally answer. Repeat until someone indicates that she has the apple.)* Good, [name] has the apple.

Who has the orange? *(Allow time for someone to answer.)* Good, [name] has the orange and [name] has the apple.

(Continue until each person has a piece of fruit. At the end, if some-one has not indicated she has a piece of fruit, ask her what kind of fruit she is holding. It's okay to repeat fruit. As each piece of fruit is chosen, keep repeating who has which so that it's firmly set in the minds of the participants.)

Now that everyone has a piece of fruit, we're going to make fruit salad. In your imagination, I now invite you to take your fruit and prepare it for the salad.

(Allow time for the participants to add their fruit into the bowl. People should be encouraged to look around the circle and imagine oth-ers working on their fruit. After a sufficient amount of time, ask if all are done. Assume so if you get no response.)

This is a lovely fruit salad. In our minds, we will now pass the bowl around the circle so that each person can smell the fruit and eat a spoonful. Who wishes to have the bowl first? *(Wait for a response.)* Good, [name] has the fruit salad. It will now be passed around the circle. *(Allow sufficient time.)*

Now that we have had our fill, it's time to return.

The Ins—Trance Induction

A vast variety of methods and ritual forms can induce alternate states of consciousness. Most methods use a combination of different sensory inputs as a cue to the subconscious that it's time to enter into trance. Used repeatedly over time, any stimulus employed in conjunction with trance will create a sort of Pavlovian response. I know of a coven that uses tangerine essence as an anointing oil for entering sacred space and trance. They laughingly tell me they have to avoid the tangerines in the grocery store because just the smell of the fruit will cause them to "zone out" in the middle of the aisle.

When inducing trance, you may want to include a suggestion that people can return to waking reality any time they choose. This will provide a safety hatch in case an emergency arises that requires an immediate return from trance. Trance returns and unexpected or quick returns are discussed at the end of the chapter.

All the examples and exercises given are merely suggestions. Once you're familiar with the techniques, you can personalize your presentation so that it addresses your own sensory strengths. You'll eventually find the combination that works to deepen your trance and heighten your experience.

AUDITORY INDUCTION

Drums People around the world and throughout time have used sound and repeated rhythms to enter into trance. I can think of no tribal culture that doesn't use percussion to help people enter shamanic ritual trance. Drums are just one of many instruments that can be used. Rattles, clicking sticks, hitting rocks, clapping hands, tapping feet—anything that can create a rhythmic pattern can also be used to help achieve trance.

Certain percussive frequencies seem to have a greater effect than others, in particular one to four beats per second. This slow and steady rhythm is calming and easy to listen to, harmonizing with the natural beating of the human heart. Many Pagans are familiar with the use of a heartbeat drum for trance induction. Its slow, steady beat becomes a focus for the participants.

Faster frequencies, such as four to thirteen per second, resonate with brainwaves. They evoke the "get up and dance" response. Both frequencies, when sustained over a period of time, can bring people into trance.

If you don't have someone who can drum for you, a number of tapes feature a heartbeat drum for trance work. If your favorite stores or Web sites don't carry trance tapes, then find a percussion instrument and tape a ten-minute continuous drum pulse at the rate of one to four beats per second. I found that the beat

> hit, hit, pause, hit, hit, pause
> 1 , 2, 3, 4   1, 2, 3, 4

works very well. After ten minutes, hit the drum solidly, one beat per two count, four times. This will indicate to your subconscious that it's time to end your journey. Increase the rate of drumbeats, changing to four beats per second, for about one to two minutes. This change in sound pattern will help dissipate the relaxed state and move you out of trance. End your session with two strong hits on the drum, one beat per two count, returning you to full consciousness.

(Make yourself comfortable and, using one of the relaxation exercises from the previous section, enter into a light state of trance. Begin the drumbeat.)

Sit with the beat of the drum. Feel it enter your body. Feel your heart beat in sync with the drum. Become one with the drum. As it beats . . . see a path form in your mind's eye. The path leads to the side of a mountain and the opening of a cave. Through the mouth of the cave, you can hear echoed in the darkness the sound of the drum. Allow the music of the drum to lead you into the cavern. Despite the gloom of the cavity, the path is clear before you and easy to follow. You follow the path as it leads you through the tunnel, down, deep and deeper into the mountain, led by the beat of the drum. Ahead of you in the darkness, you can see light. As you continue walking, the light of the entrance grows stronger, until you step out of the tunnel and find yourself on the other side of the mountain. The sound of the drum vibrates the air around you. Before you is the source of the drumbeat. If you'd like, go sit beside the drum and experience this moment, at one with the drumbeat. If you prefer, continue to wander and explore the land of the drum. *(Pause until you hear the strong single hits on the drum, indicating that it's time to leave.)*

It's time to return. Thank the drum and walk back to the path. Following it back through the mountain . . . up and up . . . climbing higher, feeling refreshed from your visit . . . walking forward until you see the light of the other side. Step through the entrance and back to consciousness. *(two hard strikes on the drum)* Awake!

Tone Tone, sounds that vibrate as compared to the single sound created with most percussion instruments, can also be used to induce trance. To understand what I mean, compare the sounds of a drum and a gong. The drumbeat lasts a moment, while the gong continues to resonate long after it has been hit.

You may be familiar with Tibetan bells or bowls. The chanting monotone prayer that Tibetan monks practice is periodically emphasized with the single ring of a Tibetan bell. The vibration intermingles with the chanting, creating an ethereal moment for those listening. Tibetan bells produce a wavering low-frequency tone that echoes within the hearts and subconscious of the listeners. A crystal wineglass can serve as a simple version of a Tibetan bowl. Just run a moistened finger around the rim until the glass begins to make a sound. My own favorite type of bells are windchimes. I have a set in my rowan tree. On a gentle windy day, I love sitting beneath the tree and allowing the tones of the chimes to take me into a light trance.

For this exercise, repeat the drum exercise, but using a tone instrument. Note the differences between the sounds and your responses to them.

Chanting Chanting is repetitive vocal toning. The chant may be wordless, as, for example, the familiar "ommm." Unstructured vocalization, a flowing of different words or sounds, is a very effective means of raising energy and entering altered states. The sounds vibrate in the unconscious, triggering an effect. Called "speaking in tongues" by the Pentecostal and other charismatic Christian religions, this method of opening to the divine has been practiced by numerous other cultures throughout time. It's used by a number of Pagan traditions. One group that I'm familiar with calls it "singing to the moon."

My coven often uses simple chants as a means of entering into trance. When we chant together, we breathe together. When we breathe together, our energies are linked and we become one. Chants with words convey meaning, and may help reinforce the intention and the purpose of the working. A good example of this is a chant that invokes a particular Goddess, such as "strong like the ocean." It does more than induce the chant—it also focuses the chant. You would not use "strong like the ocean" to enter into trance and then do a working to Demeter for good crops.

Chants that are no more than three or four lines and within a simple musical scale work best. The idea with chant trance is to lose yourself in the sound and rhythm. This is difficult to do if there are numerous words to memorize or if the complexity of the piece forces you to keep part of your attention focused on the music. Because of their melodic tones, I find that chants in a minor key allow me to enter alternative states more easily than those in the major scale.

Sit comfortably. Relax your body, and allow yourself to enter into a light trance state. Breathe gently and deeply . . . steadily and rhythmically. Allow your mouth to open slightly. Breathe in through your nose and out through your mouth. Continue breathing until you feel the energy build within your chest and throat. When you feel motivated to do so, allow a bit of sound to come with your exhalation. Express another noise with your next out-breath. As your vocal cords warm, allow more sounds to spring out. What they are doesn't matter. It could be simply "ah" or "oh." Just let it out naturally. Continue making sounds. As you relax further, experiment with moving your mouth and tongue to produce different tones and noises.

Continue with the exercise for five to ten minutes. Allow your mouth to close. Breathe only through your nose or gently through your mouth. Sit in silence for a few minutes. When you're ready, return to full awareness.

Environmental Music Environmental music is made of sounds found in nature: ocean waves, falling rain, forest sounds, bubbling brooks, waterfalls, and so forth. It may, or may not, include instrumental music that blends with or mimics the environmental sounds. Environmental music is sometimes used as background noise to heighten the senses and give greater dimension to a pathworking. It can, however, be used on its own for inducing trance states. Thunderstorms, the crackling of faraway thunder, and the sound of rain against my window can effectively put me in trance. I'm sure it brings up some long-forgotten memory of childhood when I would sit in my bedroom listening to the storms moving through my valley home.

Environmental music can be thought of as a form of "white noise." It's pleasant to listen to and blocks out any unwanted noise. The repetition of sound allows your mind to slide away into an altered state of consciousness.

You can make your own environmental music tape, although this is actually fairly difficult. There are a number of commercial lines that feature different environmental sounds.

Pick your favorite environment: ocean, stream, thunderstorm, brook, or what have you. Sit quietly. Relax your body. When you're ready, turn on your tape. Sit with the music for at least five to ten minutes. When you're ready, return to full awareness.

You might also try some meditative music, either from indigenous cultures (for example, Navaho flute music) or New Age composers. Unlike simple tones, music will set a specific mood. Carefully chosen, this can support and augment some of the specific meditations that you'll find later in the book. Just be sure the mood in the music and the pathworking are compatible.

Structured Music

⌘ Two different pieces of music, each about three minutes in length. Both pieces should be soothing, full-bodied, and rich in tone, but noticeably different from each other.

Instrumental music, which contains a recognizable melody that may be modified by harmony or counterpoint, can be used as a background for meditation or for pathworking exercises. Consider how a film's background music supports and amplifies the emotional undertones of the plot. Music can easily do the same for ritual or magic.* Different types of music will trigger different emotional reactions. Some covens use a particular piece of music to play in the background whenever sacred space

---

*Alwyn Rees and Brinley Rees, *Celtic Heritage: Ancient Tradition in Ireland and Wales* (London: Thames & Hudson, 1961), p. 137.

is being created. Just like the repetition of a particular scent of oil, the music reminds us to shift consciousness. Choose your music carefully. It can either heighten or detract from the experience.*

Are you sitting comfortably? Let yourself feel this state of relaxation and deep comfort, all your body at ease, completely relaxed and comfortable.

In a moment, I'm going to play some music for you, some very sensuous music, but first you should know that it's possible for you to hear music very differently from any way you've probably ever heard it before.

It's possible—and this is what you will do—to hear music over the entire surface of your body. Your entire body can be stimulated by the music, so that your entire body will hear. Your body is able to experience music as touch sensations, music touching you everywhere.

Now, when I play this music for you, you are going to use this capacity of your skin to hear the music with your whole body, and to be touched by the music, all of your flesh caressed and excited by this music.

It will be an extremely pleasurable experience, the music swirling around you, passing in and out of your body, as your sensitivity increases, as you become more and more sensitive, more and more responsive to the music, until you are experiencing the music with complete joy with all of your body, your flesh, your skin, your muscles. All will become totally aware and involved with the music. And I will play it for you now!

(Play music, then pause.)

And now I will play some more music for you, and this time all of your senses will participate in the music.

You will see the music, taste the music, smell the music, as well as hearing and being touched by the music. All your senses

---

*Masters and Houston, *Mind Games,* pp. 8–18 (excerpted and modified).

will become involved, each responding in its own way to the music. Each response adding another dimension to your enjoyment of the music . . . your senses coming together creating an orchestra of sensation. And I will play the music for you now. *(Play music, then pause.)*

Know that you can always listen to music this way, look at a flower in this way. You can enjoy the many facets of the Mother Earth, at any time, on your own or with a group. You can worship her by the offering of your appreciation. And this act of loving contemplation is also very good for you. You can do this as often as you like.

VISUAL INDUCTION

As any psychology student can tell you, using a visual focus to help change consciousness is a widely known and used technique. Physical impressions have touched the human psyche since the beginning of time. Paintings and statues predate writing and are the oldest records we have of human cultures. The inner need that motivated our ancestors to physically express emotional or religious constructs remains central in modern art and music. Art touches us on deep levels and moves us in many ways. Most Pagans and Witches have statues on our altars. The images representing the Gods and Goddesses bring us closer to them, providing a focus for our devotion and for our magic.

Visual trance work uses an object as a point of concentration for the purpose of altering perception. An exercise using a candle flame introduced earlier in this chapter is a popular form of using a visual focus to induce trance. Almost any object, from statues to rocks, can be used to reach into the unconsciousness. This is the heart of many divination forms: focusing attention on a particular image and allowing imagination to flow.

Many Witches use some sort of light source as their point of concentration. In addition to candles, the full moon, light reflected on water, and a black mirror are quite appropriate for magical workings. Some gaze at their reflection in a handheld mirror. A candle placed just below the line of vision between you and the mirror may heighten this technique. Others prefer to look into something blank, like a solid-colored wall.

Visual Induction Exercise
⌘ A handheld mirror.

Begin by relaxing your body and your face. Place or hold a mirror away from your face and at eye level. Allow your eyes to go slightly out of focus. See the immediate surroundings around your mirror, then slowly bring your vision in closer to the reflection. Allow your eyes to relax in whatever way feels most comfortable or easiest. You will probably see your image "swimming" in and out of optical focus. Your eyes will be making micromovements to track the image.

At this point there are a couple of methods used. The first is to allow yourself to "fall" into your point of focus so that it completely engulfs you and you are drawn into trance. The second is to make a conscious effort to stabilize the image in the mirror, which will then move you into trance. Try them both and see which works for you.

Abstract Patterns Abstract geometric, nonstructured shapes or runic patterns are used as a visual stimulus that works on the subconscious. One form, called sigils, is used in many magical systems as a sort of shorthand, a method of translating complex concepts or entire essences of a spell into a single symbol that can easily be focused upon. The subconscious mind converts the symbol back into its original full form, sort of like a "Zip drive."

Physically tracing patterns can be effective. In one Wiccan study group in New York, each student creates a finger maze out of clay, and then uses it. Slowly tracing the spiral form with a finger helps teach the student how to bring focus inward and enter into a light trance. Physically walking a maze uses the same principle. It becomes a form of moving meditation. Finding a maze to walk or a room to construct one in, however, can be difficult.

A mandala is a geometric pattern that represents the cosmos. While it's easy to purchase an already existing mandala, creating your own will develop a deeper connection with the image. The crafting integrates into your mind your personal associations with the various colors and symbols. These meanings are later unleashed during focused meditation upon the mandala. If you cannot draw, try creating a God's Eye out of colorful yarn and two sticks. Another alternative is to find coloring books with mandala imagery that you can fill in with paints or crayons.

Pick one of the previous examples of abstract, geometric, patterned inductions (finger spiral, mandala, sigil) and create your own. As you are fashioning your symbol, keep its intended purpose clearly in your mind (to instill calm, induce light trance, open intuition, or what have you). When you're done, verbalize the image's intended use. This will help solidify the connection within both your conscious and subconscious mind.

When completed, put it to one side for at least twenty-four hours. When you're ready, go through the normal steps to prepare yourself for trance: stretching, grounding, relaxation technique. Then, while in a light trance, spend time lightly focusing on your pattern.

THE BODY-DANCE AND MOTION

With their right arms pointed to the sky and their left turned down, white robes flowing around them as they slowly twirl around and around, the swirling dervishes of the Sufi have trance dance down to an art form. Trance dance, a form of kinesthetic induction, uses breath control and physical motion. With exertion, blood—along with increased oxygen—surges throughout the body. Ecstatic movement puts the brain into overload as it tries to keep the body standing upright. Put the two together and you have a powerful induction into trance state.

Note: Those who have a history of heart disease or other medical concerns where physical exercise may be dangerous should *not* attempt this form of trance. This doesn't mean that, if working with a group, you have to sit on the sidelines while others have all the fun. Whenever we do a public ritual that includes a spiral dance or other form of dance, we extend an invitation for people to come sit in the center of the circle, where they will find percussion instruments such as drums and rattles. We even provide a few chairs for any who might need them. All voyagers get to participate fully, according to their own ability and inclination.

Stillness, as found in Hatha Yoga, is another familiar form of trance technology. Certain meditation postures affect muscle tension and blood flow, while stimulating nerve points. These postures have a direct physiological effect. When placed in a religious or ritual context, a psychological connection arises. The mutual reinforcement of the physical and spiritual aspects helps heighten the experience among believers.

Body-Dance
⌘ Music, preferably continuous, with a strong enough beat to dance.

First follow the standard pretrance steps. Have people standing. Turn on the music. You do not need to use complex steps in order to enter trance. Simpler is actually better, especially if it's a participatory dance. A grapevine, which is an easy cross-step, or a skipping step, works well with a group. If you're alone, let your body decide its own movements. Focus on the music, not your physical expression of it. Allow your mind to let go of all thoughts as the music and the motion take you into an altered state. When done, record your experiences.

ॐ

As you can see, there are many methods for releasing daily issues and entering into a light trance. Each individual or group
will develop unique methods and practices, based upon their
beliefs, that will bring clarity of purpose and allow participants
to slip easily into a trance state. Just as some people like rock
and others classical music, different people have different tastes
and require different stimuli to induce trance. And some people like both kinds of music in different situations. The wider
your personal range of choice, the better.

PATHWORKING INDUCTIONS

When using a pathworking, the participants are verbally guided
into a trance state and brought to a particular inner environment. Any of the previous methods mentioned can be incorporated into the induction. For example, you could do trance
dancing until a heightened sense has been achieved. The pathworking would then build upon the experience, bringing participants deeper into a trance state and leading them to the
journey work.

While other methods can be employed, guided meditation is
traditionally used as the primary method to enter trance when
the goal is a pathworking journey. One reason for this is that simultaneously using too many differing methods will cause sensory overload. Too much and you'll find yourself unable to
enter trance at all.

Below are a number of different trance induction scripts.
They are meant to immediately follow relaxation exercises.
One should slide right into the next without a pause. Those
listed are suggestions. Once you have the general idea of how
one is fashioned, experiment, be creative, and write your own.

The end of each trance induction has been intentionally left open. It should continue with the entering of the safe home or coven temple. How to create this sacred space will be discussed later.

When an exercise is completed, remember to discuss and record your experience in your trance journal.

General Introduction A general introduction indicates to the journeyer that the trance induction is beginning. From here you should continue into one of the various methods: the staircase, elevator, escalator, slide, whatever works for you or your group.

Empty your mind of all thoughts and cares. Feel your body become relaxed. Breathe gently in . . . and out . . . and find the rhythm of your breath . . . Move comfortably with it. Relaxing into the darkness behind your closed eyes, and the gentleness of your breathing.

As you continue to breathe, a light begins to form in your mind's eye. And in the warmth of this light, before you a doorway forms. It stands open and waiting for you. You feel no fear as you approach it because you know that this opening leads to wonderful adventures. You look forward to passing through it. You cross the threshold of the doorway and find yourself . . .

Going down the winding staircase. You cross the threshhold of the doorway and find yourself at the top of a stone staircase. It is a very old staircase. You can smell the deep, musty scent of wet rock. The ancient stones spiral their way down and around and into the darkness below. You cannot see where they end. But you are not afraid. Eagerly you begin your descent down into the darkness . . . Moving down and down . . . One step at a time . . . going deeper . . . and deeper . . . down deeper, . . . descending the stairs . . . moving lower . . . and lower . . . deeper . . . and deeper . . . with each step into the darkness below . . . the stairs winding their way down . . . and down . . . descending lower . . . and lower . . . one step at a time you make your way down.

Below you, in the dark, you can now see a warm glow of a

light. It is the outline of a large ancient door. There is a brightness on the other side of the door. The strength of that brightness is pushing its light through the cracks, etching the door's
outline in the darkness. You step off the last step of the staircase
and approach the door. When you're ready, turn the handle
and open it. It swings open to your touch, and you step forward . . .

The Elevator   You cross the threshold and find yourself . . .
before an elevator door. On one side it has a big button with an
arrow pointing downward. When you're ready, reach forward
and push the button. The elevator doors slide open and the car
stands waiting for you. You feel no fear as you approach the entrance because you know that this elevator will take you to wonderful adventures. You look forward to passing through the
doorway. You cross the threshold and enter the elevator.

As you look around the inside of the elevator, you can see a
button with a big downward arrow on it. Reach forward and
push the button. The doors slide closed and the elevator begins
to move downward. Above the doors numbers are reflected.
They show you the progression of your descent. A red number
7 appears. It slowly fades away as your car continues move downward. It is replaced with an orange 6. It slowly fades and is replaced with a yellow 5. Your elevator continues to descend
down and down. The 5 disappears and in its place is a green 4.
Still lower. The 4 slowly disappears. A blue number 3 appears.
Moving still down and down. The 3 evaporates and a deep purple 2 is displayed. Transforming into a violet number 1. The
elevator slows . . . and . . . 10 . . . 9 . . . 8 . . . 7 . . . 6 . . . 5 . . . 4 . . .
3 . . . 2 . . . 1 it stops. The doors slide open and you step for-
ward . . .

Going Up? The Escalator   You cross the threshold of the doorway and find . . . before you is an escalator, the steps and the
handrail mechanically and slowly moving upward. You cannot

see where they end. But you are not afraid. I invite you to step forward onto the moving stairs. You can feel the movement as the escalator glides forward and you begin your climb. Up and up the escalator carries you. Higher and higher . . . Continuing to move slowly . . . climbing up . . . and up . . . climbing higher . . . carried by the escalator stairs . . . Moving up . . . and up . . . higher . . . and higher . . . you still cannot see the top, but you move farther upward . . . the stairs slowly climbing, carrying you on them . . . moving up . . . You can start to see the top of the escalator. You are almost there. Continuing up. The top coming closer into view as you move toward it. Up higher and higher . . . until the stairs reach their highest point. You let go of the railing and step forward onto the platform.

All Aboard!—The Subway Train

👬 This trance induction is meant to help develop a group mind. Participants will be asked to vocalize during this working. While the exercise is group-oriented, it can be used equally well in individual practice. Just remove the suggestions of the other members of your party. *A note of caution:* The imagery used in this exercise may not be suitable for those with epileptic conditions.

You cross the threshold and find yourself . . . at the entrance to a subway station. You can see stairs making their way down into the station. Beneath your feet you can hear and feel the rumbling and squealing of train wheels. The scent of fuel is on the air. The entrance stands open and waiting for you. You feel no fear as you approach it, because you know that this opening leads to wonderful adventures. You look forward to passing through it.

You put your foot on the first step and eagerly begin your descent into the dark . . . moving down . . . one step at a time . . . going deeper . . . and deeper . . . with each step into the darkness below . . . Below you, you see the glow of the platform lights. Each downward step takes you closer to it. You reach the last step and find yourself at the token booth on train level.

Before you is a turnstile, the entrance to the train platform. You realize that you have a subway token in your hand. I invite you to step forward and place your token into the turnstile, push the bar, and enter the lit platform. At either end, you can see the dark entrance to the subway tunnel. Before you stands a subway car—but the doors are closed. It is waiting for everyone to meet on the platform. Who has arrived?

(Wait for responses.) Can you see [name] on the platform? *(Wait for responses.)* Good. Can you see [name] on the platform? *(Wait for responses. Continue with the names and reinforcements of seeing all participants until you are sure that all are present in and at the same stage of trance.)*

The doors of the train open. Everyone, make your way across the platform and into the car. Find a seat. Sit and be comfortable. This train is going to take us on an adventure together. When we arrive at our destination, together we will all get off the train. Together we will share and experience this adventure. Is everyone on the train? *(Wait for responses.)* Good. The doors of the train close and it begins to move slowly forward into the dark tunnel opening ahead. You can feel the train moving down into the darkness.

Look out the window. You can see the darkness through the window; then, a flash of light as you pass by a signal marker. Darkness again. A flash of light. You keep your eyes looking out the window as darkness . . . light . . . darkness . . . passes by. The train moves faster . . . light . . . darkness . . . light . . . dark . . . light . . . it speeds up faster . . . light . . . dark . . . light . . . dark . . . flickering light moving faster and faster, like a strobe. Keep your eyes on the flashing light. Feel your train moving faster as it moves you deeper . . . down . . . moving you deeper . . . until . . . there is only light. You feel the train slow down . . . and stop. The doors open. All stand and make your way to the threshold . . . and move out onto the platform.

The Outs—Returning From Trance

It's every bit as important to take care in returning or bringing your participants back from trance as it was entering or leading others into that state. Although it's true that people will eventually return to full consciousness, not doing a return sequence can leave folks out wandering around ungrounded. You can be assured that aftereffects will occur. An individual who has had an incomplete return may show atypical behavior, which doesn't relate to any current life situations. Some of the possible symptoms are:

- Spaciness, lack of concentration, lapses in memory.
- Flashbacks, emotionality, mood swings.
- Disturbing dreams or visions, persistent unwanted thoughts or daydreams.
- Nausea, dizziness, unfocused eyes, difficulty with balance or mobility.

RECALLING SOMEONE FROM TRANCE

The return should not be rushed. The same graduated steps that were taken to enter into trance should be used to return. This means that it takes the same amount of time to come back from trance as it did to enter into that state. Failure to allow this time may cause an incomplete return, leading to the above-mentioned problems. Take your time, and reentry will be much smoother.

The best method is to come back the way you came in. If you traveled down a staircase, then walk back up those stairs. If you took the elevator, then enter it, push the up button, and watch the colored numbers go back up to ten. If you took the up escalator, then take the down ten. If you took the train, then gather your troops and get back on it to return home. Repeat the induction exercise but in reverse, returning to your original location.

Reinforce the knowledge that with each step, number, movement, or what have you, you are becoming more awake. Also
emphasize that the voyager will return refreshed, relaxed, and
looking forward to the next adventure. This will help set up a
subconscious familiarity and comfort with trance states, making
it easier to return with each journey.

Here is an example of a return. The staircase method was
used to induce the trance, so it's applied for the return. You'll
notice that I begin the return from the individual's safe inner
home, which is where the traveler would be leaving from. The
creation and purpose of your inner safe space will be discussed
in chapter 3.

Take one more look around your inner home. Know that it will
be here waiting for you whenever you choose to return, but for
now it's time to return to ordinary consciousness. Turn around
and see the large ancient door. When you're ready, turn the
handle and open it. It swings open to your touch. This has been
a good journey, but it's time to return home. You know when
you awaken you will feel refreshed, with no aches or pains. Just
relaxed and looking forward to the next adventure.

Step across the threshold and into the darkness of the stair-
well. Find yourself at the bottom of the stone staircase. The
door closes behind you. The ancient stones spiral their way up
and around and into the darkness above. You cannot see where
they end. But you are not afraid. You begin your climb up into
the darkness . . . Moving up with each step, climbing higher
and higher . . . One step at a time . . . With each step you are
becoming more awake . . . climbing higher and higher . . . feeling fine, feeling relaxed as you journey upward . . . with each
step easily moving up the stairs . . . becoming more awake . . .
moving higher . . . you can see a light above you . . . each step
taking you up toward the light . . . as you move closer to it, you
can begin to feel your body . . . with each step becoming more
awake . . . as you get closer to the top of the stairs, you can begin

to hear noises around you . . . becoming more awake . . . you reach the top and see the doorway before you . . . take a deep breath . . . step through the doorway . . . open your eyes and . . . become fully *awake!*

ADDITIONAL METHODS FOR RETURN

Just because a person has his eyes open doesn't mean that he has fully returned from a trance state. It's a good idea to check in with everyone to make sure all have returned. If there are indications that someone still has one foot in the other realm, use one or a combination of the following additional measures to help him return.

- *Count-up:* This is a simple counting upward from one to ten that helps bring the consciousness to full waking reality. It can be incorporated as a regular part of any of the trance return techniques or, as will be seen later, as a method for a quick return.
- *Repeating of Name:* Say the individual's name several times. Have her repeat her name back to you and identify others in the room.
- *Movement:* Light stretching and gentle movement to get the blood flowing can also help.
- *Sound:* A bell or other common sound can often fully return someone from trance.
- *Touch:* Physical touch, either a hand lightly placed on a shoulder or a full body hug, helps ground individuals back into their bodies.
- *Food:* Like touch, food is very grounding. Something solid like dark bread is a good grounder. I have a friend who swears by meat (of course, this doesn't work for vegetarians). It's one reason why sharing nourishment is included as a part of ritual work.
- *Imagery:* Similar to the exercises that brought relaxation to

each portion of the body, in this version voyagers imagine themselves climbing up through each portion of their body, filling it with awareness as they go.

Even when it appears that all have returned to waking consciousness, it's always a good safety measure to still use one of the simpler methods, such as name recall, on top of the trance return.

HELPING HAND

If you're facilitating a trance in which a participant is in distress and gentle reassurances fail to calm him, or if he's nonresponsive, you may need to go in and help bring him back to waking consciousness. Again using imagery, gently tell the trancer that you're going to help lead him back to consciousness. With reassurances that no matter how far he travels, he can never really lose himself or his physical realities, explain that you're standing beside him and are taking his hand to help him return home. Physically touching or taking his hand may be used as a reinforcement. Use your own judgment on whether this would help or not. Verbally lead him first to his safe space and then to his stairs, elevator, or whatever method was used to enter into trance. Use the word *we*, reinforcing that he is not alone. "We are beginning to climb the stairs . . ." "We are entering the elevator . . ." Switch back to the *you* pronoun as you finish the ascent to full waking. "You can feel your body . . . you can hear the noises around you . . ."

If you're working with a group, the members will need to decide before they enter trance whether, if a problem arises, to return along with the troubled individual or remain in trance. If the decision was to remain in trance, suggest that they continue exploration while you attend to the one who is experiencing difficulties. Once you feel that individual has returned and is all right, return to the group. Reaffirm that they are still in trance and continue with their adventure.

UNEXPECTED OR QUICK RETURN

A few years ago, I facilitated a workshop at a pagan festival that included a guided meditation. All the participants were sitting or lying on the carpeted floor of the hotel in a comfortable state of trance when suddenly the fire alarm went off. This, of course, jarred everyone to consciousness. Because of the abrupt return, however, they were left half in trance, unfocused and spacey. Before running out the door, I did a ten-count to help bring them back to a wakeful state.

A ten-count is one way of quickly bringing someone back from an altered state. A short version would be something like:

Return to breathing evenly. Focus on your breath. I am going to count upward from 1 to 10. With each number you are going to feel yourself returning to consciousness feeling refreshed and awake . . . 1 becoming more awake . . . 2 awakening more . . . 3 returning to consciousness . . . 4 refreshed and awake . . . 5 with every number . . . 6 coming more awake . . . 7 feeling your body . . . 8 hearing the noises around you . . . 9 opening your eyes . . . 10 fully *awake.*

It can take less than a minute. This method acts as a cue to the consciousness, which was put to sleep through the trance induction, that it must return. The quick count-up should be followed up with physical touch or other method for trance return. I had people repeat their names and mine before leaving the room. Thankfully, the hotel wasn't on fire; someone's lit incense had been put to close too a sensor, triggering the alarm.

☙❧

CHAPTER THREE

We Send a Voice Seeking a Sign—Meditations for Learning

By now, if you've completed the work in chapter 2, you're familiar with entering into and returning from trance states. Each time you cross the threshold, you strengthen your familiarity with trance. As your skills develop, you'll find it easier to slide into and out of alternative states of consciousness at will. When you begin to trust your abilities, you'll allow yourself to enter into deeper states, opening up more creative possibilities. With practice, you'll become more adept at your active imagination. This will add greater dimension to your adventures. You'll find it easier to grasp and retain more of the details of your visions. Even those individuals who have difficulties or are resistant to entering into an alternate state will eventually learn, through practice, how to easily move into and out of trance. It takes perseverance.

We intentionally enter into trance for many reasons. One purpose is to look inward for guidance and answers. This chapter is devoted to journeys into trance for the purpose of learning and gaining insights: about trance, yourself, your environment, your beliefs, your Gods and Goddesses. The exercises are meant to reveal, without being confrontational. As you travel, remember that no matter how far you wander, you can always return home. You have power and control over your own inner environment.

Before beginning, remember to prepare your environment (turn off the phone, predict and prevent other distraction) and be emotionally ready for the journey. Trivial stresses and worries that you don't plan on working with in the circle should be packed away. You should also have already completed the pre-trance steps (stretching, grounding, relaxation, and induction) and be in an alternate state.

At the completion of each of the pathworkings, remember to discuss and record in your trance journal your experiences and reactions to them. Also, pay special attention to your dreams for the next few days, and record them. Review your journal before the next meeting to see whether you notice any patterns worth examining further.

There's No Place Like Home: Your Personal Space

When I was a child, we used to play a form of nighttime freeze tag. The goal of the game was to walk around the outside of our house without being tagged by the one child who was "it." This trickster was allowed to hide anywhere in the yard waiting for the other players to walk by. In the dark, in a yard filled with heavy foliage, she could be difficult to spot until she was right on top of you. When this hidden child sprang out from the darkness, usually with some growling and other monster-type noise, we would all run screaming with excitement. We would head as fast as we could for our sanctuary, which was our open porch. As soon as we jumped on the cement floor, we were safe. The "it" person wasn't allowed to touch us when we were in our "safe space." She would have to return to the shadows and wait until we ventured out again.

For most trance journeys, you begin and end your adventures through your personal space. It's your sanctuary. It acts as a portal between the worlds—sort of a waiting room where you can change your clothes and your mind and get ready for play. It's a platform from which you spring out to other worlds, and a place for quiet reflection. As in my childhood game, nothing can harm you in your "safe space."

Each person's inner home is as unique as the person is. Mine looks like a small study in an old castle. It contains a very large fireplace (with a warm crackling fire) and a big, comfortably overstuffed green chair just right for curling up in with a good book. Lots of old books fill the dark wooden bookcases that stand around the room. A serving chest sits to one side near the chair. It usually has on it a hot pot of coffee or tea ready for me. The room feels warm, comforting, and inviting. There is the pleasant scent of old books and dry stone floors. A big ancient door with heavy metal hinges is the entrance to my inner home. It always opens easily with a light touch of my hand. Although I don't always see them, there are other doors on different walls in my castle room. They make themselves known to me when I'm adventuring. These are the doors that I take when I go off on my vision journeys.

The point of an inner space is that it's a place where you can feel completely safe, comfortable, and at home. It's your own personal and private location. It needn't be a room. It can be a cottage filled with herbs and cats located at the end of wooded path. It could be a stone circle, with the spaces between the stones being entrances to different worlds, or perhaps a garden, walled or not, from which you can travel. This is your personal space, a place where you feel comfortable and at peace. Creating this space is your first task before walking any farther in the realms.

CREATING YOUR INNER HOME

Before you do a personal sacred space pathworking, sit down and think about what your ideal space might look like. Is it indoors or outdoors? If indoors, is it a room or house? If a room, what kind of room? If outdoors, what kind of environment? A seaside retreat? A forest glen? Sunny skies or nightfall? What kinds of things would you expect to see in this space? What would you expect to smell? Taste? Hear?

If a facilitator is guiding you to your space, before entering trance discuss with him what you think your inner home might look like and the objects that you believe you'll find within it. If you're working with someone who needs help on creating this space, have her remember and talk with you about times and places in her life when she felt completely safe and happy. Ask her if she'd like, in her mind, to revisit one of those places and claim it as her inner home. For example, I know someone who spent many happy hours as a child playing by the seaside. Her safe space is a portion of that beach.

While within your safe inner home, you'll be asked to find a "marker" that represents your connection to this inner space. One suggestion is to see if there's an object similar to one in your waking world that can act as a material-world anchor. For example, I really do own an oversized green chair; however, it's not exactly the same chair that's in my inner home. Still, it reminds me of my connection. I also know someone who has a small, crystal ball. It sits on the windowsill of both her inner and her outer space, reinforcing her link between the two.

The following exercise was given to me by my friend and covener Hare as an example of how to find and claim your inner sanctuary.

When you're ready, do the relaxation and trance induction as usual, then . . .

Open your inner eyes. You find yourself in a forest glade before the mouth of a large cave. The warmth of the day is wearing upon you, and you find yourself drawn by the cool darkness—and the mystery of what lies within sparks your curiosity. Would you like to go in? *(a presumed yes)*

You enter the cave and let the coolness enter in and sweep away fatigue and worry. Your eyes quickly adjust and, though it's dimly lit, you're able to see well enough to find firm and comfortable footing.

Near the back of the cave, you see a tunnel with a staircase leading down into darkness and feel yourself drawn toward it. Calmly and without fear you begin your descent, quietly sinking deeper and deeper into stillness as you take each step downward into the Earth. *(The bottom is reached.)*

Stepping off the last step, you peer forward into the darkness around you. Far ahead is a pinprick of light that calls to you. The light calls with all the promise of comfort that you seek. It draws you with all the conviction of courage you wish to find. It offers the sanctuary of safety that allows you to exist as you truly are, without need of mask or manipulation. You find your steps quickening as you rush forward to fulfill that promise and accept that offer.

As you draw near, you see the light is actually the opening of the tunnel. You step into *(insert the general location type that was indicated in the prepathworking talk)*. You find yourself totally at comfort here, well at ease and relaxed, yet filled with the knowledge and conviction that this is where you are meant to be. Look around you. Etch every detail of this newly found haven into your memory.

(Give the journeyers a few minutes to quietly explore the world they have found.)

You are totally at home and at ease here. Do you wish to claim this area as your home? *(If yes, have them interact with their landscape. For example, if it's an outdoor location, they can plant a tree or herbs; if indoors, they might rearrange or bring in furniture.)*

Look around you for a small marker or token that you feel best represents the tie between your space and yourself. Touch it: Pick it up and cradle it if you can. Take in the texture, the scent, the color and sounds that it brings forth. Now caringly and respectfully place your mark, sigil, or just your intention into your token. Let it key into you and your special place. Set it down lovingly in a spot that seems meant for it. This is your token; this is your key. This marks this spot as yours and yours only. Everything that loves you will recognize this as your claim and mark. Nothing that can harm you will ever chance to be in its presence. This is now truly your home and sanctuary. Sit quietly in your new home now, and when you're ready, start walking back toward the tunnel that gave you entrance.

Reverse the tunnel journey back to consciousness.

A COVEN SPACE

Covens that are working toward forming a group mind may want to create a shared coven meeting space or sanctuary as a base for group explorations in the inner realms. This is a mutually agreed-upon and collectively created environment where the members meet before heading off into adventures. The subway platform in the "Subway Train" trance induction in chapter 2 is a great example of this concept. This is the location where the group formed and recognized each other as participants in the same vision.

Careful thought, conversation, and compromise should go into creating this inner location. All members must be in agreement in order for it to work to its fullest potential. It needn't be a complex space. I know of one coven whose inner sanctuary is the coven temple room. When in trance, they enter the space through "doorways" and see the space just as it is (minus their physical forms). They then travel together though a tapestry previously hung up on one wall for this purpose. They return through this same portal when their adventure is done. Finally, they leave the temple through their individual "doorways" to return to full consciousness in the temple room.

Another variation on this theme is to see your circle in your physical temple in your mind's eye. The room grows darker and darker until you are in complete blackness. Then a warm light forms in a portion of the room. Within this light, a doorway is revealed. This is the portal to the astral realms.

Some groups create very elaborate temple structures of crystal and topaz. Others prefer the stone circle at night. I know one that meets in a meadow under an old oak tree. Another has a castle where they meet as a group in the common room. Different rooms within the castle lead to adventures. In addition, each person has his own personal room or space within the castle walls. What your space will be depends upon the nature and abilities of your group and its members. The point is that it should be a space where all feel comfortable.

Once the group sanctuary is formed, there are a number of possibilities for group travel. Participants can choose to meet in their astral space but then travel the realms separately. Think of it as arriving in the hallway of an office building that's lined with doors. Each door leads to a different room. The group can meet in the corridor and then choose individual doors through which to walk. A group mind is still being formed in that everyone is entering and leaving together, but each person is encouraged to have her own experience.

Another alternative is similar to the subway scenario. The group meets in the coven sanctuary and then leaves together on a journey. While on this journey, the group members may wander around the same environment and interact or not, depending upon the nature of the trip.

Another possibility is to follow one participant, allowing that person to have an adventure supported by all circle members. The key to all of this, whether the group goes off exploring together or separately, is the mutually agreed-upon starting point, the group's shared space in the inner realms. The following is just one suggestion on how to form this very important collective resource.

Stretch, relax, and do your trance induction as usual, then . . .

Open your inner eyes . . . and you see nothing. It is gray all around you, flat and dull. Above you it is gray. Below you it is gray. Around you it is gray. It's as if you have walked into a sterile, gray fog. You are not frightened. You know that this cloud is an illusion. Behind the emptiness you know there is form. Although you cannot yet see them, can you sense the familiar presence of others near you? *(a presumed yes)* You realize that what you feel is the love of your friends. Allow yourself to open to the trust-filled connection that you share, one that does not need a mask or manipulation.*(Wait a moment.)* You are relaxed and ready for whatever occurs in this formless space.

You notice a small table. It sparks your curiosity. Would you like to go look at it? *(a presumed yes)* The table is empty, but you instinctively know that there is supposed to be something resting on it. The table has attracted all who share this space with you. You can feel them forming a circle around this table, all staring intently at its surface. This is your group altar, the center of your dreams. It is a point for gathering. Around this altar, you will form your coven temple.

One at a time, come forward and speak the name you wish to be called by in this sacred realm and offer a gift of self to this place and to this group. Begin when you're ready. *(After each name and gift, group members should be asked if they can clearly see the group member.)*

> Example: *Aurora. My gift is laughter.*
> *Can you see Aurora?* (Wait for response.) *A rush of fresh air blows past you. It tickles your nose and ruffles your hair. You can hear laughter upon the winds. Your hearts fill with joy.*
> *RompWell. My gift is dance.*
> *Can you see RompWell?* (Wait for response.) *Feel the warmth of the sun shining, warming your bodies. Feel your energy surging through you.*

Join hands, if you will. You can feel your circle of friendship. Close your inner eyes. Take three breaths together in this space. As you open your inner eyes again, you see it is no longer gray, but transformed. (*Replace with the general environment location previously discussed.*)

You find yourself totally comfortable here—at ease and relaxed. You look around and see the faces of people you know well, of friends. Everyone look around you at your temple. Etch every detail of this newly found haven into your memory.

(*Give the journeyers a few minutes to quietly explore the world they have found.*)

You are totally at home and at ease here. Do you wish to claim this area as your coven temple? (*a presumed yes*) Look around you for a small marker or token that you feel best represents the tie between your space and yourselves. What have you found? (*Allow different people to find things and make suggestions until all present agree upon one object.*) Pick it up and pass it around if you can. Take in the texture, the scent, the color, and sounds that it brings forth. Now caringly and respectfully place your individual marks, sigils, or just your intention into your token. Let it key into you and your special place. Set it down lovingly on the altar table that was meant for it. This is your group's token. This is your key. This marks this spot as yours. Everything that loves you will recognize this as your claim and mark. Nothing that can harm you, individually or as a group, will ever chance to be in its presence. This is now truly your home and sanctuary. Sit quietly in your new home. (*Allow them to sit for another minute.*)

It's time to return. Start walking back toward the tunnel that gave you entrance.

Reverse the tunnel journey back to consciousness. Everyone should discuss what they saw as soon as they return.

A few variations on the theme:

• Create or choose a symbol. It could represent the group or have some magical significance. Take apart the symbol—

for example, a pentacle—giving a portion to each member of the group. Each person will have one of the points and the center. When all have come together in trance, each member presents his piece. The symbol is reconstructed, each joined piece adding energy to the creation of the space.

• Have people bring gifts of Earth, Air, Fire, and Water. Each element as it is added brings with it greater dimension to the space. For example, Earth can start. Participants would be able to see the space—but it would be flat, like a photograph. Air could add noise and scents. Fire could instill life energy. Water would open the intuition or emotions.

• All participants meet on a boat dock in an underground passage. At the dock is a boat. Each member takes a seat in the boat. The boat drifts down a river and out in the sunshine, finally drifting ashore in the environment that was previously discussed. This works best, of course, if the boat can take you to an outdoor location.

Learning to Work Your Environment: Your Tool Kit

Things may sometimes appear frightening or confusing, but everything that occurs within your trance environment is under your control. How you wish to deal with a situation is up to you. Imagine that a lion springs out in front of you: Some of the things you could do are turn and run, call for help, fight, transform her into a kitten, or extend a hand and see if you can make friends with her.

The following pathworkings are a "tool kit" for increasing your options in trance. Each adventure will provide you with additional methods for working within pathworkings. I'm assuming that you have already gone through the pretrance steps (stretching, grounding, relaxation) and a form of trance induction.

The adventures all start after you have entered your inner temple.

The journeyers should be allowed a moment to relax and re-connect with their safe space. When they are ready, they will leave this space and begin their adventure. The following is an example of a good general segment that moves the participants from their inner safe space and into the adventure:

Relax as deeply as you can. You are completely comfortable. As you stand in your temple, your inner home, you feel completely safe. You have all the time you need, and this knowledge lets you relax even more, going deeper and deeper as you relax and open yourself to the possibilities. When you're ready, you will leave your sanctuary and begin your journey.

EXERCISE 1

You see before you the mouth of a cave and find yourself drawn by the cool darkness. The mystery of what lies within sparks your curiosity. Would you like to go in? *(a presumed yes)*

You enter the cave and let the coolness sweep away fatigue and worry. Your eyes quickly adjust, and although the light is dim, you're able to see well enough to find firm and comfortable footing.

Near the back of the cave, you see a tunnel leading into darkness and feel yourself drawn toward it. Calmly and without fear, you enter into the deep stillness of the Earth. Far ahead of you is a pinprick of light that beckons. You are drawn to it . . . moving faster as you climb toward the light. It becomes brighter and brighter.

You step out of the cavern and find yourself standing on the edge of a high precipice. Before you is nothing but blue sky. Peering over the edge, you see a straight drop down a cliff wall into the clouds below. You turn around and look up. Above you is an ice wall reaching up to a snow-covered peak. You look back to where you came, but your entrance is no longer there.

Once again, you face the empty sky around you. You shout "hello" to the wind and wonder, *What now?* The sun shines down upon you. The wind blows your hair. Your heart and mind join as one with the wildness of this place. As if in response to your call, an eagle's cry hits your ears. He comes swooping down, emerging from the brightness of the sun. His immense wings spread out like a glider as he plunges downward toward you. You jump back, not from fear but in respect of his size, as he lands on the edge of the cliff next to you, taking up most of the available space. The eagle cocks his head to one side to peer sharply down at you. Slowly, he lowers his body, bending to the ground and spreading his wings, offering you a perch upon his back. Would you like to fly with the eagle? *(a presumed yes)*

Once you have made yourself secure between his wings, he pushes off the ledge. His wings spread wide as you rush to greet the wind. Together you climb high into the sky, experiencing the joy and freedom of the air. He turns and swoops, drifting in a slow spiral down and down through the clouds. You see the Earth spreading out below you. Gently, he continues his spiral, down to the Earth, until finally, with a great flurry of wings, he rests on the ground and you climb from his back. You bid him thank you and offer him a gift. *(Pause for personal interaction.)* He gives a cry of parting, lifts his wings, and takes off back to his home, which is the sky, disappearing into the clouds.

You look around you. Behind you is the mountain, as unscalable as ever. You notice before you a path picking its way through the rocks. You continue on your way, following the path as it leads you into grassy plains. The plants grow high enough to tickle your fingers as you walk. You caress their tops as you pass and feel the pollen between your fingers. After walking for some time, you come to an incline in the landscape. You climb to the top of the rise and stare out at an endless sea of grass rippling before you. You stop to catch your breath and again wonder, *What now?*

You feel the Earth beneath your tired feet. Your muscles sore from the journey, you can feel your heart beating. Each beat thumps into the ground. As you stand listening, you realize that the sound has been joined by the pounding of hooves across the plain. Out of the vastness comes a stallion as golden as the grass. You give him greetings as he dances before you. He stops and kneels, offering you a mount upon his back. Would you like to run with the horse? *(a presumed yes)*

You climb on and feel his muscles grow taut beneath you. As you grasp his mane, you feel his legs again move and pound the earth. Together you gallop out onto the plains. The grasses part. Dirt is ripped up from under his hooves, flung to the sides of the path as you go, spreading the seeds. You experience and become one with the strength of the beast as the stallion races across the plain.

After a while, the grass becomes shorter. The horse slows and comes to a stop before a small stream. You slide off, give him your thanks, and offer a gift. *(Pause for personal interaction.)* After receiving the gift, the horse goes to drink his fill of the cooling water. You hop over the stream. Stop to take a taste of its refreshing waters. *(pause)* Feeling renewed, you turn and begin to follow the stream as it burbles through the countryside. After a short time, the stream widens into a small river and trees start to spring up along its banks. You continue to follow the river as it makes its way through the forest. The waters swell and pick up speed. Soon you find yourself on the edge of a cliff. The stream you've been following travels over a falls and empties into a larger river. You carefully follow the path as it makes its way alongside the falls and down to the river's edge. You sit down on a large rock, allowing the cool water to gently rush over your feet, soothing them, and wonder, *In what direction do I go now?*

Again your call is heeded. The rock you are sitting on slowly rises beneath you and you realize that your perch is actually the shell of a large turtle. She pokes out her head and looks back to stare up at you in greeting. Would you like to swim with the turtle? *(a presumed yes)* You reach down and take hold of the rim of her shell as together you wade into the river and plunge into its depths. As the water rises over your head, you find that you have no problems breathing underwater. Your body floats and you experience the pull of the currents, but you hang on tight to the turtle as she makes her way down the river.

After a short time, you feel the water begin to warm. The turtle rises to the surface and comes to shore. In front of you, you see steam rising from pools and realize that you have arrived at a hot spring. Turn and thank the turtle and offer her a gift. *(Pause for personal interaction.)* She leaves you standing in a warm, shallow pool as she slides back into the cool depths of the river.

You take a moment to relax and allow the warmth of the spring to refresh you. It has been a long journey. *(pause)* After you feel relaxed, you notice a spout of water dance into the air nearby as a geyser erupts. With curiosity, you climb out of the pool to investigate. Walking toward the geyser, you notice a path leading through the rocks. You take the path. Suddenly, the Earth opens underneath you. You slide into a large pit and you find yourself standing on the edge of a lava flow. Feeling the heat of the lava, you try to scale the walls, but they are too sandy and give under the weight of your body.

As you cry out for help, you notice something squirming across the lava. It walks out onto the rocks in front of you and scuttles across your foot. Although you are startled, and you can feel its heat, you realize that you are not burned. It looks up at you and you recognize that it is a salamander. Would you like to pick it up? *(a presumed yes)* You reach down and pick up the salamander. You can feel its warmth fill your body. While attempting to hold on to the squirming entity, you discover you have inadvertently stepped into the lava flow, yet you are unharmed by its intense heat. Suddenly the ground gives beneath your feet, and you feel the flow draw you down into the Earth . . . and down through the rock.

The downward motion stops. For a moment you are completely embraced in the warmth of the Earth. Then Earth around you shivers in response to some inner force. You feel a shift and you find yourself being pushed upward. Faster and faster, carried along with the current of liquid rock, you are hurled up and up as the lava in front of you explodes into the sky.

You find yourself deposited on the inside rim of a volcano. The rocks beneath your feet are no longer searing. The salamander squirms out from your hand and jumps back to its fiery home. You offer it thanks and toss it a gift, which is greedily consumed. *(Pause for personal interaction.)* You climb up over the rim and into the sun.

The clouds spread out below you. You find you are on a small path that winds its way down to a ledge of an ice-covered precipice. Carefully make your way down. Above you, you hear the call of an eagle and you realize that *in your journeys, help is always there for the asking.*

When you reach the ledge, you see before you the entrance to the cave that leads you home. Enter the cave, allowing the cooling darkness to refresh you, taking away your tiredness. Follow the path through the Earth as it makes its way toward your home. Ahead, you can see a pinpoint of light. As you come closer, you find that you are leaving the cave. The path in front of you leads straight to your home. You follow it, knowing you had a good journey . . . back to home.

For Contemplation Upon Your Return Discuss and record in your trance journal your experience and your reactions to this adventure. Describe your reactions to the different types of environments and the helpers found within them. Which was your favorite and why? Which did you dislike and for what reason? What other kinds of helpers do you think you would find in each of the environments?

EXERCISE 2

You step from your home space and find your feet on the path of a sandy dune on an ocean shore. Stand and look around you. You can hear, on the other side of the dune, the sea washing onto the beach and receding. Seagulls fly overhead, calling to each other as they play above the waves. The scent of salty brine is on the air. The sun is bright and warming; the breeze, cooling and refreshing. You are wearing your swimsuit. It's a perfect day for a picnic on the seaside.

With that thought, you notice a picnic basket sitting waiting for you at the base of one of the dunes. You recognize this basket and realize that it is yours. The warm sand finds its way between your bare toes as you make your way over to the basket and pick it up. You can feel the weight of it in your hands. You hear the crying gulls and ocean waves beckoning. The desire to see the ocean builds in you. It is only on the other side of the dune.

Carrying your basket, you begin climbing up the sand dune. With each step, the sand breaks under your feet, and you slide back to the base of the dune where you began. Looking around you, you see nothing but a continuous line of tall dunes. There is no way to the other side except over the slippery slope of sand. The gulls' cries, which seem to mock your attempts, only strengthen your determination to find a way. Place your basket down and sit down beside it. *(pause)*

A movement on the ground catches your attention. You notice a rabbit hopping along, nibbling at the low greenery. You observe her as she easily makes her way up and over the dune. Her big, wide feet provide stability for her weight on the fragile sand. Watching her, you realize that you have packed something in your basket that can help you. Open your basket and look inside. You find within it a pair of swimmer's flippers! You pull them out and put them on. Picking up your basket, you face the sand dune and climb to the summit. *(pause)*

The sea breeze washes over you in greeting as you stand on

the top of the dune. The scents of seaweed and seashells washed up along the shore fill your nostrils. The waves of the ocean churn into foam as they hit the shore. You make your way down the sand dune and to the ocean's edge. You no longer need your flippers, so you remove them and put them back into your basket. Walk along the beach, and look for the perfect place in the sun for your picnic. When you see it, make your way over to it. *(pause)* It is a perfect spot. Place your basket down and open it. Inside you find a blanket. You pull it out, spread it on the ground, and sit down.

You feel the weight of the sun and begin to feel very hot. Perspiration runs down your face. There is no shade. The sun feels scorching on your exposed skin. You begin to wish that you were under your blanket instead on sitting on top of it. You see a collection of large sticks washed up by the ocean tides. You realize that you have rope packed in your basket. If you wish to build a shelter, go and collect the sticks, then lash them together and throw the blanket over it to create a small lean-to to block the sun's rays. Enjoy the protection of your shady space for a moment. *(pause)*

The sun's warmth diminishes, and a cooling ocean breeze blows the intense heat away. Go and take a short swim in the ocean or just walk along and dip your toes in the waves. *(pause)*

The sound of laughter touches your ears. You discover a young child along the seaside. The child is trying to scoop wet sand and carry it to the shore to create a sand castle. The child runs back and forth from the water to his play site, but the water and sand run out between his fingers as he moves, leaving him with little to use for his castle. If you'd like, go and help the child create his castle. There might be a plastic bucket in your basket that could help carry the wet sand. *(pause)*

The day draws to an end. If you helped the child, you receive a hug of thanks before he disappears, running along the shore back to his home. The sun begins to set, and you realize that you're getting cold. Return to your blanket lean-to. Remove the blanket, shake out the sand, fold the blanket, and replace it in your basket. Untie the rope from the sticks, roll it back up, and put it back into your basket, too. The sea breeze has a chill to it. Before you close your basket, you reach in and find a dry, warm sweater. Put the sweater on. Feel the fabric warming your skin.

It's time to go home. Pick up your basket, turn once again to the dunes, and begin walking toward them. The journey over them is much easier from this side of the shore. You make it to the top without any difficulty. Turn around and take one last look at the ocean. It was a good adventure. Take one last deep breath of salty air before you head back to the base of the dune where you began. You leave your basket where you found it. You realize that *in your journeys, the tools that you need will be there whenever you need them.* Put your feet back on the path. You can see the doorway that leads to your home. Step through the threshold and back into your safe space.

For Contemplation Upon Your Return Discuss and record in your trance journal your experience and your reactions to this adventure. When you looked into your basket, did you notice anything other than what you were looking for within it? Did you have any difficulties building your lean-to? Finding what you needed in your basket? Who, or what, was the child? What kind of castle did you build? If you chose not to help the child, why not?

Additional Exercises With this exercise, the tools are all things that you can find or do on the physical plane. To strengthen these skills, choose other scenarios: a walk in the woods, up a mountain, swimming in a lake, even walking though your current work environment. Allow yourself to explore the environment using both tools and creative ingenuity.

EXERCISE 3

You step out from your inner home and find your feet on the sidewalk, on a corner of a busy city street. The city traffic—cars, buses, and bicycles—speeds by you. You hear horns honking, voices calling to each other, the crashing and banging of construction, and other noises of the city all around. You smell car and bus exhaust. There is also the faint smell of roasting peanuts from an unseen sidewalk vendor. People on their busy way walk by. They do not notice you as they hurry along. Tall buildings line both sides of the street, their concrete, steel, and brick structures reaching up to the bright sky above.

Walk along the sidewalk, past the many buildings with stores and apartments. You pass by interesting cars, people, and animals, until you come to a break in the scene. One of the buildings is missing, torn down in some long-forgotten project, leaving behind an ugly, empty lot. The ground is brick dust and rubble, devoid of life. Trash and big pieces of concrete are scattered all around. Yet here, the Earth calls to you. Picking your way carefully through the debris, you enter the lot and make your way to the center.

There you find a single plant. It is determined to somehow survive in this world. You realize that you have the ability to help it. Ask the plant if it would like you to help it grow strong. *(a presumed yes)* Focus on the plant. Believe it to be . . . large, strong, and beautiful. Touched by your love, the plant slowly grows. The concrete and trash that had been holding it back fall to one side and disappear. The plant grows . . . and grows . . . until it is large, lush, and healthy. But it is the only live thing in the old lot. Would you like to help create growth on this piece of Earth? *(a presumed yes)*

Look around you. Think of a small, beautiful garden. A place of peace and growth. You stretch out your hands. From your fingertips come tendrils of light. The light spreads and grows, moving over and under the debris, until soon the whole lot is filled with light. Within the light, there is movement and change. As the light dissipates, you find that you are now standing in the middle of your garden vision. Sunlight shines here. Your plant, still in the center, is surrounded by others. As you leave the lot, the plants all thank you for your help.

You continue your walk along the sidewalk, past buildings with stores and apartments. You come to a very, very tall building and suddenly feel the desire to go inside. You enter the lobby and see a row of elevators. Take one of the elevators to the top floor. *(Pause to allow travel to the top.)* You step out of the elevator onto the roof of the building. The city stretches out before you. Up here the wind is strong. It tugs at your hair and clothes. As you walk around the roof, you see something moving in the corner. When you approach, you see that it's a small bird. The winds must have blown it against the building, breaking its wing. It runs from you, obviously in pain, dragging its damaged wing behind it. You sit down on the roof so that you will not frighten the bird any more than it already is. It shivers in the corner, making small sounds. Would you like to help the bird? *(a presumed yes)*

As you sit there, you realize that you can speak the language of birds. You call out to the bird. It responds by slowly making its way over to you. You ask the bird if it would like you to heal its wing. It answers with a pain-filled yes. The bird allows you to pick it up and gently hold it. You envision the bird healthy and strong, soaring out over the buildings and into the green forest beyond the city. As you do so, you lightly stroke the broken wing with healing energy. Under your caress, the bone begins to move back into place and mend. Soon the bird struggles in your hands. As you let go, it bursts up into the skies with a loud song of gratitude. It circles around you once, thanks you for your help, then soars away.

You stand up, return to the elevator, and take it back down to the lobby. *(Pause for travel.)* Return to the street and continue your walk. You pass by more buildings and more people. Subway stations and buses. As you walk, look around and notice the architecture. Some of the buildings you pass appear to be very old. Interesting and fanciful statues stand guard on the platforms extending from building corners and roofs. A few buildings have statues of Gods and Goddesses serving as sentry figures at their entrances.

As you continue down the sidewalk, one particular figure on a building ahead of you catches your attention. Make your way toward it. As you stand looking at the statue, you realize that you recognize this figure—it's a spirit friend who has somehow become stone. You call to your friend. Although difficult to understand, your friend responds. Would you like to help this captured spirit? *(a presumed yes)* Decide how you wish to go about it, and do it. *(Pause to allow time to free the friend.)*

Your spirit friend gives you a hug of gratitude and leaves you. It is also time for you to leave this city. As you look around, you realize that you are on the corner sidewalk where you began. Take one more look around at the magic that can be found here. You realize that *wherever you may journey, the magic within you will be there whenever you need it.* You can see the doorway that leads to your home. Step through the threshold and back into your safe space.

For Contemplation Upon Your Return Discuss and record in your trance journal your experience and your reactions to this adventure. When you looked at your plant, what did you see? What kind of plant was it? What did the lot look like when you arrived? When you left? Did you feel the magic move through you when you transformed it? What kind of bird did you find? Did you feel the energy move through you when you healed its wing? What was the figure that held your spirit friend? How did you release it? What did it look like once it was released from the stone? If you didn't help your spirit friend, why not?

EXERCISE 4

You step from your home and find your feet on . . . snow. You are blinded by snow. You can't see the path—it's covered by snow. It swirls around you, teasing you with its harsh bitterness. You are cold. Your feet are cold. Your body is cold. You have stepped into winter. It appears as if there is nothing but whiteness all around.

You think of going back but hesitate for a moment. What would bring you to a world of snow? What can you learn among the snowflakes? Allow these and other questions to spark your curiosity. *(pause)*

Instead of running, you stamp your feet to get the circulation moving through them. As your feet strike the Earth, you sense of bit of warmth. You repeat the motion. Yes, your feet are getting warmer. It feels as if an invisible pair of boots have been put on your feet. Another strike. You can feel your toes again. A few more times and you feel the heat rise from your feet up to your thighs, as if you've stepped into a pair of snow pants. If you will, start dancing with the snowfall. Each swirling movement bringing up warmth from the Earth, covering you with its heat until a barrier of warming protection covers your entire body. You are no longer cold.

Dance until, like a snowflake, you fall gently to the Earth to lie upon the snow. The snowflakes continue to float down, landing on your body and face. You stick out your tongue and catch one. It tastes and smells like Yule. You catch another. It tastes of hot chocolate and cinnamon. And another. It reminds you of fresh peppermint leaves. Catch a few more snowflakes and enjoy the tastes that they bring. *(pause)*

Stick your arms and legs out into the snow. Simultaneously moving them up and down, you create a child's "snow angel." And you realize that, right now, you are a child. The snow is something to play in. Allow the laughter and the joy of the moment to rise in you. With your child's eyes, I invite you to explore winter. See the beauty of the flakes. Wonder at their individual splendor. Enjoy a slide down a nearby incline. Skate on a frozen lake. Build a snow fort. Spend time with the wonderment of winter. *(Pause for a reasonable amount of time for people to explore.)*

It is almost time to return home. Stop your play and find your way back to where you began. Even with the snowfall, you can still see the path you are meant to tread. Before you cross the threshold, turn and look all around you. Across the snow-covered Earth, you see movement. A woman as white as the snow, Her hair and gown shimmering and glittering as light strikes them, makes Herself known to you. She has been quietly watching you since you arrived. She is the Winter Queen, the Lady of Snow. It is She who offered you this opportunity. You realize that *in your journeys, sometimes you have to change your view of a situation, even one that may appear challenging, in order to experience what you need to know from it.* You can see the doorway that leads to your home. Thank the Lady. She smiles at you and bids you good-bye as you step through the threshold and back into your safe space.

Searching for Answers: Exploring Paths and Decision Making

One of the gifts of guided meditations is the possibility they offer us to gain insights into our own hearts and minds. This knowledge can help us make or understand difficult life decisions. In magical practice, we call this far sight—seeing the various possibilities of the future.

The following are just a few pathworkings that allow for exploring possibilities. Travel those that call to you. Once you understand the concept, draw on your own creative sense to adapt them to fit your own personal needs.

Again, I'm assuming that you've done all the pretrance and trance induction work. Unless otherwise noted, the scripts all begin with you leaving your safe space.

CAREER PERSPECTIVES—WHAT WILL I BE
WHEN I GROW UP?

Before you do a personal career-choice pathworking, sit down and think about some possibilities, ranging from the impractical to the possible.

You are comfortable in your inner space, feeling safe and relaxed. In your relaxation, turn your mind to careers. What would you like to be when you grow up? Allow any and all possibilities, from the fanciful to your current job, to form in your mind. Do not accept or reject any. Like waves upon the shore, allow them to gently rise and recede, one replaced by another.

Look now, if you will, and notice an opening that a veil *(door, or path)* is beckoning to you. Would you like to see where it leads? *(a presumed yes)* You approach the threshold and step over.

You find yourself entering a tunnel. Your eyes quickly adjust and, though it is dimly lit, you find you are able to see well enough to find firm and comfortable footing. Without fear, you follow the tunnel down into darkness. Far ahead is a pinprick of light that calls to you. As you draw near, you see that the light is actually an opening. You step out into a bright, white room.

Before you stands a table so large that it takes up almost the whole space. As you come closer, you realize that it's covered with a variety of objects—from a computer to a blackboard, snorkel gear to a basketball. *(Replace with the general objects associated with careers previously discussed.)* You realize that each object is associated with a different career choice. Look at all the possibilities.

You reach forward and pick up one of the objects, a stethoscope, and place it around your neck. As you do, the room dissolves and you find yourself in the busy corridor of a hospital. You can smell the various medicinal hospital smells. You look down, and although your physical form has not changed, you are now wearing a nurse's uniform. You can feel the cushioned soles of your shoes as you walk through the corridor. Stop and go into a few of the rooms. Go and speak to the patients in their beds. Take their vital signs. Change a bedpan. Wander down to the nurses' station where conversation and paperwork wait. Take in all the sights, sounds. Feel what it's like to be a nurse. Do you like what you are experiencing? Does being a nurse feel comfortable? Interesting? Is this something you would like to do in your life? When you are done exploring, you take off the stethoscope. You are once again standing in the white room.

Reach forward and pick up another object. As you do, the room disappears and you find yourself experiencing what it's like to be in that career. Continue with as many different possibilities as you wish to explore. *(Allow sufficient time to explore.)*

During your search, you may find one career that's a perfect fit, or you may not. This space will be here whenever you wish to visit to offer you various possibilities.

When you're ready to leave, turn and find the entrance to the tunnel. You step into the darkness and stillness of the Earth. Follow the tunnel to the staircase and climb upward until you reach the top and find yourself at the doorway to your safe sanctuary and cross the threshold.

Spend some time now, in your safe space, thinking about your experiences in the white room. If you found a career path that fits you, you may want to spend time contemplating how you can make this happen in the outer world.

For Contemplation Upon Your Return What were some of the various objects on the table? Which ones were you drawn to? Were there any that you avoided touching? Why? Make a list of things you liked and things you didn't like within each exploration. Do you see any correlations? Focus on the thing you liked, and perhaps a new possibility will emerge. Take your list and do research in the physical world to see if you can find a position that matches your interests.

Discuss and record in your trance journal your experience and reactions to this adventure.

Additional Exercises Focus on one career path. Do a trance journey that takes you through an entire day.

EXPLORING SPIRITUAL PATHS

Wicca is just one of many paths to the sacred. By experiencing other faiths, we can gain greater understanding of our neighbors who practice them. Comparison may also offer insights into our own beliefs, symbols, and rituals.

This voyage has been broken up into many different trips, one journey for each spiritual tradition you wish to explore. This will allow you time to fully integrate each experience before you move on to another one. You will find that each time you travel to the same location in trance, you reinforce the association and deepen your connection to it. Symbols perhaps previously unnoticed become clearer, and the details of the image solidify.

Note: In order for this exercise to work, the facilitator or the traveler should either be familiar with, or have done prior research on, the faith to be explored. This exercise could also become a wonderful learning opportunity. At the end of each journey to the stone circle, a symbol for the next adventure is identified. This faith or tradition should first be researched, and can then experienced during the next trip to the stone circle. I highly recommend that, whenever possible, your research include an actual visit to a worship service.

Introduction You find yourself stepping into the center of a large stone circle. The ancient gray stones show wear from weather and time. You can tell by looking at them that they are very, very old . . . as old as the ground beneath your feet. As you stand looking around you, you realize that you are in the center of a giant wheel, with each stone representing a spoke. When you look closer at the rocks, you notice that each pillar has a different symbol carved into its surface. As you slowly turn around, looking at each of the stones, the symbols begin to glow. You see

a pentacle on one pillar, a crescent moon on another, a triskelion (a triple spiral that, in the Druidic tradition, represents the
connection of land, sea, and sky), runes, primitive designs, a cross,
a Star of David, and many more symbols representing different
spiritual paths.

Part I You approach the pillar with the triskelion carved on
it. It glows brightly as you get closer. Reach out, if you will, and
touch the triskelion. Feel the hard, rough rock under your
hand, the smoothness of the carving. When you have the mark
clearly in your mind, a doorway on the stone reveals itself to
you. Without fear, you step through the opening.

You find yourself on a forest path. You can smell the scent of
pine and fallen leaves. Birds play overhead. Before you stands
an old oak tree. You can tell by its size that this is a very ancient
tree. The bark is thick and bumpy. If you wish, place your hands
on the tree and feel the life within it. The sun is shining down.
The light creates patterns on the forest floor. You notice a small
natural spring burbling up from the ground near the oak. If
you wish, go and take a drink of fresh springwater.

As you stand, you see a group of people making their way
through the forest toward you. They are wearing hooded white
robes and are carrying staffs. A person who seems to be the oldest member of the group bears a golden sickle. You realize that
they are Druids, coming to harvest the white berries of the
mistletoe, which you can now see cling to the branches of the
mighty oak above you.

The Druids either do not notice or do not care about your
presence as they form a circle near the base of the massive tree.
Watch as they light a sacred fire and begin singing in Gaelic to
the spirits of the land. Stay and watch the Druids for as long as
you like. While you observe them, also take note of the feelings
their ritual brings up in you. Do you wish to join their rite? Or
are you satisfied just to watch? Would you prefer to leave?

When you're ready, turn back to the path that brought you
here. As you begin to walk, you see the portal marked by the

triskelion. You step through it, and find yourself entering back into the stone circle. The triskelion still glows on the gray stone.

It's time to return. This circle will be here to offer you various possibilities whenever you wish to visit it. Take one more look around. Thank the stones for their guidance and wisdom. The path that brought you to this place becomes visible. Walk toward it. As you put your feet upon the path, you can see the entrance of your sanctuary before you. Step through the doorway and enter into your inner home.

Part II Walk again to the center of the stone circle. You turn to the stone with the triskelion. It still glows on the gray surface of the rock, and you remember your encounter with the Druids. Look around you for other possibilities. A glowing pentacle calls to you from one of the pillars. Would you like to explore that realm? *(a presumed yes)*

You approach the rock and touch its hard surface. Run your fingers over the carving of the pentacle. Feel the hard, rough rock under your hand, the smoothness of the carving. When you have the mark clearly in your mind, a doorway on the stone reveals itself to you. Without fear, you step right through the opening.

You find yourself entering into an open field at night. A light dew is on the grass. The scents of fresh grass and hay rise with each step. A full moon shines overhead, giving light to the ritual that you realize is occurring before you. A group of people, all skyclad, stand in the center of the field. You hear them as they bid hail and welcome to the Elements: Earth, Air, Fire, and Water. The priest then steps into the center of the circle and calls to the Lord of the wild wood. As if in response, somewhere in the distance, you hear the howl of a coyote. The priestess raises her arms to the full moon above so that it looks as if she has captured it between her outstretched hands, and begins her invocation to the goddess of the moon.

Stay and watch the Wiccan full-moon circle for as long as you like. While you do so, ask yourself what feelings their ritual evokes in you. Do you wish to join the Witches in their rite? Or are you satisfied to simply observe? Would you prefer to leave?

When you're ready, turn back to the path that brought you here. As you begin to walk, you see before you the portal marked by the pentacle. You step through it and find yourself entering back into the stone circle. The pentacle still glows on the gray stone.

It's time to return. This circle will be here to offer you various possibilities whenever you wish to visit it. Take one more look around. Thank the stones for their guidance and wisdom. The path that brought you to this place becomes visible. Walk toward it. As you put your feet upon the path, you can see the entrance of your sanctuary before you. Step through the doorway and enter into your inner home.

Part III Walk again to the center of the stone circle. You turn to the stone with the triskelion. It still glows on the gray surface of the rock, and you remember your encounter with the Druids. You turn and see the pentacle shining on its pillar. Think back to your experience with the Wiccan coven. Look around at the stones and their possibilities. Find the pillar with the cross. *(Proceed as with the other pillars.)**

You find yourself in a large open room. Above you, the high arched, vaulted ceiling disappears into shadows. Light shines through great windows of vivid glass, filling the room with many colored rays. The air is filled with sweet incense and chants that reverberate through the lofty arches.

In front, at the altar, a priest invokes the spirit of their God into the bread. Then the bread is broken and shared. As people come forward, they take the Holy Spirit into their own bodies, as their great teacher taught them centuries ago. Thus, as so many times before, sacred union becomes real for them. Many return to their seats with glowing auras; some are weeping for joy.

---

*Judy Harrow contributed to this section.

Stay and observe the Christian Eucharist as long as you like. Notice what you perceive and feel as you do so. Would you like to go forward, and share their bread and wine? Are you content simply to observe? Do you feel uncomfortable here? Would you like to leave? *(Return as before.)*

On other trips you could choose the runes and enjoy an Asatru blot, toasting the Viking gods and the ancestors. Go listen to the song of the Jewish cantor in a synagogue, or the call to prayer from the tower of a Muslim mosque. Take the path to an exploration of tribal shamanism, or the crescent moon of the Dianic Witch. See the Latin inscribed on a pillar that leads you the temple rites for the Greek and Roman Gods and Goddesses. Alchemical sigils will bring you to the ceremonial magician's circle. Spend time wandering the paths that call to you. While you observe them, also take note of feelings their rituals bring up in you. Do you wish to join the rite? Or are you satisfied just to watch? Would you prefer to leave? Look at the symbols glowing warmly on the ancient stones. Choose one and go explore.

Come back to the stone circle as many times as you wish to experience other spiritual paths.

For Contemplation Upon Your Return From Each Journey Which symbols called to you? Were there any that you did not want to explore? What color(s) were the symbols? How did they feel when you touched them? Make a list of things you liked and didn't like in each exploration. Do you notice any correlations? Focus on the things that you liked and see if any new possibilities emerge.

Discuss and record in your trance journal your experience and reactions to this adventure. Research in depth one or more of the paths that you enjoyed.

THIS OR THAT—GAINING PERSPECTIVES

This is an exercise in far sight. This guided meditation offers you an opportunity to see where a particular path or decision might lead; to take a quick glance at possible outcomes of your choices. This pathworking can be used for a wide range of possibilities, from relationships to decisions on purchasing a home. It's applicable to any situation that requires a decision between two or more choices.

To help you within this working, you will be meeting the keeper of the crossroads, Hecate. She is a Greek goddess who was often worshiped where three roads come together. She is the crone within a sacred triad; the other two are Persephone, the Maiden, and the Mother, Demeter. Hecate is associated with the dark moon, magic, fertility, endings, and beginnings. She is often depicted with a large dog.

Before you begin, spend time thinking carefully over what your situation is and exactly what your choices are within it. The more clarity you have, the more successful this exercise will be. As with all of the previous exercises, I'm assuming that you have done all the pretrance and trance induction work. The script begins with you leaving your safe space.

You find yourself standing outside at an empty crossroads at night. The stars shine brightly down upon you. The road smells of dry dirt, moistened with night dew. You can hear crickets chirping around you. They are the only sound in this desolate place. There are no other signs of life . . . no buildings, no cars, just a dirt path. You can feel the crunching of stones and dirt under your feet as you walk forward. Ahead of you, the road forks out in two different directions: one to your right and another to your left. Both roads lead into darkness.

As you contemplate the roads, you hear a gentle sound. You turn and find an old and stately woman standing behind you. A black veil covers Her head, with wisps of white hair visible beneath it. Her dress is a black robe that drapes over Her entire body. When you look into Her eyes, you can see the span of creation, and you realize that this is Hecate, ancient Mother and Crone goddess. Take a moment to give Her honor. *(pause)*

She thanks you, takes your hand, and leads you to the split in the road. She bids you to turn around and look at the path from which you came. As you do, you see your life flash before you. You observe other times when you stood at the crossroads and made decisions. *(Pause to experience life's decisions.)* You see how each of those previous decisions has brought you here, to this point in time, and to the decision that you now must make.

Hecate turns you around again to face the two paths before you. Each will lead to a different resolution, a different future. You have two roads, two possible choices, two different outcomes to your decision. Think of the choice that you need to make. Make a choice. Hecate takes your hand. Her hand is strong, warm, and comforting. She leads you to the left, and together you walk down the path. You can see yourself making this decision. As you continue to walk, you see the steps that are needed to complete the decision. *(pause)* You see the reactions of others—your friends, family, and those who are affected by your choice. You can feel the ripples of cause and effect as they extend away from you. *(pause)* Continue walking and watch the future unfold before you. Follow the chain reaction of events caused by your decision. *(pause)* When you are done, stop. Hecate looks at you knowingly. You gaze into Her eyes and realize that you are back at the crossroads.

This time She takes your hand and leads you to the right. Imagine now the other choice. Together you walk down the other path. You can see yourself making this decision. As you continue to walk, you see the steps needed to complete this decision. *(pause)* You see the reactions of others—your friends, family, and those who are affected by your choice. You can feel the ripples of cause and effect as they extend away from you.

(pause) Continue walking and watch the future unfold before you. Follow the chain reaction of events caused by your decision. *(pause)* When you are done, stop. Hecate looks at you knowingly. You gaze into Her eyes and realize that you are once again at the crossroads.

Now She points to a place between the two paths. As you watch, a third path begins to materialize. This is a choice that you have not yet realized. It is another possible future. Hecate looks at you questioningly. Would you like to explore this alternative possibility? *(If no, go to the end of the pathworking. If yes, continue.)*

Hecate takes your hand again and leads you to the middle path. The way is rocky and unsure. But you step forward. As you do, a new idea begins to form. You see yourself making a decision. As you continue to walk, you see the steps needed to complete this decision. *(pause)* You see the reactions of others— your friends, family, and those who are affected by your choice. You can feel the ripples of cause and effect as they extend away from you. *(pause)* Continue walking and watch the future unfold before you. Follow the chain reaction of events caused by your decision. *(pause)* When you are done, stop. Hecate looks at you knowingly. You gaze into Her eyes and realize that you are once again back at the crossroads.

Hecate steps back onto the path from which you came. You give Her your thanks and offer Her a gift. She smiles at you and accepts. A big, black dog runs up beside the Lady. She lovingly pats his head. Hecate turns and walks away down a path of her own. Her dog glares a warning at you. You are not to follow. He then races to catch up with Her. She disappears, leaving you alone at the crossroads. When you look back at the paths, you can still see your three choices and how each will affect your future. Take one more look and etch them clearly in your mind. As you turn back, you see the doorway that leads to your sanctuary. As the crickets chirp a farewell, you step over the threshold, returning home.

For Contemplation Upon Your Return What did you see on the left path? The right path? Did you take the middle road? If not, why not? If yes, what did you see? Did you notice any similarities within the different futures on the two or three roads? What does that suggest to you? Did you notice any major differences? What was the gift you gave the Goddess? Discuss and record in your trance journal your experience and reactions to this adventure.

Additional Exercises When you believe you know which path you will choose, take a trip to visit Janus, the Roman god of time. He is pictured with two heads that face in opposite directions. He represents both past and future knowledge. You can ask him of the wisdom of this decision and perhaps request a glimpse into the future.

WHAT IS MY ROLE IN MY COMMUNITY?

Your community is made up of the individuals with whom you share a common bond or identity. This link could be your town or neighborhood, spiritual beliefs, religious practices, or ethnicity, to name just a few. It takes many people to make an individual whole, and it takes many different people to make up a whole community. It takes friends and family all loving and supporting each other.

I remember my first Pagan gathering. It was held in a campground in western Massachusetts. Seeing people wandering around in capes, hearing the drums, breathing in the smell of the fire circle, partaking in the conversations that went on until the sun rose—for me, it was a coming home. I had found my community. I also realized that passively observing could never make me a full member. As with any relationship, to be fully part of a community, you need to contribute and to be open to receiving the contributions of others. It's love and support and the everyday sharing of our talents and skills that make community real.

Just as we each have our personal strengths and weaknesses, interests and abilities, so this offering will be different for each individual. For example, you might be a wonderful teacher and choose to pass down the traditions and beliefs of your religion to a small group. You may enjoy creating the children's activities for your community get-togethers. You may be a quiet home-body who creates wonderful works of art or music to delight people you may never actually meet. Or you may be one of those who has the vision to organize an entire community event.

Before you do this exercise, think about what you like to do and how it might benefit your community. Do you like to keep history? Sing? Bake bread? Engage in interfaith contact and community outreach? Teach our traditions to others?

This exercise is to help you gain clarity and focus in the ways you can best serve your community so that your community can best serve you.

Helping you with this working will be the Greek Goddess Athena. She is the protector of cities, a friend to communities and those who live within them. She is skilled in the arts and crafts as well as in war, justice, wisdom, and strategy. Her sacred symbols are owls, olive trees, and the intertwined snakes whose image is on Her helmet and shield.

This journey is meant to be worked over an extended period of time. On your first visit, you will meet with the Goddess and begin exploring. Each time you return, She will take you to another location. Contemplate what you might like to explore and allow Her to take you there.

As with all of the previous exercises, I'm assuming that you've done all the pretrance and trance induction work. The script begins with you leaving your safe space.

Part I You find yourself on the streets of Athens in ancient Greece. People pass by you, all on their busy way. You hear the screaming of horses and smell the odor of manure. Chariots rumble by, soldiers in armor at their reins. The buildings are all short. Most of them are white, but many have dimmed from the dust of the street. You reach out and touch one of the rough plaster-covered surfaces and the pillars holding up their entry-ways. If you peer in, you may see a small, open courtyard with bright paintings on the walls. Many of the homes you pass have small, elaborate mosaics. These small individual bits of color combine to form an intricate work of beauty. For a brief moment, allow your fingers to touch their small pieces, then continue your way down the road.

Ahead of you, you see a very large temple complex. Huge, fluted columns hold up the roof's apex, which is decorated with scenes of Gods and Goddesses. Priests, priestesses, soldiers, men, and women are hurrying up and down the stairs of the temple. As you stand and watch, a large bird flies past you so close that its wing tips stroke your check. As the bird moves away toward the temple, you realize that it is a large owl. Will you follow the owl, up the steps and into the temple itself? *(a presumed yes)*

A mixed blend of incense flavors greets your nose when you enter into the cool interior of the temple building. The inner pillars and floor are of smooth marble. You can feel where portions of the floor have been worn away by the thousands of feet that have walked here. You hear the owl's calls echo off the walls. You follow the sound as it leads you deeper into the temple.

Torches line the hall as you wander farther into the center of the structure. The smell of their suet is harsh next to the sweet scent of perfumed incense, but you are thankful for their light. You turn a corner, and there before you is a seated, life-sized statue of Athena, Goddess of wisdom, protectress of Athens, friend to community. Her helmet rests on Her head; Her shield lies at her feet. The owl is perched upon Her shoulder, softly cooing.

Her face draws you. You are unable to take your eyes away from the delicately carved features of the Goddess. As you watch, the statue slowly moves. Her head turns to look at you,

Her eyes open, and Her mouth forms a slight smile. Take a moment to give homage to the Lady. *(pause)*

She slowly stands. Her perch shaken, the owl makes annoyed noises. Athena approaches you and beckons for you to follow Her. Will you follow? *(a presumed yes)*

She leads you out of the temple and down the stairs. No one notices as you walk among the people on the street. She leads you to a row of small buildings. She points to one and bids you to enter. You step through the door and look around.

A loom sits in the center of the room. Yarn and wool are scattered in baskets on the floor. You can tell that this is the home of a weaver. Bunches of raw wool lay on a table. You pick up one of the bundles. You can feel and smell the lanolin held within the fiber. You look around. Beautiful tapestries line the walls. Each piece contains pictures of Gods and Goddesses that visually tell their stories and myths. This person is both an artisan and a teacher in his community. He passes down the stories, myths, and lessons of this faith in a way that can easily be understood. You realize that you could teach others your spiritual tradition and beliefs, passing down your knowledge. Or you could become an artisan, using your hands and talent to create works of beauty and utility that will bring joy to their owners. Or you could do both, like the resident of this place. Or you might be a weaver of Internet technology, supporting your community through working the threads of communication. You nod at the Goddess, indicating that you understand. Stay for a while and explore the home of the weaver. *(pause)*

It is time to leave. Athena leaves the home of the weaver and heads back to the stairs of Her temple. Her owl flies in front of Her. When you arrive at the base of the steps, She stops and points to the floor on which you stand. You look down at your feet and see a large, beautiful mosaic—thousands of small, individual pieces that, when brought together, create this beautiful whole.

You thank the Goddess Athena and offer Her a gift. She accepts and, with a slight smile, turns and makes Her way back up the stairs to her temple home. You follow the street back the way you came, past the white buildings, the horses, and the people, until you see the entrance to your portal. Turn, if you will, and say good-bye to ancient Greece, then cross the threshold back to our own time.

Part II You find yourself back on the streets of Athens in ancient Greece. You hear the horses and the people. You see again the buildings and the temple of Athena. Before you is the beautiful mosaic. Reach down and touch the small pieces, then continue your way up the temple stairs. Enter the temple and again meet the Goddess Athena.

Athena slowly stands, and She beckons for you to follow Her. Will you follow? *(a presumed yes)* She leads you out of the temple and down the stairs. No one notices as you walk among the people on the street. She leads you to a row of small buildings.

You walk toward the house of the weaver. You can see someone inside working away at the loom. He gives you a nod of greeting as you pass by. Athena leads you to another building. She enters, and you follow. As you enter, your nostrils are filled with the scent of herbs. Hanging bunches of dried herbs line one wall. Another is covered with shelves holding neatly labeled jars. Before you is a table and on it a bowl of crushed herbs. More herbs waiting to be prepared lay beside it. You pick up one of the dried plants and feel its roughness between your fingers. This house belongs to a local healer or midwife. She offers her knowledge to her community, relieving their pain and helping them regain their health and strength.

You realize that you could help those within your community by comforting those in sorrow, providing strength to those who will accept it, and taking care of those in need. You nod to the Goddess that you understand. Stay a while if you would like to explore the home of the healer. *(pause)*

It is time to leave. Athena turns and heads back to the stairs of Her temple. Her owl flies in front of Her. When you arrive at the base of the steps, you stop and look down at the beautiful mosaic and all of its small pieces.

You thank the Goddess Athena and offer Her a gift. She accepts and, with a slight smile, turns and makes Her way back up the stairs to her temple home. You follow the street back the way you came—past the white buildings, the horses, and the people until you see the entrance to your portal. Turn, if you will, and say good-bye to ancient Greece, then cross the threshold back to home.

Part III *(Enter Athens as before and meet the Goddess Athena.)*

Athena slowly stands, and She beckons for you to follow Her. Will you follow? *(a presumed yes)* She leads you out of the temple and into the streets.

You walk toward the house of the weaver. He is inside working away at the loom. He stops and gives you a wave of greeting as you pass by. You pass by the healer. She is busy preparing her herbs, but she smiles at you as you continue down the street. Athena leads you to another building.

You follow Her into a small temple. In the simple room you find an altar to a local deity. Incense is burning on the brazier, and offerings have been left before the altar. You can see a small table that holds a stone tablet. You go and pick it up. It is surprisingly heavy in your hands. Although you cannot completely make out the writing, it appears to be an order of worship, a ritual script. This person helps organize the local community for group worship of the Gods. You nod that you understand, and the Goddess takes you out again into the sunshine.

It is time to leave. Athena turns and heads back to the stairs of Her temple. Her owl flies in front of Her. When you arrive at the base of the steps, you stop and look down at the beautiful mosaic and all of its small pieces.

You thank the Goddess Athena and offer Her a gift. *(Return as before.)*

Part IV *(Enter Athens as before and meet the Goddess Athena.)*

Athena slowly stands and beckons for you to follow Her. Will you follow? *(a presumed yes)* She leads you out of the temple and into the streets.

You walk toward the house of the weaver. He gives you a wave of greeting as you walk by. You pass by the healer who is tying her herbs to dry. She gives you a hello as you pass. You continue past the small temple. You can see the priestess giving offerings to the deity.

Decide what you would like to explore, and Athena will take you. See how other people serve their neighbors and the community. As you explore, allow yourself to consider each as an option for your role within your own community. *(Allow time for exploration and return as before.)*

Know you can return as often as you like to explore the possibilities found within the community. Cross the threshold back to home.

For Contemplation Upon Your Return What was the mosaic a picture of? What do you believe the picture represented? What other buildings did you enter? What insights did they provide? If you found a direction, what will you do to help it manifest?

Discuss and record in your trance journal your experience and reactions to this adventure.

The Answers Are Within

Many of the answers that we seek are already within us. They can be found by looking deep within our own hearts.

The following are just a few pathworkings designed to help you explore and open your own heart. Travel those that call to you. Once you understand the concept, draw on your own creative sense to adapt them to fit your own personal needs.

Again, it's assumed that you've done all the pretrance and trance induction work. The scripts all begin with you leaving your safe space.

FLOWER BLOSSOM OPENING

As you step across the threshold, you find yourself entering into, and becoming a part of, the Earth. It feels natural to be a part of the Earth. You breathe the Earth, smell the Earth, taste the Earth. You can hear it shift and move. It is not threatening. You feel calm and content.

You realize that you are a seed within the Earth. You have been sleeping, but now you are awake. Feel your seed-self crack open. Your roots form and grow deep into the Earth. A stalk emerges and pushes its way out from under the ground, to stretch up to the sky. Leaves open and a big, beautiful bud forms.

You are a many-faceted flower. Feel the outer petals slowly open to the sun. Then the next layer of petals gently unfolds. And the next layer slowly opens. With each unfolding layer, feel yourself opening . . . to possibilities . . . to healing . . . to change . . . to growth. Allow each layer of petals to spread open, until all your petals are exposed to the sun, taking in its warmth. Allow yourself to sit and experience this feeling for a while. *(pause)*

When you're ready, see the portal before you. You are no longer a flower, but you remember its essence as you step across the threshold to home.

For Contemplation Upon Your Return How many layers of petals did you need to unfold until you were completely open? Were you able to open all your petals?

MEETING PARTS OF YOURSELF

You find yourself on a familiar path. The sun shines down on you. You can hear the birds flying above. A gentle breeze blows by. You are comfortable and relaxed. It is not difficult to walk this path. You enjoy the feeling of your feet connecting to the ground with each step. A familiar scent on the winds, the warming sun, the movement of life—all is right with the world.

Far down the path you see a house. The road leads toward it. You feel drawn to the house. Something within you hears a call from this dwelling, and you can't help but respond. You feel your feet picking up their pace, moving faster toward the house until you reach the front of the building. As you gaze at it, you realize that the building is very familiar to you. Stop for a moment and take a good look at this house. Take in the doors and window, corners and roof, every part of this house. Etch it into your mind.

As you stand in front of the house, the door before you opens. Your curiosity is sparked.

You make your way to the threshold and step over. Slowly start looking around the inside of this house. It is filled with lots of unusual and interesting things, most of which, you realize, are familiar to you. Some of the objects and pieces of furniture that fill the house you remember from your youth, others are from more recent times.

As you wander around you notice a number of doors. You realize that no two doors in this house are alike. One door in particular captures your attention. You feel yourself drawn to the door and the mystery of what lies behind it.

You reach your hand forward and knock on the door. It opens, and a familiar person greets you. You suddenly realize that this person is you . . . but only a portion of you. It is one of the many aspects—one of the parts of your personality—that make up who you are. Spend a moment getting to know this facet of yourself. *(pause)*

It is time to leave this persona. Before you leave, this facet offers you a bit of advice. *(pause)* You give thanks, and the persona closes the door. Another door beckons. Spend time meeting various aspects of yourself. *(Pause for interaction.)*

Now it's time to go. Make your way to the door of your house. Take another look around you. In this space, you can meet all the various individual parts of yourself anytime you wish. You want to return here again to continue to exploring. You step outside and onto the path. As you walk away, take one more look so that the memory is etched into your mind. When you turn back, you find your portal back to your safe inner space. You step through to ordinary consciousness.

For Contemplation Upon Your Return What does your house look like? Because the house represents yourself, what does it suggest to you? Who did you meet in the first room? What advice did this persona give you? In the second room? Who did you meet in other rooms? What objects did you find inside the house? Does this suggest anything to you?

Discuss and record in your trance journal your experience and reactions to this adventure.

CULTIVATING GROWTH

What parts of me need to open and grow? This question is the focus of this meditation. It looks at the areas of your self that need to be fertilized so you can grow to your fullest potential.

To help you with this working is the Green Man. Covered in green leaves from head to toe, He is the European agricultural God of unbound growth, fertility, and change.

As with all of the previous exercises, it's assumed that you have done all the pretrance and trance induction work. The script begins when you leave your safe space.

You find yourself in an overgrown green garden filled with lush vegetation. The sun is shining above you, and a gentle breeze touches your checks. The wind brings the scent of spring, a damp, clean smell of wet earth and new growth. You can hear birds singing and playing in the branches of the trees and in the thick foliage around you.

You feel drawn to one particular large green bush. As you stand before it, looking at the green leaves and vines that make up the plant, a pair of eyes pop open and you see a big green grin. Sets of arms and legs appear from under the grin. This is the Green Man, otherwise known as Jack-in-the-Green. He springs up with a gleeful laugh, pleased with Himself for having startled you. He dances around you, giggling with merriment. You can see the mischievous look in His eyes, but you are not afraid.

Jack wanders over to a group of small plants. He reaches down and caresses their little leaves with His green fingers. He then stands up and wanders off as the plants explode into growth and life. You watch him move from one plant to another, each responding to his gentle touch with a flurry of growth.

He beckons for you to follow Him. Will you go? *(a presumed yes)* He leads you into the center of the garden. There you see a pool of water. He points to the pool, indicating that you are to go look into it. You walk over and gaze in. To your amazement, the image of yourself reflected back is almost completely green with growth. You can see vines twirling around your hair, and shades of green covering portions of your skin. As you look at yourself, you realize that there are also parts of you that are completely bare and empty. You look over to the Green Man. He shakes His head sadly and, pointing to the barren sections, makes little clicking noises. These are the areas of yourself that need to be tended.

Look carefully at your body and note what parts are lacking green growth. What do the areas represent? Is your head bare? Maybe it's your mind that needs to opened. Your chest? Does your heart need to allow in love? Your feet can indicate lack of support; your genitals fear of sexuality. Look at what parts of you need some tender loving care in order to explode with the full potential of life. *(Pause to allow observation and reflection.)*

You look back at the Green Man, who gives you a big grin. Knowledge is the first step toward growth and change. His eyes dance with merriment. Give Him your thanks, and offer Him a gift. He smiles wildly at you again, gleefully accepts it, and, with a laugh, dances away into the foliage. You look down at your body. The magic of the pool has faded, and you are your normal color again. You turn and see your doorway before you. Take one last look around and step across the threshold back to your inner home.

For Contemplation Upon Your Return What parts of your body were barren? What do you believe this represents? Knowledge is the first step, action is the second. How do you plan on helping them grow?

THE HEART OF LOVE

This guided meditation explores self-love and self-acceptance. Joy and love are not given to you by others. They come from within your own heart, your own spirit. Born of the foam of the ocean, Aphrodite is the Goddess of love and beauty. She will help you on this journey to touch your heart and open yourself to loving yourself.

You step from your temple and find your feet on the path of a sandy dune on an ocean shore. Stand and look around you. You can hear the sea washing onto the beach. Seagulls fly overhead, calling to each other as they play above the waves. The scent of salt is in the air. The sun is bright and warming; the breeze, cooling and refreshing.

The warm sand finds its way between your bare toes as you make your way across the beach. You find a hollow in the sand of the dune, a private alcove just the right size for your body. You lie down within it. The sand molds to your body beneath you. The sun shines down from above, warming and relaxing you. You are very, very comfortable, content, and relaxed. The ocean's rhythm lulls you, and you dream.

In your dream, you see a beautiful woman emerge from the ocean. Her hair, wet with sea foam, clings to her naked body. You marvel at Her beauty as She slowly, with a sensual motion of her hips, makes Her way toward where you lie sleeping in your earthen womb.

She softly kneels down beside you. You smell the salt and rose scent of Her body. You can hear Her soft breath rising and falling with the ocean waves. She leans forward and softly whispers in your ear: "Joy." In response, you feel your heart open and fill with abandoned joy. "Tickles." Every memory of happy, innocent play fills you. *(pause)* "Delight." *(pause)* It fills your heart. "Laughter." It fills your heart. *(pause)* "Wonderment." *(pause)* "Patience." *(pause)* "Acceptance." *(pause)* "Union." "Love." It fills your heart. Your heart is bursting with joy and love. You feel at peace with yourself.

You feel Aphrodite's hand rest lightly upon your chest and your heart responding; it dances with love. You can feel love circulating within every part of your being. You are love. You are joy. She lightly touches your check, and softly says, "I love you . . . I love you . . ." Like a mantra, you embrace it, "I love you . . . I love you . . ." If you allow Her, She will caress your body, enjoying all of you, those parts that you are proud of and those you keep hidden. *(pause)* "You are beautiful." "You are special." "You are love." You open your eyes and look into Hers. You see yourself reflected in their depths . . . "I love you . . . I love you." Feel the love moving within you. *(pause)*

You awaken from your dream hearing "I love you," and realize that it is your own voice. The hands that were so lovingly touching you were your own. You brought joy and love to your heart and filled it. Allow this knowledge, this self-love, to move within you and continue to repeat for a few moments your mantra . . . "I love you . . . I love you." Let it become part of your being. *(pause)*

You sit up and stretch, still smiling from the love that has filled you. As you get up to leave, you look down. In the sand right next to where you lay, you see the imprints of two knees and drops of water. Was it a dream? Walk down to the shore and offer your thanks to the lovely Goddess Aphrodite and throw a gift for Her into the ocean.

It is time to leave. Remember that you can return here as often as you like, but for now it's time to return to your inner home. Find your feet on the sandy path. Before you is your portal. Take one more look, then cross the threshold to home.

Communication With the Gods

WHAT'S IN A NAME?—YOUR MAGICAL NAME

You find yourself in a forest glade before the mouth of a large cave. The warmth of the day is wearing upon you, and you find yourself drawn by the cool darkness. The mystery of what lies within sparks your curiosity. Would you like to go in? *(a presumed yes)*

You enter the cave and let the coolness sweep away fatigue and worry. Your eyes quickly adjust and, though the cave is dimly lit, you're able to see well enough to find firm and comfortable footing.

The tunnel narrows as you make your way down into the Earth. The walls begin to become damp with condensation. The tunnel smells of wet stone and cold fresh water. The tunnel continues moving farther down and down, into the quiet stillness of the Earth. You reach your hands out to touch the wall to help you with your balance lest you slip on the damp surface. The wall is hard, wet, and smooth under your fingers. The light dims as you continue your descent, but you are not afraid. With calmness and determination, you continue into the darkness.

Far ahead is a pinprick of light that calls to you. The light calls with the promise of comfort. As you draw near, you see that the light is actually the opening of the tunnel. You step out into a huge, well-lit cavern. The walls are all of pink rock. There are stalagmites reaching upward from the floor of the cave.

Stalactites jut down from the ceiling, drops of water dripping down them to merge with the pools of water on the cavern's floor. The floor is uneven. It rolls like gentle hills with small pools of water forming in their valleys. It reminds you of a mother's womb, and you find yourself totally at peace here.

As you take in the sight of the room, you realize that what you thought was a rock formation in the center of the room is something else. You step into the cavern and slowly make your way toward it, realizing that seated on a rock bench is a Goddess. As you come before Her, you kneel in homage. She smiles and bids you welcome. If She chooses, She will reveal Her name to you.

She invites you to come, sit close to Her. You sit at Her feet. She reaches out Her hand and begins to stroke your hair, as a loving mother does to her young child. You can hear Her softly singing to you. You place your head upon Her lap and allow the peace and love to fill you. *(pause)* As She continues to lightly stroke your hair, you hear Her call you by a new name, one you have not heard before. This is not is the name you use in the waking world. This is the true name of your inner being. She whispers words of endearment and speaks your name again. And a third time. You feel your new name fill your heart and being.

Before you is a shallow pool. She invites you to look into Her pool of knowledge. You move over to the pool and look in. At first, you only see your face. Then your features begin to blur as visions rise to the surface. Perhaps the pool will reveal why you have been given this new name. Spend a few minutes with the pool. *(pause)*

You feel a light touch on your head. The Lady stands beside you. She touches your shoulder. As you rise, She whispers your inner name again in your ear. You can feel your body tingle.

It is time to leave. You thank your Goddess for Her many gifts to you and offer a gift to Her. She accepts it and returns to sit on Her throne. You make your way across the floor and to the opening of the cavern. Take one more look at the beauty of this inner place, then turn to make your way up the tunnel.

Using the sides for leverage, you climb higher and higher up through the tunnel. It begins to slowly widen as you continue your ascent, moving higher and higher. The rocks begin to dry. The ground is more steady. You can see the light growing, until you step out of the cave into the forest glen and onto the path. Before you is the portal to your sanctuary. Take one more look around and step over the threshold to home.

For Contemplation Upon Your Return Did your Goddess reveal Her name? What did She look like? What name was given to you? What were your visions in the pool? Did it explain why this name was chosen for you? Discuss and record in your trance journal your experience and reactions to this adventure.

Additional Exercises Trance journey to a mountaintop, where you listen to the winds whispering your name.

THE TEMPLE OF THE GODS

Connection and communication with your Gods is the goal of this two-part pathworking. In Wicca, we honor many Gods and Goddesses, yet many of us find ourselves drawn to working with one or two primary deities. Exactly which deity may vary with each person, or even at different phases of our lives. For this reason, the imagery in this exercise will be very generalized. If you know the Goddess or God who currently guides your path, please weave in His or Her specific symbols. If not, watch which symbols emerge as you journey, as it may help you discover your diety.

If you know which deity is focal for you right now, then do some research first. Read up on the mythology associated with your deity and the lives of His or Her worshipers. In which cultures did He or She originate? In what time period? In what environment would you most likely find Him or Her? You would not look for Poseidon, God of the Ocean, in the middle of a meadow, nor for Artemis in the sea. What kind of temple do you think your diety might have? What do you think He or She would look like? What are His or Her favorite colors, flowers, scents, foods? Is He or She associated with a particular animal or symbol? You can incorporate all this imagery into your journey (or ask your trance facilitator to do so).

When you feel ready, begin.

Part I—The Home of the Gods

You find yourself on a dirt path that winds its way through a meadow. You can feel the soft earth beneath your feet as you walk along it. Many others have walked this path before you. It is well worn from many, many feet. You can smell the scents of the meadow: warm sweet hay, meadow flowers, and rich earth. The path leads into a forest. The sunlight shines through the trees, creating patterns of light upon the ground. You follow the path, in the footsteps of thousands before you, as you make your way through the glen. The path opens, and ascends to the top of a hill. As you reach the top, you can see an ancient temple.

You stop and stare at what you know is what you've been looking for: the home of the Gods *(or insert name of deity)*. You can feel the great power within this sacred place as it flows out from the temple. You stand and feel the energy as it washes over you. Look at the environment around you. Absorb it with your being so that you can find this place again.

Make your way to the temple *(pause)* and enter it. It's empty, but it resonates with the unseen presence of its occupant(s). Look around you. Examine every nook, every stone, every little detail. Touch, smell, and, if possible, taste this place. Do you see or feel any symbols? Perhaps you will find the answer to a question or discover a message that will teach you something you need to know. Explore this place and its secrets. *(pause)*

It's time to leave. Leave an offering to the deity. You take one last look so that this place is etched into your memory, then return to the hill. *(pause)* You can still feel the energy coursing through you as you follow the path down the hill and into the forest, through the forest and back to the meadow, until you see your portal, your threshold to your inner home.

Part II—The Gods Therein
You find yourself back on the dirt path that winds through a meadow. You can feel the soft earth beneath your feet as you walk along it. You can smell the smells of the meadow. You remember where this path leads, and you walk it joyfully. If you wish, pluck some flowers or harvest a handful of grain to take with you as a gift.

You follow the path into the cooling forest and make your way through the glen. The path opens, and with anticipation, you make your way up to the top of the hill. As you reach the top, you can see before you the ancient temple. You stop and stare at the home of the Gods *(or insert name of deity)*. You can feel the great power as it flows out from this sacred place. You stand and feel the energy.

Make your way to the temple *(pause)* and enter it. It resonates with an unseen presence. Place your offering in the appropriate place and wait. Stand and feel the energy of this place. Wait and see if the deity whose home it is would like to reveal Him- or Herself and speak with you. If He or She does, listen carefully and respond if appropriate. Remember, the Gods can communicate in many different ways. *(Wait an appropriate amount of time.)*

It's time to leave this place. If you were given a piece of wisdom from the God or Goddess, take it with you. If not on this trip, remember you can return here whenever you choose. Take one last look so that it's etched into your memory, then return to the hill. *(pause)* You can still feel the energy coursing through you as you follow the path down the hill and into the forest . . . through the forest and back to the meadow . . . until you see your portal, your threshold to your inner home.

For Contemplation Upon Your Return What was the first thing you noticed about the temple? Did you notice any differences in the temple between trips? Was something missing or added? Were there animals present? Did your deity make Him- or Herself known to you, and if so, in what manner? What message were you given?

Additional Exercises If you expected a particular deity, and the vision or the symbols of the temple did not match up with what you believed you would see, take the clues and research. Another deity may be calling to you at this time.

CHAPTER FOUR

ༀ༰

By Our Will: Creating Change—
Meditations for Transformation

When we enter trance states, we enter into a magical realm. In this domain, we are able to communicate with the Gods and Goddesses. We can look inward for guidance and insights to learn and to find answers. When we enter trance with the intention to transform something within ourselves, our lives, or the lives of others, we are working magic—the art of creating change in accordance with will.

This chapter is about how to use trance for inner change, change that will eventually bring about change in the outer world as well. When we change our consciousness, behavior follows. When we act differently, we elicit different responses from the people and things around us.

In most cases, you'll know what changes you seek before you enter trance. Sometimes, the exercises may help reveal issues or goals you had not previously recognized. Difficult memories or long-repressed feelings may surface. You'll need to integrate or release these to clear the way for new growth and adventure. As you act on these insights, you may find yourself in confrontational situations. Remember what you learned from the previous chapter: You have power and control over your inner environment. As you travel, remember that no matter how far you wander, you can always return home.

A ⌂ indicates those workings that I believe deal with difficult issues. Still, everyone has their own issues that trigger powerful responses. You should always read a script before setting off on the journey to identify any potential problems before they arise. Group leaders who are facilitating the journey may have a general sense of what areas will be difficult for those they're working with, but it's impossible to predict what may bring back a repressed memory, causing a severe emotional reaction. If this occurs, bring the person out of trance, allow him time to process what occurred, and, if appropriate, suggest that he seek professional counseling.

In some cases, tools or supplies will be needed or suggested in order to fully participate in the experience. This will be indicated with a ⌘ at the beginning of the exercise. If you like, you can enhance your ritual space and altar with items that can help you focus on your intent—candles, colors, scents, and statues of appropriate deities, for instance.

The journeys included in this chapter are only suggestions. Many more possibilities exist. Use your own creative sense to adapt and change what's here to fit your own needs, visions, and practice. As with any magical working, remember to keep your intent clear and your ethics in mind. Forcing another to your will is coercive and unethical. In addition, remember that any magic needs to be followed through on the physical plane. A trance journey to help heal your body is wonderful, but if you don't follow up on it by taking care of yourself, you've defeated your purpose.

If the working is with an unfamiliar deity, spend time researching Him or Her before taking the journey. This will give you a clearer sense of whom you're working with and will add greater depth to the experience.

Before beginning, remember to prepare your environment (turn off the phone, create sacred space, and so forth) and be emotionally ready for the journey. Trivial stress and worries that you don't plan on working with in the circle should be packed away. I'm also assuming that you have already completed the pretrance steps (stretching, grounding, relaxation, and induction) and are in an alternate state. The workings begin with you leaving your inner home.

At the completion of each of the pathworkings, remember to discuss and record in your trance journal your experiences and reactions to them. Also, pay special attention to your dreams for the next few days and record those. Review your journal before the next meeting to see whether you notice any patterns worth examining further.

Magical Journeys for Magical Change

GET OUT OF MY WAY! REMOVING OBSTACLES

What blocks your way to change? Money? Location? Time? I've often found that my greatest obstacle is myself. This is a very short and simple pathworking. It can be done as often as is needed.

Find yourself in the middle of a field. The sun shines above you. A cooling breeze plays with your hair. The only thing visible in this field is a large stone. You walk toward it. As you stand inspecting the boulder, you realize that beneath this stone lies the solution to removing a current blockage in your life. You need to remove this stone in order to receive the gift. As you stare at the stone, the desire to find out what is underneath it builds in you. You want more than anything to find out what message is beneath its weight.

You place your hands upon the rock and feel its cold, rough surface. You give it a push. It doesn't move. But you must move this boulder. Look within yourself and around you at your environment and figure out a way to move the rock, and then do it. *(Pause for sufficient time to accomplish the task. If successful, then continue. If not, return another time and try again.)*

As the rock is moved away, you can smell the raw earth beneath it. Where the rock stood, you find a hole, and you see that there's something inside the cavity. This is the answer to your current perplexity. Retrieve it. Look closely at it. Turn it over in your hands. If it has any written words, read them carefully. If it's a symbol, engrave it into your mind. This is your answer, but you realize that by moving the stone you already began the work of removing your obstacle.

Return now to your inner home, bringing with you your hard-won answer to your problem.

For Contemplation Upon Your Return What kind of stone was it? How large was it? What was its shape? Do you notice any connection between the rock and your current situation? How did you move the boulder? What did you find underneath it? What form did your answer take? How will you follow up in the outer world in the next week, month, and year? Discuss and record in your trance journal your experience and your reactions to this adventure.

LIKE A ROCK—STRENGTH AND SLOW
TRANSFORMATION*

⌘ A rock—either a sedimentary (sandstone, limestone, or shale) or an igneous (granite) rock.

Many people have told me that they can feel the energy within crystals and minerals—but from a rock, a plain rock, they pick up nothing. This may be because rocks work at a much slower pace than their flashy siblings. You need to quietly sit with a rock, slowing yourself down to the rate of the stone, before you can understand the stories it tells. Rocks can teach us a great many things, especially insights into magical transformation. Not the one-two-three quick change. Rocks move very slowly. Their transformation may take longer, but it's solid.

This is a working for transformation, but its focus is the strength and patience that are required to break down and re-

---

*Based on conversations with Ted Tarr.

structure what needs to be changed. Have your intention, the transformation you seek, clear in your mind before you start. In order to create a strong connection, hold your rock throughout the entire working.

Go to your safe inner home. Sit there, holding your rock. Relax as deeply as you can. In your inner space, you feel completely safe and comfortable. You have all the time you need, and this knowledge lets you relax even more. You feel yourself slowing down . . . slowing even more . . . time holds no meaning . . . slower . . .

You begin to feel the rock in your hand getting warmer. Focus your attention on the rock. As you do, you realize that you and the stone can communicate. Tell the rock what you would like to transform. Ask it if it's willing to help you. If yes, an opening will be revealed to you.

Go through it, if you will. It is a doorway into the distant past, where the rock will show you where it has been, what it has seen. As you step through the doorway, you become the rock as it was centuries ago. Experience the life of the rock. Allow yourself to be slowly transformed with the rock.

If You Hold a Sedimentary Rock You find yourself as a rock in an ancient riverbed. Water continuously rushes over you. Slowly worn away by the waters of time, you feel yourself breaking into smaller pieces, becoming sand and mud. Other rocks and sand cover you. And they are worn away, becoming sand and mud . . . becoming layered on top of you. More rocks and sand . . . more layers. And more layers. The weight of the sand, rocks, and mud above you is immense. Still more layers. You feel the intense pressure of the weight bearing down on you . . . then the weight begins to re-form you. Slowly, very, very slowly, the mud and sand are fused together . . . transformed into rock . . . the rock you hold in your hand.

If You Hold an Igneous Rock You find yourself as a rock on the edge of the immense heat of a volcano in the inner core of our world. The Earth shifts, and you slide into the red mass. You begin to melt, broken down by the intensity of the volcanic heat, slowly becoming liquid rock . . . melting . . . becoming lava. You merge and join with other rocks. The Earth shifts again. You are slowly pushed upward toward the airs of the world above. Away from the heat, you cool, transformed into a rock . . . the rock that you hold in your hand.

Transformed, you find yourself returned to your inner home. If you wish, you can continue talking with the rock, asking for advice, listening to its stories. *One word of warning:* If the rock tells you that something is going to occur soon, remember the rock is talking in stone time, not people time.

Take the rock home with you and keep it handy. When you feel the need to slow down, make a nice cup of tea and sit quietly with your tea and your rock. Or try placing the rock in your bathtub while you enjoy a soothing soak.

For Contemplation Upon Your Return What stories did the rock tell you? What advice, if any, did it give you? The change that has begun here will take time and effort. It takes time, patience, to be worn away or melted so that another form can emerge. How will you follow up with this work in the outer world in the next week, month, and year? Discuss and record in your trance journal your experience and your reactions to this adventure.

IT'S OFF TO WORK I GO . . .

⌘ On your altar, place an object that represents your general occupation, or one you would like to enter (not a specific job). Also, have a copy of your resumé and any small tokens of your talents and skills. Use green or gold candles for prosperity, or whatever color seems to represent your chosen career. If you like, you can also have an image of a God or Goddess (or saint) who has been regarded as patron of your particular line of work.

This working is to help find work. It is not meant to focus on one job in particular, but instead to be used as a general call for employment or advancement within your chosen career field. If you are unsure of what career you wish to enter, go back to chapter 3 and redo "What Will I Be When I Grow Up?" (see page 136).

As a part of this guided meditation, you will send your resumé out to the universe. Here are some suggestions on how to imagine doing this:

- If your career choice is office work, create a paper airplane and let it out onto currents of air, or send it by fax.
- For computer technology positions, use the magic of the World Wide Web. See the information running along the wires and into the world.
- For transportation, put it into a model of your preferred method of travel and send it out down the road.
- For manual labor, use one of the pieces of equipment.

Remember, you must also follow through on the physical plane. Working magic for a new position without sending out physical resumés or making phone calls defeats your purpose. You need to give the magic a "landing pad" in the material world. Follow up the energy with some commonsense action.

Go to your inner home; you may find a work space there. Or you may find a door or archway leading to an adjoining space. This space will be either indoors or outdoors, depending on the activity that's going on there.

You find yourself in a work space typical of your chosen career. Feel yourself moving through a day . . . doing the day's work . . . and . . . returning home when the day is over. Hold in your heart the desire to do this type of work. Continue your creative imagination of your career until it's clear and vivid in your mind.

When you're ready, send forth your call in whatever way is appropriate. Feel the paper of your resumé, the keys of your computer, or the telephone in your hands. Know that it will go to those who should receive it.

You may want to dedicate your work to the relevant deity, or to the Earth and Her children. Give thanks, and return to ordinary reality.

For Contemplation Upon Your Return How will you follow up in the outer world in the next week, month, and year? Discuss and record in your trance journal your experience and your reactions to this adventure.

THE GIFT OF ABUNDANCE

The Gods' sense of humor sometimes leans to the ironic. I've a friend who owns an occult store. A customer came in one day asking for a prosperity spell, which she helped him create. A month later he came back to her, annoyed. He hadn't won the lottery. Instead he'd been bugged by his boss to work overtime. This brought him additional income, but wasn't what he'd expected. Maybe he should have done a spell for leisure? But then, he might have found himself unemployed.

Money is not the only form of wealth. Wealth can also be the abundance of friends and family loving and supporting you, the free flow of creativity that allows your soul to dance, a garden where you can feel the Earth between your fingers, or a work environment that you enjoy going to every day. You can be very rich while owning very little, and very poor while living in a mansion.

Laksmi, the Hindu Goddess of wealth and prosperity, will help you with this working. She is often depicted standing on a lotus blossom, being showered by two elephants.

You find yourself on a dirt path in a tropical forest. Large-leafed and lush vegetation lines the path on either side of you. The warm air carries the sweet scent of fragrant flowers. Above you are the noises of the forest, the chattering of birds and small animals. The path is clear and easy to follow. It has been well traveled. The passages of many feet have pressed the Earth into a hard surface. You follow the path through the growth. The foliage begins to thin as you approach the edge of a clearing. The path leads you into the brightness of a grass meadow and to the edge of a lush pond filled with white lotus blossoms. The large pads cover portions of the pond.

Brilliant-colored flowers and rich plants edge the water. As you admire the beauty of this place, a shimmer of reflected light catches your eye. You notice that on the shore of the pond stands a luxurious and brightly decorated canopy. A thick, soft cloth covers the Earth beneath the elaborate cover. There are comfortable reclining pillows and a low table holding bowls of sweets and nuts. A golden cup and pitcher contain drink. It all looks very inviting.

You notice movement on the pond. A large lotus bud is floating toward you. As it moves, the petals of the flower slowly unfold to reveal in its center a beautiful woman dressed in colorful silks and sparkling jewels. She steps from Her flower onto the shore and walks toward you. This is Laksmi, the Hindu Goddess of wealth and prosperity. Give homage to the Lady of abundance. *(pause)*

She smiles and invites you to come sit with Her under the canopy. You make yourself comfortable on the soft pillows. Laksmi offers you refreshments. Will you eat and drink with Her? *(a presumed yes)* As you enjoy what is offered to you, tell the Goddess in what ways you would like to prosper. *(Pause long enough for the task.)* She asks you what you are willing to do in order to make this happen. *(Pause long enough for the task.)*

A warm breeze drifts through the air. The pillows feel so

comfortable. You find yourself growing sleepy. Your eyes become heavier. Soon you find that you can no longer keep them open. You drift off into sleep and begin dreaming.

In your dream, you experience your request granted. The steps required to attain your desire are revealed to you. You become prosperous. Feel what that is like. *(Pause long enough for the task.)* Now ask yourself if there is anything missing. What did you leave behind in order to succeed? *(pause)*

You awaken, retaining the knowledge gained in your dream. You find that Laksmi has returned to Her home, but She has left you a present. On the table you discover a single lotus blossom and a necklace of gold. Take the one that you need. *(Pause long enough for the task.)* As you pick it up, it is absorbed into your being. You feel the abundance that surrounds you.

It is time to return. Go to the pond, thank the Goddess Laksmi, and leave an offering for Her in the waters of the pond. Now retrace your steps into the forest and back to your inner home.

For Contemplation Upon Your Return What insights did the dream provide? In the dream, what was missing from your life? For example, did you find that you had wealth, but had lost your closeness to friends and family because you had no time to nurture these relationships? Was it worth the sacrifice?

Which of Laksmi's gifts did you take? The lotus represents an abundance of intangible things such as friendship, love, and growth of spirit, while the necklace is the symbol of material prosperity. Did you take the gift that you think you need? If not, what might that indicate to you?

What are you willing to do on the physical plane to help fulfill your desires? Discuss and record in your trance journal your experience and your reactions to this adventure.

WHERE IS LOVE—A CALL FROM THE HEART

Many people call for love. They beg for love. They cry for love. They search for love in the face of everyone they meet, hoping that they will see their soul mate in another's eyes. But as much as you may long for love in your life, you cannot make it happen.

First, you need to be whole within yourself, so that you desire a partner instead of needing one. Then, you must have love in your own heart before you can share it with another. If you cannot truthfully say that love is a request, not a requirement, go back to chapter 3 and work with Aphrodite and self-love.

This pathworking is a heart-call, meant to be heard by someone who is out there looking for a partner like you. As with any magical act, it is unethical to direct this working toward any one person in particular. Think of it as more like a radio broadcast than a telephone call.

Aphrodite, the Goddess of love, will again be helping you with your working. You may want to turn back to pages 157–59 to refresh your connection with Her before beginning.

You find yourself on the dunes of Aphrodite's beach at night. Your picnic basket is where you left it. You go and collect it. You climb the sand dune and make your way to the beach on the other side. The ocean washes against the shore. Above you the stars are bright jewels on the black sky. You can see the constellations, and note the brightness of the star Venus.

Small shells and mica rocks glitter in the moonlight on the beach. A waxing moon is overhead, moving toward the horizon, providing enough light for you to see where you're going. A salt breeze is coming from the ocean.

The sand still holds warmth from the long day as you walk across it. You find a hollow in the sand of the dune, a private alcove just the right size for your body. Open your basket, remove your blanket, place it in the hollow, and sit. Feel the sand move beneath you as it shifts to mold to your body. Feel the sea breeze lightly touch you. Listen to the waves wash onto the shore. You are completely at peace here.

Reach into you basket and find paper and a writing instrument. Think about all the attributes you would like in a partner.

Funny? Cheerful? Supportive? Write them down on your piece of paper. *(Pause long enough for the task.)* Think about your list. Think about what it would be like having such a person in your life.

Take another piece of paper and write a letter to this person. Tell him or her about yourself, your life, the life that you hope you will have together. Use as many pieces of paper as you need. *(Pause long enough for the task)*

When your letter is complete, reach into your basket and pull out a bottle with a cork stopper in it. Remove the cork. Roll the letter up and place it into the bottle. If you were unable to write your note, whisper into the bottle what you would like to say. Replace the cork. Pick up your bottle and your list and make your way to the ocean shore.

Step into the tide and feel the cool water wash over your feet. Each wave takes away care. It helps you focus on your purpose. A heart-call can only be done with an open heart, not one filled with need and fear. Feel the weight of the bottle in your hand. The smooth surface of the neck, the roughness of the cork top. You look up again at the waxing moon. It shines brightly, sending down silvery light to aid you. You think again about your unknown partner. In your heart, call to your beloved. Feel the emotions of love rise with each wave of the ocean. Allow the desire to find this person, or to have this person find you, build. The sea responds, the waves building in strength and intensity to match your emotions. When you're ready, send forth your heart-call by throwing the bottle as hard as you can out into the depths. *(Pause long enough for the task.)*

The ocean accepts the charge. Your bottle with its call is engulfed and carried off in the tide. Stand and watch the ocean as it returns again to calm seas. *(pause)*

You notice movement along the shore. A beautiful woman approaches you. Her long hair cascades down her naked back. Her hips sway in sensual motion in time with the ocean's waves.

She moves along the water's edge toward you. She has been watching you as you stood on the beach sending your call. Greet Aphrodite, the Goddess of love, and pay Her homage. *(pause)*

She looks at you with a gentle smile. You find your attention drawn to Her eyes. You can't help but gaze deeply into them. You may glimpse your beloved in their depths. *(pause)*

If you like, give Aphrodite your list so that She can help guide your bottle through the tides to the right partner for you. *(pause)* When you're ready, thank Aphrodite and offer Her a gift.

The Goddess leaves you with a gentle kiss and returns to Her home by the sea. It's time for you to return as well. Go back to your hollow. Pick up your blanket, fold it, and replace it in your picnic basket. Remember to leave your basket in a place where you can find it again when you return. Take one more look at the ocean and the moon above it, then make your way back to your inner home.

For Contemplation Upon Your Return How did it feel return to the beach site? Did you find it easier to enter? Was your basket any different? What was your bottle made of? Does that indicate anything to you? Were you able to write in trance? Did you see a person in the Goddess's eyes? How will you follow up in the outer world in the next week, month, and year? Discuss and record in your trance journal your experience and your reactions to this adventure.

FEELING NO FEAR—PROTECTION

This pathworking is to strengthen your psychic and inner defenses. Remember, protection can be anything from a good lock on your door to a change in attitude. Always make sure to do what you need to in the material world so your magic has a channel to manifest through. Take the normal commonsense precautions. Lock your house doors and windows. Lock your car when you leave it, and check inside the car before getting back in. And if you feel threatened, notify the authorities.

The Greek God Hephaistos will be aiding you with the creation of a suit of personal protection. He is the God of fire and smithies. The metal objects he creates often possess magical qualities.

Slowly let your eyes become accustomed to your surroundings. It is night. A waxing crescent moon shines overhead. Before you stands a volcano. The summit glows red and orange in the night sky. The smells of sulfur and raw heat permeate the air. The steep, rocky landscape is rugged and bare. In the distance, you can hear the methodical pounding of hammers playing against the rumblings of the fiery mountain.

A path winds its way along the side of the steep slope. You make your way up that path, drawn by the hammer's call. The way is difficult. The small stones of the path occasionally slip beneath you. But you continue on, your feet keeping pace with the stroke of the hammer. You climb until you reach the large mouth of a cave.

Inside the opening, you see Hephaistos putting the finishing touches on a magnificent suit of armor. In the bright light of a massive forge, you see him raise his hammer and strike the metal before him on the anvil. The sound echoes off the walls of the cavern. Satisfied with his work, he thrusts the hot metal into a large bucket of water. Hot, acrid steam billows upward from the water's surface.

He looks up, sees you standing at the entrance, and beckons you to enter. You walk in staring at the armor, knowing it will protect the wearer from anything. Hephaistos smiles at you and says, "This armor is not for you; it belongs to another. But if you wish, I will teach you how to make your own." Would you like him to teach you to forge a protective suit of armor? *(a presumed yes)*

Hephaistos puts you to work keeping the immense forge. You stoke the fire by hauling buckets of charcoal from the depths of the mountain. The contents of the buckets are so heavy that you must drag them to their place beside the forge. The wooden handles of the buckets raise blisters on your hands and palms. Eventually hard calluses form. As your body grows strong, the buckets grow lighter with each trip to the inner core.

You pump the huge bellows for the God, forcing out air to keep the embers hot. The searing heat of the forge reddens and hardens your skin. As you grow accustomed to the heat, you learn to enjoy and respect the fire spirits found within the heart of the furnace.

From a spring in the mountain, you collect the water to cool the metal. At the spring, you also pour the healing waters over your hot and tired body to temper and refresh your spirit.

All the time, you watch Hephaistos as He works His skill.

After what seems to be a long time, He brings out a hammer and two large sheets of metal. They glitter in the light of the furnace. He hands you one of the sheets and a hammer. The metal is heavy and sturdy. You place it on Hephaistos's workbench. The hammer fits well in your callused hand. You feel the heaviness of the mallet and the rough wood handle. You bang the anvil once . . . twice . . . three times, feeling its weight and balance.

Hephaistos turns to you and says, "Now that you've watched me, we will work the metal together. Watch and do as I do."

You follow Hephaistos. Matching his moves with your own, you cut out pieces of metal and begin making the armor. The metal works like clay under your strong hands. First, you make the helmet. You hammer out the piece of metal and thrust it into the center of the furnace. When it glows red, you remove it from the flames and work it again with your hammer. Your hammer creates sparks as it strikes. Sweat from the heat and exertion drips down your nose and runs down your body. Continue heating and molding your metal under the watchful eyes of Hephaistos until you're ready to immerse it in the cooling water. *(pause)*

Next, you turn your attention to the breastplate and skirt, heating and hammering until they are complete. *(pause)* Then to the greaves to cover your legs. *(pause)* Finally, the vambrace for your arms. Hephaistos nods his head and smiles at your accomplishment. You have fashioned a beautiful suit of protection. You run your hands along the smooth, cool surface and feel pride at your work.

When it's complete, you carry your newly formed armor to the edge of the lava pool in the center of the volcano. You look into its fiery depths. The lava swirls below you. Clouds of smoke and gas rise in the air. Call upon the power of Earth and Fire to empower your armor with protective energy. *(pause)* A spark leaps out of the lava and sinks deep into the armor. You can feel the suit vibrate and hum with energy.

Hephaistos bids you to don your suit of armor. You start with the greaves. They wrap tightly around your legs. You add the breastplate and the skirt. They feel snug against your skin, as if molded to your body. You put on the vambraces and finally the helmet. You stand there for a minute and feel the effort of their making, and your pride in the result. *(pause)*

More and more, you feel the energy of the armor, which is made of your own focus and effort, Hephaistos's blessing and guidance, and the power of the volcano. Your body seems to vibrate in time with the armor. Then the armor begins to disappear. It is absorbed into your body. You can feel it as it's pulled way down deep inside of you. You stand, experiencing the flow of energy from the suit. It feels like an invisible, impenetrable barrier. Hephaistos smiles.

He says to you, "Now everywhere you go you will be protected, whether it be from physical, magical, or spiritual dangers. Go now, knowing you are protected."

Thank Hephaistos and offer Him a gift. When you're ready,

make your way back down the mountain and return to your inner home.

For Contemplation Upon Your Return Why do you think you were required to labor for Hephaistos before constructing the armor? What did you learn through the efforts and your time with the God? What form did your armor take? From what metal was the suit constructed? How will you follow up in the outer world in the next week, month, and year? Discuss and record in your trance journal your experience and your reactions to this adventure.

Variations on Creating Protection
- For your home or place of work: From you inner safe space, you step out and find yourself in your home or at your job. Walk around the outside of the building, creating a protective circle of glowing light. The energy can come from your hands, from your body, or from a magical instrument as you walk. Repeat on the inside of the space, creating a double circle. You can also bring spirit guardians into your circle and ask that they remain at each of the quarters to help keep you and the space safe from harm.
- Create an invisible bubble of protection that encapsulates your home, your work, or yourself.
- Create a cloak of invisibility. Fashion it while in trance, as you did the suit of armor, then use it in the same fashion. Be sure to leave yourself a way to remove it when you want to be noticed.

Healing the Body, Healing the Heart

THE COMPASSION AND MERCY OF KWAN YIN
Kwan Yin, the Goddess of mercy, is the bodhisattva of compassion. As She was about to enter nirvana, She heard a child crying and turned back to comfort him. Hence She is called by the

Buddhists "She who harks to the cries of the world." She has the power to heal; all you have to do is ask. The following healing work with Kwan Yin was written by Ashta'ar Arthura.

Look up at the full moon, or imagine the sight. It glows brilliantly silver. Its markings seem to suggest a beautiful young woman dressed in the ornate robes of ancient China. In one hand, She holds a blossoming lotus; in the other, She holds a flask, tilted down to pour out healing for all beings. Her lovely face bears an expression of compassion and care. You address Her respectfully: "Kwan Yin, please heal me!"

As you continue to stare at the moon, it seems to contract into a brightly glowing white pearl, which begins to move swiftly toward you. It lodges at your very center, and you feel it filling your entire body with silver radiance. The glowing energy spreads out from the pearl, driving out all pain, all illness, all imbalance, and all impurities. As the silver glow fills you to the tips of your fingers and toes, to the very ends of your hair, everything negative that was driven out collects in a pool of black fluid at your feet.

You look down and see that the dark puddle has attracted a swarm of small monsters and demons. To them, it is delicious and nourishing food, and they lap it up eagerly until they have consumed it all. Once sated, they depart, and you wish them well. You are filled with strength and well-being, and you feel no fear. Your entire body radiates purifying moonlight, cleansing the space around you.

Presently the glowing pearl in the center of your body rises back into the sky, but you are still filled with its pure silver radiance, which leaves no room for pain or disease. When you look up, the pearl has once again become the moon in the sky. The beautiful Lady in the moon smiles at you, and you whisper to Her: "Thank you, Kwan Yin!"

Return to your inner home.

THE HEALING GARDEN

You find yourself entering a garden filled with flowers, plants, and vegetables. The sun is shining. A cooling breeze fills your lungs, refreshing and relaxing you. You smell the fragrance of the flowers, the earth, and vegetables ripening around you. The dirt path is soft beneath your feet. As you walk, you reach out and touch the leaves and petals of various plants. Some are velvety soft, some waxy smooth, others rough. A few are fuzzy like feathers.

Small pathways weave around the garden, bringing you from one bed to another. You pass a small pond. Its cooling waters twinkle in the sunlight. Wander your garden for a moment, enjoying the growth and the life within it. Feel the life energy surging through this sacred space, moving through the roots of the plants beneath your feet and blowing on the air. Feel it wash through you and around you. *(Pause to allow exploration of this place.)*

You come to one section of your garden that is in distress. The plants are wilted and weeds fill the beds. Here is illness. You need to tend and nurture this area to make it strong again. Put your hands into the earth. Pull out the weeds and remove any dead plants. Loosen the soil so that new roots can easily spread and grow. Add compost or fertilizer and, if needed or if you wish, weed killer.* Plant new seeds or plants. Offer support to frail plants by staking them with sticks and twine. Retrieve water from the pond and water the growth. Take time to care for your garden. *(Pause long enough for the task.)*

---

*Weed killer is a metaphor for chemotherapy and other invasive drug therapies, and may be used for those who are seriously ill. Use if appropriate, or leave this sentence out. You may also want to consider inserting other gardening methods that correspond with medical treatment. "Staking" a plant can also be seen as setting a bone; washing the leaves to remove parasites, for skin conditions; covering the plants to shade them from the sun, for burns; and so forth.

Finish with your section of the garden bed. You can see how much better it looks already. Before you leave, soak up the beauty and energy of the rest of your garden. Let it build in you, then channel some of that energy into your newly tended bed. See the plants within it respond. A leaf opens, buds form on one of the flowers, a small sprout pokes its head out of the earth. It will take time until it blossoms into complete health, but you've begun the process toward healing. You can return here as often as you like to continue helping your garden grow strong.

It's time to go. Retrace your steps back to your inner home.

For Contemplation Upon Your Return What was in your garden? What kinds of plants were predominant? What bed was having difficulties, and where in your garden was it located? What might that indicate to you? What did the weeds look like? What kind(s) of seeds or plants did you plant? How will you follow up in the outer world in the next week, month, and year? Discuss and record in your trance journal your experience and your reactions to this adventure.

Variations on Healing Your Body
- Find yourself in a miniature submarine inside your body. Take your sub to the location where you're experiencing illness. See what's causing the trouble and either zap it with you sub-gun, killing the bad cells, or send it a jolt of healing energy from your sub's healing ray.
- Find yourself beside a car that isn't running properly. Spend time under the hood repairing the car. Look around it for other dings and dents and repair those, too.
- Or find yourself inside a house. Look around and see what problems you can find. Maybe the roof needs to be repaired, a support replaced, or the plumbing unclogged. Spend time repairing your house.
- Find yourself in a home or apartment. Redecorate the space. Recover or replace the furniture that looks old and

frayed. Mix up some heavy-duty, kill-germs-on-contact cleanser and wash the floors and walls. Wash the windows and let in some light.

HELPING OTHERS HEAL

⌘ Although it isn't required, a picture of your loved one would be useful as a focal point during the trance induction. This will help you keep his or her image and essence clearly in your mind.

There are many ways to use pathworking to help heal a loved one, human or animal, who cannot be physically present for the working. The vast majority of healing work involves using your creative imagination to "see" the subject happy and healthy. While keeping that vision clear, you send him or her healing energy. Here is a simple suggestion that works on this idea.

You find yourself in a place that you associate with your loved one. It's a place where you created and shared happy moments together. As you explore, your loved one joins you. Bid him welcome and, if you desire, give him a hug.

As you experience being with your loved one, you notice that he is ill or hurt. You can sense the sickness and the afflicted area. Ask him if he will allow you to do magical work to help strengthen and heal his body. If he indicates yes, reach deep into the Earth and draw up its healing energy. You can also pull in and use the energy of the environment around you.

Feel the healing energy build within you, like a capped volcano. Keep pulling the energy up and up. Fill your body with energy until you cannot fill it anymore. Reach your hands forward and touch your loved one in the area that needs this healing energy. Allow the healing energy to explode outward from you and into your loved one. Feel it streaming out of you, to fill your loved one. As it does, see health begin to return to him. See him becoming stronger.

Your loved one stands before, you smiling with thanks. Hold

this vision of your loved one—healthy and happy. Do something together that you both enjoy: dance, talk, laugh, make love, play a sport, take a walk. Feel life and joy within and around your loved one.

Your loved one gives you his deepest thanks and leaves this familiar environment. When you're ready, return to your inner home.

For Contemplation Upon Your Return In what environment did you find your loved one? Was there anything within the environment that you could use to help heal your loved one? How will you follow up in the outer world in the next week, month, and year? Discuss and record in your trance journal your experience and your reactions to this adventure.

Meeting the Challenge

FACING YOUR DEEPEST FEAR Ꭷ

Fear is a strong emotion. This can make it difficult to find what's at the heart of the fear. Through allowing yourself to feel and release your fear, and other painful associated emotions, you can gain insight into aspects of the frightening situation that you can change, and make a realistic plan of action.

When my husband was dying, I was terrified of losing him. When I allowed myself to face and experience the fear, pain, grief, and anger, I reached a deeper insight: It was not his death that terrified me, it was being left alone. Naming my fear eventually allowed me to transcend it.

It can be difficult to confront your deepest fear. At different points, you will be given opportunities to leave this working. Doing so is not a failure. You can return as often as you need to, until you're able to face and work through the thing that frightens you the most.

You step from your home your find your feet on the dirt path in the middle of a dark forest engulfed in fog. Above you, you can see the glow of what you know to be a waning moon through the branches and clouds. The air is damp and carries the scent of rotting leaves and dark earth. Very large and ancient trees, their bark thick and knotted with age, line both sides of the path. The trees are leaning forward over the path. Their branches intermingle and merge above you, forming a dark tunnel. The path leads into the fog and the darkness.

Ahead of you on the path is the sound of running water. An owl calls somewhere above you. You feel fear. Fear is an energy around you, moving through you. Every fiber of your being feels fear. You smell your fear. You taste your fear. Will you move forward onto the path?

(If yes, continue. If no, return to your safe inner space.)

You walk down the path. There is no noise except the sound of your feet on the hard dirt path and the soft sound of water flowing. You can see the path ahead of you in the fog. It leads you toward the sound of the water. Soon you approach a dank and murky swamp with a shallow brook running through its center and stop.

On the other side of the mire, emerging from the fog, a figure forms. As it becomes clearer, you realize that on the other shore stands your greatest fear. It faces you from the other side of the water, but it cannot cross. Spend some time safely observing it. What does it look like? What does it represent to you? *(pause)*

Your fear stands glaring at you, daring you to cross. Looking at the flowing water beyond the mud of the banks, you realize that you are at a ford. At this point the brook is shallow, and you could easily walk across. Will you go forward to walk through the swamp, to stand in the middle of the brook and confront your fear?

(If yes, continue. If no, return to your safe inner space.)

You step into the muck of the water. The mud catches your heels, sucking and dragging them down. You must work to free yourself with each step. You slowly make your way toward the shallow brook. When you reach the flowing water, you find that its undersurface is sand and small rocks, and it is sturdy beneath your feet. The gentle water cascades over your ankles, washing away the mud. You walk easily to the middle of the stream. You can smell the stagnant water around you. Your fear continues to stand and watch you from the other shore.

When you arrive in the center of the flowing brook, you stop. Your fear is closer to you now. What is this thing that scares you? Speak to your fear. Yell, scream, or cry at your fear. Allow all the emotions that feed your fear to pour out of you. Let the water take these emotions and wash them away. The anger . . . it is taken away . . . the pain . . . it is washed away . . . the uncertainty . . . the grief . . . the stream takes it away . . . any other emotions you have associated with this fear, allow the water to wash them away. *(pause)*

Your fear still stands on the shore. Perhaps it looks different now that the layers of emotion that have fed it have been removed. Can you name your deepest fear? It stands daring you to finish your journey over to where it stands. Will you finish crossing the brook to stand and face it?

(If yes, continue. If no, return to your safe inner space.)

Stepping forward, you continue to the other side. Each step brings you closer to that fear. You realize that as you come closer, your terror is lessened. When you arrive on the shore, you walk to face your fear. Stand so that you are looking directly at each other. What does it look like now? If you will, reach your hand out to touch it and, as you do, name your deepest fear. *(pause)*

With your touch, your fear slowly evaporates before you, dispersing into the fog. In its place, you can see and feel a beautiful pillar of glowing energy rise up from the ground where it stood. If you will, reach out and touch the column. *(pause)* You feel healing energy fill you, filling the areas where the fear once lived. The pillar vanishes and you find yourself alone in the forest. The fog is lifting. You can see the beauty of the landscape around you. With a lighter heart, follow your steps back across the brook, past the trees, and return, with a new sense of self, to your inner home.

For Contemplation Upon Your Return Were you able to face your fear? What form did it take? How did your fear change after the emotions feeding it had been washed away? How will you follow up in the outer world in the next week, month, and year? Discuss and record in your trance journal your experience and your reactions to this adventure.

REWRITING THE PAST—RECLAIMING POTENTIALS* 🔔

As we go through life, we make choices. Every time we choose, we open one door and close one or more others. While we may fantasize and wonder about the "what ifs," we cannot go back in time, change our minds, and choose the other road. But we *can* go back to that point and reclaim some of the potential that we left behind.

When I was in college, I used to sing. I was very good at it and had toyed with the idea of a career in the music industry. One day a fork came in my life, and I had to choose. I chose the other road. I left the potential of a singing career and even my voice behind. For many years I didn't sing at all.

Then, during a coven ritual, I participated in a working similar to the one included here. I went back in time to remind myself of what my childhood dreams had been. It was then that I remembered my singing. With this realization, I went forward in time to the moment when I made the decision that took me away from my music and seized back the potential for my voice.

---

*This is based on conversations with Penny Novak.

Soon afterward, I came across a box in my attic containing sheet music from my college days. Today I sing, not for large adoring crowds but for my friends and at times my community. Doing so gladdens my heart. I am told that I still have a lovely voice.

In this working, you will go back in time to a moment when you made a decision that intentionally or inadvertently closed out some area of potential growth. You will then be given the opportunity to alter that choice slightly so that you can reclaim the portion of yourself that you left behind with the decision. Remember that whatever you reclaim will be lost again unless you integrate it into your current life.

Not everyone had a wonderful childhood. In this guided meditation, you will have the choice of returning to your youth to rediscover a dream. You will be brought to only those times when you felt happy and safe enough to dream. Those of you who, even in this framework, find remembrance difficult, or who already have a clear idea of what you would like to reclaim, will have the option to skip directly to the timeline portion of the working.

Janus, the Roman God of time, will aid you in your search. He is seen as an older man with two faces or heads, looking in opposite directions. One gazes into the possibilities of the future, and the other to the wisdom of the past. According to Roman mythology, Janus is present at every major occurrence in your life.

You find yourself on a very straight path in the middle of nothing. There is darkness above you, below you, all around you. There is no noise and no wind. It is as if you stepped onto the empty sound stage of a movie studio. The only thing visible is the path before you. It is hard and sturdy beneath your feet. Although you cannot tell whether you would fall if you stepped off the path, you feel no fear.

As you look straight ahead on the road, you see someone approach. As He comes closer, you see it is an older man with a heavy beard wearing a white toga. Although you do not see the back of His head, you know that when you do, you will see an identical face. He stops before you. Give homage to the Janus, God of time.

Janus offers to take you back in time, to happy moments in your childhood so that you can rediscover your dreams of what you had hoped to become as an adult. Will you allow Janus to bring you back to only the safe and happy moments in your childhood? *(If yes, continue. If no, skip to going back to the moment a potential was lost.)*

He offers His hand. As you come up beside Him, you see His other face smiling at you. With a wink, you find yourself at your own birth. Walk with Janus as he brings you through your younger years and back to the present. Experience being a young child for a moment . . . an older child . . . an adolescent . . . a young adult . . . remember what brought you joy. Rediscover your early dreams. *(Allow enough time for the task to be completed.)*

You stand back at your present with the memory of a dream that you relinquished in order to pursue other interests that, at that time, seemed more important. Janus offers to take you back to that moment when you made the choice. Will you go? *(a presumed yes)*

Take the hand of Janus again and walk backward in time. You see your life in reverse. What you did today . . . last night . . . yesterday morning . . . afternoon . . . the hours and the days move by quickly. With each step, a week passes. Skip over those times you do not wish to reexperience; just let them slide by without noticing. *(pause)*

Janus slows as He approaches the moment of choice. You find yourself back at the moment the decision was made—whether consciously or consciously—to turn away from the potential that you now seek. See it clearly. *(pause)* Reach into that moment and grasp hold of what it was that you left behind. Pull it from the fabric of time. Feel it as it's absorbed back into your being.

Janus returns you to the moment you began your journey with Him. You can feel the reclaimed portion of yourself as it settles within you, possibly already tugging at you to begin exploring the potential it brings. Thank the God and offer Him a gift. When you're ready, return to your inner home.

For Contemplation Upon Your Return What potential did you recover? Were there other dreams that you would someday like to reclaim? How will you follow up in the outer world in the next week, month, and year? Discuss and record in your trance journal your experience and your reactions to this adventure.

IT TAKES COURAGE

Say the word *courage* and perhaps a firefighter or police officer comes to mind. But courage does not mean just unselfishly running into a burning building. Courage is going forward even when you fear failure. It is the willingness to test your abilities and the faith that the outcome will be what you need. Courage is failing but trying again and again until you accomplish your goal or accept with grace that there is another path you're meant to walk.

You find yourself in a large empty parking lot. Beside you is a young child with a bicycle. She looks so small next to the bike. When you look at the bike, you see it has training wheels on the back tire. The child looks up at you with expectation and trust. You feel a sense of love and connection to this child. You are there to help her learn how to ride the bike.

The child climbs on the bike and pedals back and forth showing you how well she can ride with her training wheels. She stops before you and gets off the bike. You find a screwdriver in your hand and begin to remove the extra wheels. The child runs around you in circles, very distressed. Take a moment to calm the child's fears *(pause)*, then finish removing the training wheels.

You ask the child to get back on the bike. She begins to cry with fear, but she approaches it. You hold it as she gets on. *(pause)* Encourage the child *(pause)* and let go of the bike. You jump forward again and catch it before both the bike and child hit the ground. Let the child try again. *(pause)*

It takes courage to do something that you have never done before, to trust in your abilities. Help her back on the bike. She is shaking, tears are spilling down her cheeks, but she is willing to try again. This time you give her a little push. She pushes the pedals, and the bike goes forward for a few feet . . . then slowly wavers and begins to fall again. Before it hits the ground, you catch and steady the bike and the child.

The child is now excited. Did you see how long the bike stayed up! She was riding! Give her a bit more encouragement. *(pause)* She gets back on the bike with determination. Hold the bike and run beside it as she pumps the pedals as hard as she can. Then let go. She is riding all by herself. You can feel a sense of pride, the exhilaration that comes when you face something that you aren't sure you can do but move beyond the insecurity to try, and then succeed. This is true courage.

You watch the child ride around the parking lot and, for a moment, you become the child. Feel the wind on your face, your body finding its sense of balance and the freedom found within courage. *(Pause long enough for the task.)*

It's now time to return. You find yourself back watching the child. See her ride the bike exultantly around the parking lot. She calls out, "Thank you!" and waves good-bye to you as you turn to find your way back to your inner home.

For Contemplation Upon Your Return What are you facing that requires courage? What skills do you already have that can help you succeed? Did you notice anything special about the child? What she was wearing? The bike? If so, what associations can you draw with your own life? What steps are you going to take on the physical plane to help manifest this work? Discuss and record in your trance journal your experience and your reactions to this adventure.

CAULDRON OF TRANSFORMATION ☽

The act of change can elicit conflicting emotions, for real change is not often gentle. Self-transformation often requires letting go of things we will miss, such as comfortable habits that conflict with our goals. Something must die in order for something else to rise and take its place. Sadness is a normal reaction. We may feel angry or frustrated, or too frightened to give up familiar patterns. We can become confused, conflicted, even resistant. Much as we may want new things in our lives, it's hard to clear the space for them.

This pathworking will continue to resonate in you long after you've returned to ordinary reality. Remember, you are not a failure if you choose not to release your burden at this time. Cerridwen and Her cauldron will be there when you are ready.

Cerridwen, who will be aiding you in this working, is one of the Welsh Mother Goddesses and is said to tend a cauldron of inspiration and transformation. Associated with the moon, Her symbol is a white sow.

You find yourself on a dark, tree-lined path in the woods. In your hands is a heavy knapsack. A full moon shines above, lighting the road before you. Without fear, you put on your knapsack and walk down the road, listening to the night sounds. Suddenly, a white sow breaks from the undergrowth, scampering across your path and then back into the darkness on the other side of the road. As you look in the direction toward which the sow ran, you notice a light far off in the woods. The light seems to beckon to you. You become aware of a small path, so slight that only someone looking for it would notice its presence. It branches off the road, heading in the direction of the light. Will you take the path less trodden? *(a presumed yes)*

Stepping carefully, you take the side trail. It takes all your concentration to follow it in the dim light as the path makes its way through the woods. It winds around trees and bushes. Your heavy pack keeps catching on branches and leaves. You push away the foliage with your hands lest it hit your face in the darkness. The light that you saw on the road grows brighter as you move closer to the source.

When you arrive, you can see the clearing through the trees and the woman who stands within it. It was the fire beneath a massive cauldron that attracted your attention from the road. The wood smoke fills the clearing. The woman stands at Her pot, stirring the contents with a large wooden spoon the size of a boat oar. She does not look up from Her work as you enter the glen, but you realize that She knows you are there. She is an older woman. Her wild black hair contains large streaks of white. Her face shows the lines of one who has lived long and seen much. The sleeves of Her robe have been pulled back, exposing arms that are thin but strong.

You quietly cross the clearing and approach the black cauldron. The woman continues to look into Her pot and stir. You can hear Her muttering words over its contents, but you are unable to understand their meaning. She does not bother to look up at you as you come closer. You feel the heat of the coals. The smell of mystery permeates the air around you. You come closer . . . and closer, until you are beside the massive container. You place your sack on the ground and peer into the dark contents of the pot. Reflected within the cauldron, you see the full moon.

You look up at the old woman. She stops Her work and levels Her eyes to look straight into yours. The wisdom and knowledge of the ages are reflected in Her eyes. You want to pull away, but you are held by Her gaze. You feel as if She can see into your very essence and that She is judging you and your worth. *(pause)* Satisfied with what She has found, She nods and slowly starts to stir again.

She begins again to mutter her incantation, then stops.

"Do you know what this is?" She asks you, Her voice strong but soft, as if She were speaking to a child. "I am called Cerridwen, and before you is the cauldron of inspiration, knowledge, and transformation."

She lets you think about this for a moment before She continues.

"You carry something you no longer need; a burden that is keeping you from fully experiencing life. I give you an opportunity to let go of it, to surrender it if you can, and let it die. In the cauldron it will be transformed into something more useful."

She stirs her mixture, in silence. Do you have a weight? Something that is no longer useful? Something that you have been unable to let go? Anger? Jealousy? Grief? Sorrow? Hope? You have been carrying it for a long time. It is with you even now, in that heavy bag beside you. Do you have something that you would like to surrender to the cauldron of change? *(If yes, continue. If no, then allow for personal interaction and return to your safe inner home.)*

You pick up your knapsack. It feels very heavy. You open it and peer inside. You find the thing that has been burdening you. Remove it from the sack, and when you're ready, drop it into the cauldron. *(Pause to allow completion of the task.)*

It lands in the cauldron with a *plop*. Bubbles form and burst on the surface. Swirls of colors emerge from the dark liquid, followed by bright sparks. Then it is quiet. As you watch, something floats to the surface. Cerridwen fishes it out for you with Her giant spoon. You take it from Her. Look carefully at what gift has been given to you. As you study it, you realize that it is just what you need. You pick up your bag (it is so much lighter now) and put it inside.

Thank the Lady Cerridwen and offer Her a gift. If you would like, stay a moment and speak with Her. (*Pause to allow personal interaction.*) You retrace your steps to the edge of the forest. As you enter the woods, you hear behind you in the glen the squeal of a sow. You leave it behind and find your way back to the road. It is so much easier without the heaviness that was in your pack. You find the road and return to your inner home.

For Contemplation Upon Your Return What did you see in the Goddess's eyes? What else was in your knapsack? What did you drop into the cauldron to be transformed, and what form did it take? What form was it transformed into? How will you follow up in the outer world in the next week, month, and year? Discuss and record in your trance journal your experience and your reactions to this adventure.

Shape Shifting

Shape shifting is experiencing life from a different perspective, that of an animal or other being. In our imaginations, we become the animal, or tree, or rock. By doing so, we expand our own awareness and understanding of our world and the things within it.

RELEASING YOUR WILD INSTINCT ♨

It's so easy in this world of automation and technology to shut off our wilder, instinctual selves. Many of us live in cities, work in cubicles, and buy our food prepackaged and precooked—far removed from the natural realms. Our behavior is often regulated, our natural, primal selves restricted.

We need every aspect of ourselves in order to be complete, joyful people. Repressing our wild-self energy may cause pressure to build—pressure that can eventually break out in inappropriate, even destructive, ways. By embracing and integrating

198 ᘓ Wiccan Meditations

this energy, we can instead channel this energy into creativity and healthy endeavors.

You find yourself in the middle of a lush, wild wood. The sun shines through the leaves of the trees above you, warming you. There is no cleared path before you, just the moss-covered forest floor, soft beneath your feet. You smell the scent of pine, green trees, and decaying leaves. Birds fly and sing above you. The wind catches the leaves of the trees and rustles them. Nearby you can hear the sounds of animals foraging for food. You feel completely at peace.

You hear a movement in the forest before you. Something is coming toward you through the bushes. A strong scent of animal musk hits your nose, followed by the sight of a pair of antlers emerging from the growth. Beneath the rack is a majestic buck.

He pushes the bushes aside with his body and makes His way toward you while His eyes scan the underbrush for danger. He stops, and levels His eyes to look into yours. You blink. No longer a deer, but a man with a set of antlers upon His head stands before you. Give homage to Cernunnos, Lord of the wood. *(pause)*

Cernunnos reaches into a bag that He has slung over His shoulder. He pulls out a wooden cup and a bottle. He pours some of the contents of His bottle into the container and offers you the cup. Will you drink? *(a presumed yes)* You take the cup. The edge is uneven; the surface feels rough in your hands. You bring the cup to your lips and take a sip. The nectar within is strong and sweet. Suddenly, you find your vision blurring. You feel your heart beating hard and fast within you as you fall to the soft earth.

Cradled on the mossy ground, your body begins to grow and change. When you rise again, it is on the four sturdy legs of a deer. You feel energy surging through your body. You have forgotten that you are human. Your senses and instincts are now those of an animal. You feel completely free. You are wild, a creature of the forest.

Cernunnos, again a buck, stands before you. The woods beckon. The Horned One turns and leaps into the growth of the forest. You follow Him into the brush. Your instincts tell you where to go in the woods. Spend time running and exploring as a deer. *(Pause for sufficient time to complete the task.)*

Suddenly, your instincts tell you danger is near. You smell the wolf before you see it. You run. Your heart pounding with fear. You feel the wolf behind you, giving chase. You feel it leap upon your back . . . the wolf's teeth ripping your soft throat . . . and you feel your mouth clamping down hard . . . You are no longer the deer. Now you are the wolf, and this deer was your hard-earned prey, the food you and your pack need for survival.

Your pack joins you as the deer ceases its struggles beneath you. You raise your head and howl for victory and pride. You feel the strength of your wolf's body. The muscles ripple beneath your fur. You see your wolf pack around you. One catches your attention. It leaps into the brush, and you give chase. Feel the forest around you, your heightened animal senses. Feel the wildness of being a wolf. *(Pause for sufficient time to complete the task.)*

Suddenly you sense danger. You smell something that is not deer, nor wolf. You can hear it moving ahead of you. You stop and crouch low to the ground. Allowing your natural instincts to guide you, you move cautiously forward. You see a creature standing on its hind legs in a clearing. A growl fills your throat, and your fur arches on your back. He turns to look at you. When His eyes meet yours, you remember who you are. Your vision blurs and you find yourself lying on the Earth's floor, human again, with Cernunnos, beside you.

If you will, allow the memory of being a deer and a wolf become part of your being. Remember the feeling of being completely wild and free. The sense of animal instinct that exists within all living creatures . . . including you. Allow the memory to merge with you. Feel the wolf and the deer run within you.

It's time to go. Give your thanks to Cernunnos and offer Him a gift. He may offer you additional words of wisdom. (*Allow a moment for personal interaction.*) Watch Him return to the wood, blending into the forest and disappearing in its growth.

For Contemplation Upon Your Return Both a deer and a wolf are wild creatures. Having experienced them both, do you have a preference between them? Why? How will you use your instincts? How will you follow up in the outer world in the next week, month, and year? Discuss and record in your trance journal your experience and your reactions to this adventure.

VARIATIONS—EXPLORING THE ANIMAL WAYS

In the last two chapters, you were given an opportunity to experience becoming a tree and a rock. What I am offering in this section is an example of how to set up a shape-shifting journey. Take it and apply it to the animal or element of your choice.

The trip begins and ends at an ancient willow tree. The willow is associated with lunar and seasonal cycles, the tides, and cycles of nature. Each time you visit, you build up the associations with this place, becoming familiar with the willow and the magic that is found within its shelter. This familiarity will add greater dimension and depth to your adventures.

The Willow Tree You find yourself journeying to a great old willow tree. The thick curtain of light green and yellow branches caresses the ground before you. It forms a living barrier between the world and the trunk of the tree, a magical enclosed space hidden by the branches from all who cannot understand our work.

The branches sway in time with the light breeze. The living scents of green growth, rich earth, and meadow flowers are carried in the air. This is a special and sacred place. You can feel the energy radiate out from the tree and through your body. You feel completely safe. You relax and open yourself to whatever experience may unfold here.

The willow senses your presence. A small opening between the branches is revealed to you. You crouch low and go inside. The tendrils of the tree brush your body as you pass, tickling you with their small leaves. When you reach the center, they close behind you, enclosing you within the treelike womb. The trunk of the tree is before you, old and thick. The layers of bark create an intricate pattern of textures. You reach out and explore the rough surface with your fingers. You find a place to sit, leaning up against the tree. The pressure of the bark with its bumps and creases feels comforting on your back. You relax and begin to meditate. You see the rhythmic patterns of life before you . . . the millions of animals and plants that coexist with us on this world . . . the Earth itself . . . all pass before your eyes. Your focus is drawn to one image. You see it clearly before you. And as you concentrate on the image, you feel your body vibrate . . . tingle . . . hum . . . and change.

Snake Your arms are absorbed into your body. Your legs fuse together, your feet forming the tip of a tail. You slide to the ground, finding it familiar and comfortable to have your belly in contact with the Earth. Your face elongates; you find your sense of smell is no longer with your nose, but has switched to your tongue. Your tongue darts quickly in and out of your mouth, its long thin surface catching the odors. You have transformed into a snake. Look at your new body.

Spend time as a snake. Follow crevasses under the roots of an old tree. Slide along the Earth, feeling the rocks, dirt, and grass on your scales. Spend time seeing the world through the eyes of a snake, smelling it through a snake's tongue, feeling it through a snake's graceful body. *(Pause long enough to enjoy the experience.)* Your skin begins to harden and itch. It feels uncomfortable.

You rub your face against the rough surface of the tree to scratch off the irritation. Your outer skin begins to crack and peel back. Very slowly, you wiggle out of the old skin. Experience the regeneration of the snake.

Look at your new skin as it emerges.

Retuning to Human Form You find yourself where you began your journey, at the foot of the ancient willow. You feel your body again vibrating with energy. Slowly your body returns to its original form. Your human senses return. Your sense of self returns. You feel the bark of the tree on your back. Before you open your eyes, you hear the spirit of the tree whisper to you. Listen to the insight or wisdom it offers to you. *(pause)*

When you're ready, the branches pull back again to reveal an opening. It takes you back to the path that led you to the arms of Mother Willow. As you leave, you know you can return here as often as you like to change your shape and explore the world.

For Contemplation Upon Your Return Did you notice anything within the patterns on the trunk of the willow? Did you enjoy being a snake? Why or why not? How was the world different from the snake's perspective? What other animals would you like to explore? How will you follow up in the outer world in the next week, month, and year? Discuss and record in your trance journal your experience and your reactions to this adventure.

∞

One important use of trance is to prepare ourselves to make changes in our lives. Animal life begins in the womb. Plant life begins in the seed. Human achievement begins in the dream.

Magic is often defined as "the art of changing consciousness in accordance with will." Entering trance itself is a willed change of consciousness. Guided meditation or trance work, known to Wiccans as pathworking, is a form of willed dream, a more intense and more specific shift.

Through metaphor and symbolism, we explore possibilities and overcome obstacles. We find insight, wisdom, and guidance. We gain access to the sources of inspiration and power that can help us keep going when the going gets tough. We discover who we really are and what we really want.

In a magical worldview, all things are connected. We say, "As within, so without." We realize that changing consciousness results in changed behavior. Then changed behavior elicits different responses. So pathworking is a tool for changing our lives. Use it well.

℃℞℥℧

CHAPTER FIVE

Walking With the Ancients—
Exploring the Cycles

Trance journeys help us strengthen our understanding of our religion and its myths and symbols through active imagination. In trance, the tale is transformed into a vivid experience, a living and real adventure. With deeper comprehension and personal connection, we can more easily take the wise lessons into our hearts and minds.

Wicca is very individualistic. Beliefs often vary with each person, or even at different phases of our lives. We may all call ourselves Wiccan, yet follow a variety of cultural myths and honor different Gods and Goddesses. Even within individual or coven practice, it's not unusual to mix pantheons as we feel the need or inclination. For example, a Wiccan may use a Celtic myth at Imbolc and then invoke Roman deities at Ostara.

We also create our own eclectic blends. A Witch might call on Hecate, a Greek Goddess of the crossroads, at Samhain, which is the Celtic high day honoring death and the ancestors.

Wicca is based on the cycles, the rhythmic pulses of life. There are many such cycles in our lives. One is the year, the cycle of Earth's seasons. Our ancestors—hunters, gatherers, farmers, and fisherfolk—lived very close to these cycles. Today, we need rituals to remind us that, even though modern technology may distance us from the Earth, our lives still depend on Her. So we mark the changing seasons with eight festivals, which we call sabbats.

In this chapter, I'm offering a small sample of pathworkings for each sabbat. It's impossible to include all the myths that might be relevant, so I've picked a few that are either very popular among Wiccans or personal favorites of my own. You can use these as pathworkings or as models to create your own journeys from the myths that you like best. Before beginning, remember to prepare your environment (turn off the phone, and so forth) and be emotionally ready for the journey. Trivial stresses and worries that you don't plan on working with in the circle should be packed away. I'm also assuming that you've already completed the pretrance steps (stretching, grounding, relaxation, and induction) and are in an altered state.

At the completion of each of the pathworkings, remember to discuss and record in your trance journal your experiences and reactions to them. Also, pay special attention to your dreams for the next few days and record them. Review your journal before the next meeting to see whether you notice any patterns worth examining further.

The Sabbats

There are eight sabbat celebrations on the Wiccan wheel of the year, each marking a major transition in the seasonal or solar cycle. They are the Yule/winter solstice (December 21), Imbolc (February 2), Ostara/spring equinox (March 21 or 22), Beltane (May 1), Litha/summer solstice (June 21 or 22), Lammas (August 1), Mabon/fall equinox (September 21 or 22), and Samhain (October 31 or November 1).

I have included a pathworking in each of the sabbats that will return you to the same location. This is to give you an opportunity to explore this environment throughout an entire cycle of the year. Each time you return to the meadow, it will strengthen your associations with it. Your trips will build on the previous experiences, forming a more diverse and full adventure. The location is one that I enjoy, but all of us have our own individual preferences and associations. I suggest that you find your own favorite spot and build your own pathworkings around it. Better yet, locate an area near where you live and spend the next year observing the seasonal changes. Take pictures, make drawings, create poetry, or write down what you see as the wheel of the year turns. Fashion your pathworkings around this location.

WINTER SOLSTICE

The sun's return is imperative in an agricultural society. Many cultures and religions around the world have stories that celebrate the longest night and the rebirth of the sun. (The one notable exception to this is the Celtic culture: Ancient Celts acknowledged the cross-quarter points on the calendar of Imbolc, Beltane, Lammas, and Samhain.) This is a time when people come together to share the warmth of family, friends, and community—a time of anticipation and hope in the face of cold, dark fear. Will the sun come back? Or will the nights continue to get longer, plunging the world into complete darkness? Solstice tales sustain us, giving reassurance in the dark.

The Holly and the Oak　△

There is some debate about the time of year at which this battle is enacted. Some traditions place it, as I do, at the summer and winter solstices. The Holly King reigns over the lengthening nights. His brother, the Oak King, rules while the light increases. Twice a year, at the solstices, They battle for dominance. The crown passes back and forth between Them.

Other traditions place this battle at the equinoxes. In this version, the solstices mark the height of the King's power. The lengthening, or shortening of the days reflect His decline, ending with His eventual death in battle with His brother. No matter where on the calendar you place this Duel of the Kings, the imagery is extremely powerful.

I have placed a warning bell on the guided meditation because of the ritual battle imagery, which may offend some readers. Although the conflict is lethal, the myth shows that the outcome of Their battle is known, understood, and even welcomed by the Brothers. Their cyclic conflict represents the eternal cycle of death and rebirth, seen in the grasses and trees all around us.

You find yourself outdoors beneath a night sky. As your eyes become accustomed to your surroundings, you see that you are standing on the edge of a snowy field. You can hear the gentle strains of a brook somewhere nearby. The winter air is cold, but you feel warm and comfortable, as if wrapped in a magical cloak. You gaze up at the stars dotting the black sky, points of light beckoning from unknown heavens, and take a deep breath. The smell of pine and fresh snow is strong around you. Take a moment to enjoy the beauty of your surroundings. *(pause)*

You hear the crunching of snow beneath heavy boots, breaking the silence. Soon, a man steps out from the dense forest and enters the meadow. He wears a dark robe, dark as the night sky. A large sword, enclosed in a scabbard, is tied to His waist. The shaft taps lightly on His thigh in time with the breeze.

His movements seem somewhat stiff and heavy. His body, once strong and muscular, is now aged. His hair is powder white. On His head is a crown of holly. It slips down from its perch covering His eyes. You hear Him sigh as He pushes it back into place. The bright green holly leaves still hold some luster but, like Him, they have dulled with age.

Yet He is a King. His piercing black eyes are clear, and His posture proudly erect. When He walks forward on the snow, His sturdy boots leave no imprint on its mantle. You recognize that this is no ordinary man. This is the King of holly, Lord of winter, and ruler of the long nights. You realize that tonight is the longest of nights, the winter solstice.

The Holly King strides into the center of the clearing and

waits. As He looks skyward in contemplation, He lightly strokes the shaft of His blade. You think of entering the field and approaching Him when a sharp noise of sticks snapping startles Him, and you, from your musing. You look across the meadow for the source of the sound. Striding lightly forward, emerging from the tall trees comes a young man. His light brown and green garments flutter in the breeze as He comes closer.

A smile crosses the face of the Holly King. "Ah," you hear Him say, His rich voice rumbling across the field, "it is time for battle!"

You hear the singing sound of metal as He removes His sword from the confines of the scabbard and strides forward to meet the approaching warrior.

There is silence around them as they meet, the young and the old. They bow their heads, honoring each other, then take up dueling positions. The sounds of metal striking metal echo off the trees. They are well matched, a reflection of each other. You watch as they fight bravely for what seems like hours under the night sky, until the dawn's rays strike the snow.

As the light ripples across the frozen meadow, the men pause in their contest and look up to see the sunrise. The Holly King looks down at the sword in His hands. The crown of holly has again slid from His brow. His breath is labored with effort. You watch as He looks at His opponent. Their gazes meet. You know that Their eyes contain a knowledge older than the mountains, or the trees, or the rocks around them. The young man raises His sword; the Holly King nods and steps forward into the blow.

As the Holly King slowly slides to the ground, the young man, with tears running down His checks, catches Him and holds Him tight. While His blood flows into the Earth, you clearly hear the Holly King say, "Good-bye, my brother. Until our next battle."

The younger responds, "Sleep well, my brother, until we meet again." You watch Him as He gently lowers His brother to the Earth's embrace.

She emerges from the woods carrying a crown of green oak leaves and acorns. She places it upon the brow of the Oak King. With a kiss, She welcomes him back to the world.

Then She kneels before the Holly King, Her King of winter. With cold, wintry tears, She covers Him with snow. You know that He will sleep peacefully until the height of summer. Then He will awaken, young and renewed. He will once again face His brother, the King of oak, in immortal combat, for thus the seasons change and the wheel of life turns.

The Oak King and the Goddess look at you. You feel Them inviting you to enter the field and pay homage to the Goddess of the cycles, the Oak King, and the Holly King. *(Pause long enough for interaction.)*

The Lady beckons you to Her side. She has a gift for you or some words of wisdom to impart. If you will, approach the Goddess, greet Her, and receive your gift. *(Pause for personal interaction.)*

The light is climbing higher in the sky. It's time for you to return. Thank the Gods and Goddess. You watch as, arm in arm, They depart from the meadow, leaving the Holly King to slumber in the Earth. You return to the edge of the field and find your way back to your inner home.

Birthing the Sun You find yourself in the inky blackness of space. It feels completely natural, floating out among the planets. You can see galaxies around you, swirling bright colors against the dark canvas of the sky. The Milky Way is before you, a cascade of millions of stars, placed in the sky as if crafted by the stroke of a master's brush. Your body is weightless and comfortable. You are completely at ease, one with the universe. You can see the blueness of Earth, its gray moon, red Mars, orange Saturn, and all the other planets of our solar system.

As you float, you notice a collection of stars in the distance. Watching, you perceive a pattern among the dots of light. It appears to be a figure of a woman. You can clearly see the stars that make up the mound of her belly and her swollen breasts. Following their line, you find the outline of her head. It is pulled back, creating a grimace of pain—or is it ecstasy?—on Her dark face. Looking closer, you can make out Her arms. They are reaching down to grasp what must be Her knees, forcing Her legs open wide. There, between them, is Her exposed vulva, open wide to the universe.

As you watch, the outline becomes clearer. The Star Goddess, Her dark form even blacker than the night sky, writhes before you in the throes of labor. The stars that make up Her body ripple with each contraction and with each breath that She takes. You find yourself breathing with Her, using your own will to help Her push. Her mouth opens in a silent moan. You can almost feel the contractions within your own womb.

Her vulva bulges and slowly splits opens. A sliver of light appears from between Her legs. She arches Her back, forcing the life to come forth from Her body. The light grows in intensity. She is panting from the effort, Her belly rippling, Her knees shaking as She strains against the constrictions of Her own body. You see Her take another breath and bear down. The light emerging from Her womb grows brighter . . . and brighter . . . and brighter . . . coming forth from the night Mother . . . the birth of a sun.

She lies back, satisfied with Her accomplishment. There, before you, is the brightness of the new sun. She gathers it to rest upon Her bosom.

The outline of Her body begins to fade, merging back into the sky. The sun continues to shine before you. Give welcome to the sun child! And give blessings to the Lady of the night sky! If you listen, you may hear Her voice across the space, whispering to you. *(pause)*

It's time to return. As you turn, you will see the entrance to your inner home. Say good night, and cross the threshold.

IMBOLC

Imbolc or *Oimelc* literally means "in the belly." The name derives from Scotland, where pregnant sheep begin to lactate at about this time, a very early sign of the coming spring in the dark of northern winter. The rays of light, growing since the winter solstice, continue to strengthen and lengthen with each day. The ground appears bare, even frozen, but underneath the frost, in the Earth and within the trees, there is already a reawakening of life energy. Seeds germinate, the sap begins to rise, and hibernating animals turn in their slumber. The crone begins to give way to the Maiden.

Brighid's Forge

⌘ If you want to use them, gather a charcoal brazier, some wood shavings, a small bowl of water, a small anvil or metal block, and a metal-headed hammer.

Brighid, Brigit, or Bride is one of the great Celtic Goddesses. Like many Goddesses and some Gods, Brighid is seen as a triple deity, Lady of smithcraft, poetry, and healing (especially midwifery). She is associated with fire—fire of the forge, inspiration, and transformation/healing.

With the onset of Christianity, Brighid was transformed into a Christian saint. Brigit's Day in the Catholic calendar is February 1, followed immediately by Candlemas, February 2, the day that the candles are blessed within the church.

The following Imbolc pathworking was written by my friend Hare for use with his coven. It uses external stimuli to heighten the internal experience. You will find directions for this during the working. If you prefer, however, you can do the working without these aids.

You find yourself on a forest path. A heavy mist swirls around you. The air holds a damp chill with the faint scent of smoke in the air.

(Place a few wood shavings onto the brazier, then keep replenishing them throughout the journey.)

As you stand, you become aware of a faint rhythmic sound coming from ahead.

(Softly begin tapping on the anvil with the hammer in a steady, slow beat.)*

The sound draws you forward.

(Slowly increase volume of the tapping during the approach.)

The mist swirls about your feet as you move quietly along the path. You pass through stands of ash and oak trees and dark patches of pine. Before long, you come to a small clearing in the trees where the mist thins. In the center of the clearing stands a small open-air smithy.

A woman is working diligently at the forge. Her arms are strong and soot-covered. A heavy leather apron covers Her front. She has tied back Her long red hair. You can see that She is completely focused on the work before Her. The glow of Her forge gives the promise of warmth and relief from the mist's chill, so you move toward it.

As you approach the fire, She puts down Her work *(stop tapping)* and turns toward you with a welcoming smile. You return a respectful greeting. *(Pause for personal interaction.)*

The smith steps back and looks you over. You feel the sweep of Her keen eyes looking deeply into your being, touching your inner spirit. When She is finished, She gives you a thoughtful smile and turns back to Her forge. Taking Her tongs, She pulls hot iron from the fire and lays it on Her anvil. She begins striking it energetically, and the sparks begin to fly.

(Start heavy, slightly faster strokes on the anvil.)

Though She works fiercely with Her heavy hammer, you find yourself amazed at the delicate intricacy with which She forms the metal.

---

*It might be easier to have someone read this while someone else hammers, or to tape record the hammering in advance.

(Continue tapping for a bit.)

Finally, apparently satisfied, She stops Her hammering *(stop tapping)* and plunges Her finished project into the tempering vat.

(Sprinkle a few drops of water onto the charcoal brazier to produce a slight hissing noise and a faint charcoal smell.)

She withdraws the now-cool work from the vat and turns to you with it in Her hands. You see a token that you realize has been made just for you. It is a symbol of the best that you can be; a token of all that you hope to accomplish. It is a promise of fulfillment for the future. She speaks to you solemnly.

"Here, in this place, I have forged the possibility. It is up to you to craft the fulfillment of that possibility in your life. Look closely at this token and carry the remembrance of its promise in your heart and into the future. As I have labored at the anvil, so must you labor in your heart and mind to complete *our* creation."

(Pause for personal interaction.)

With a final smile and a small wave, the smith turns back to Her fire, and you realize it's time for you to return to start your work.

(Start tapping again, this time gradually fading as the exit is being made.)

You turn your face toward the path that led you here and walk back into the mist, carrying the heat of your new understanding to keep you warm and dry.

Breaking of the Ice You find yourself beside an ice-covered stream on a bright, cold day. You feel completely warm and comfortable in this environment. Behind you on your side of the water stands a forest of maple, pine, hawthorn, and oak trees. All are covered with a heavy blanket of snow. The weight of the snow on the young branches of the saplings causes their slender bodies to bend and touch the Earth. The air is crisp and fresh. The scents of the snow and ice mix with those of the forest. Other than the occasional chirp of a bird, it is quiet. The sun shines down. Reflections of light sparkle off the ice crystals and dazzle you with their brilliance.

Look into the clear ice covering the brook. Perhaps you will see some parts of yourself that have become frozen, waiting there for the spring's release. Are you ready for them to change with the season?

On the other side of the frozen water is an empty, snow-covered pasture. You can see the wire fencing that keeps the animals safe within its confines. You realize you have seen the open meadow before, but it was under a night sky. Take a deep breath and enjoy the serenity of this moment. *(pause)*

You look down and notice a bit of color by your feet. Carefully, you move the snow back to reveal a trace of green . . . and white. It's a snowdrop flower that has been emerging from the cold Earth. Its small white petals shine against winter's background. A sign of spring in the snow.

A young woman emerges from the woods. She quietly walks toward you. It does not seem strange to see Her. Somehow you knew that you would meet Her here. She greets you with a sweet smile. *(pause)* She sees the flower and reaches her delicate hand down to lightly caress the green stem. As She stands and moves away, you see that there are now two snowdrops stretching their heads upward toward the sun.

She gracefully walks away from you and crosses the frozen stream. When She reaches the other side, She turns to look back at you. The world is in complete silence. As your eyes meet, you hear an enormous cracking noise. It echoes like a firecracker off the trees. Then another . . . and another. A network of cracks spreads across the frozen surface of the stream. The ground seems to quiver beneath your feet. You hear the rushing of water. You watch as the ice covering the stream crumbles and breaks, carried downstream by the quickening waters. The water, once released from its confines, finds an even, gentle flow. You can feel the breeze on your skin caused by the sudden release of pressure.

You hear the call of a sheep and the clanging of a bell. A

small herd of sheep have entered the pasture. You can see that many are heavy, almost ready to give birth. You look at the Goddess of renewal. She places Her hand lightly on Her belly and gives you a shy smile. You notice that there is a swelling beneath Her fingers. She is not ready to give birth, but the seed is growing and quickening within Her, unseen.

As you look back up from the water's edge, you see that the Lady has gone, but you can still feel Her smile. It's time to return. Take with you the knowledge that you gained from the water. Turn, and find your way back to your inner home.

OSTARA/ECESTRE/SPRING EQUINOX

As we continue around the wheel, we come to the spring equinox. The days and the nights are of equal length, and spring is fully on the wind. The Green Man, the spirit of vegetation, has awakened, bringing us His first gifts: crocuses, hyacinths, and daffodils. You can taste the spring in the maple syrup, made from the sap that runs freely in the trees.

Dancing With Rabbits Eœstre is an Anglo-Saxon Goddess of dawn and spring. She loaned Her name to Easter. As a Goddess of fertility, Her symbols are the hare and the egg. It was said, during the Scottish witch trials in the Burning Times, that the hare was one of the forms that a witch could take. If so, it was to dance among the meadow grass, leaping high toward the full moon on hare feet—perhaps accompanied by the lovely Eœstre.

This pathworking was also written by my friend Hare. His inspiration comes from the music and lyrics of Maddy Prior's "The Fabled Hare" Suite.[*]

It is spring and you find yourself in a wide, windswept meadow dotted with little patches of wildflowers. The sun has

---

[*]Maddy Prior, "The Fabled Hare," *Year.*

barely risen above the eastern horizon, and a thick dew still covers the field. As you look around, you see several hares silently going about their morning business, nibbling on the fresh green growth that abounds here. Dotted about almost invisibly on the ground are small nests in which mother hares nurse their young, called leverets.

One of the largest hares hops toward you, and without quite realizing how, you find yourself gazing into a deep brown set of wide, round eyes. Behind them you sense an invitation.

> I shall go now into the hare*
> With joy and dancing and little care
> I shall go in the Horned One's name
> Aye, and come home safe again.

You feel a brief moment of dizziness and disorientation. When you regain your focus, you find yourself staring out of the hare's eyes. The morning colors are crisper, and the images in the field leap into sharp focus. The air brings you the sweet scent of hay and the musky odor of the other hares around you. The tang of half-chewed clover fills your mouth, and you find it quite possibly the best thing you have ever tasted. A sense of wonder fills you; you begin to understand the wisdom that the hare offers.

Time passes and day moves to night. The full moon rises. It calls you out from your nest in the grass. You dance under the light of the moon, the symbol of the cycles. You see the hare pictured within the moon and leap up to join with it. You are the symbol of rebirth, of spring and life renewed. Your body is lithe, nimble, and fertile, capable of bearing numerous young.

---

* This is based on the Isabel Gowdie spell, from the Scottish witch trials, that she reputedly used to transform into hare shape. Margaret Murray, *The God of the Witches* (London: Oxford University Press, 1952, 1974), p. 142, adapted by Black Lotus.

Another hare catches your eye and joins you in the meadow. Together you dance, leap, and play the among the grasses under the Lady's glow. *(pause)*

The night turns again to day. As the sun rises, we run. We run. And the sun becomes warm again. And again the leaves are beginning to turn green and sweet. Our young lie in our nests. For we are hares and our promise is that of renewal, resurrection, and triumph in the face of hardship and death.

You are the hare. You have been feared as a witch in disguise. You survive. You have been hunted by dogs and humans for food. You survive. You have danced in the meadow full of hay and clover and shivered in the cold under a snowy moon. You survive. You are the fields. You are the clover. You are the moon in Her cycles. You are rebirth and endurance. You will run forever.

Triumph and joy overwhelm you, and the rising spring sun fills your vision and blinds you for a moment.

> Hare, hare, Goddess send thee care[*]
> I thank you, hare, and set you free
> Return to human, and blessed be.

When your eyes clear, you find yourself once again human, face to face with the hare. There is a sparkle in his brown eyes now, and he playfully rears up and gives you a few gentle bats before turning and running off into the dewy hay fields. As you stand erect, the field where you found so much knowledge slowly fades from view. Turn and return to your inner home.

The Children of Spring   Kore, also known as Persephone, is the Maiden of spring. As a young woman, She was abducted by Hades, Lord of the underworld, and brought to His kingdom beneath the Earth. When Her mother, Demeter, Goddess of

---

[*]This is also based on the Isabel Gowdie spell and Murray's *God of the Witches*, adapted by Black Lotus.

growth, found out what had happened to Her daughter, She went into mourning. All the vegetation stopped growing and died.

In time, a bargain was made. Now, Kore spends half the year here in our world. During the other half of the year, She joins Hades. Her descent and return cause the changing of the seasons. Her return, and the return of life along with her, is what we know as spring. In Her joy, She is a young child, laughing and dancing upon the Earth.

You find yourself beside a stream. You have been here before, when the winter's hold first broke. Now it is early spring. Behind you stands the forest of maple, pine, hawthorn, and oak trees. The saplings stand tall, their snowy burden shed. The buds on the trees and flowers are just beginning to form— streaks of light greens and yellows on a brown background. The ground is still cold and wet beneath your feet. The scent of the forest, the rich moist earth, and the running brook are all around you. The air feels cool and fresh. You feel completely comfortable in this environment. The sun shines down, and you can feel the Earth awakening around you.

Across the stream, you can see the pasture. The sheep are wandering in it, eating the new growth. The young lambs dance behind their mothers and play among the adults. You watch as the youngest runs to her mother to nurse.

You notice a very large rock outcrop nearby and walk toward it. A few young trees have grown up around its sides. Green and gray mosses cover a portion of the stone's rough surface. You put your hands on the face of the rock and feel the warmth of the sun stored within it. There are small indents on the stone, just the right size for the ball of your foot to catch and hold your weight. Using the young trees for leverage, you climb to the top of the rock and sit on its warm surface. *(pause)*

As you lean back, enjoying the breath of spring, you hear the sound of children's laughter. From your perch, you see a young girl emerge from the woods, laughing and giggling. Her long hair flows and bounces as she skips. She turns and looks back to the woods with an expression of expectation and abandoned joy. A young boy runs out after her. She shrieks with laughter. Running and ducking behind trees, she scampers across your field, the youth following her in a playful game of tag. The boy catches her as she reaches the edge of the stream. They collapse on the ground in a fit of giggles.

The boy produces a set of reed pipes and begins to try to play them. The music is hesitant. He repeats the piece, hitting a few wrong notes that cause the young girl to cover her ears and make a sour expression. You would, too, except that you find the sounds not that unpleasant. It's obvious that, given time, the boy will someday master his pipes.

As they sit at the shore, you look back to where the children played. Wherever the children ran, the ground is covered with thick, bright green growth. The trees that she touched are opening their leaves to the sun. The flowers around where the children sit are bursting into bright-colored bloom. The birds are singing along with the boy's pipes. He's getting better already.

Kore, Maiden of spring, stands again. She lightly skips from stone to stone, crossing the stream. The boy leaps up to join Her. As he lands on a river rock, you notice that what you thought were mud-covered feet are actually hooves. He turns to look back at you with a mischievous glint in His eyes. You realize two small nubs on either side of His brow are the beginning of horns.

The young Pan follows Kore, continuing Their playful game. They climb under the fence and run through the pasture, causing the sheep to scatter before Them. Behind Them, where Their feet tread, They leave a swash of green. You can still hear Their playful laughter on the wind even after They leave your view.

The sun is starting its descent. Using the footholds and the saplings, you climb down from your rock and walk over to where Kore and Pan sat. If you look, you may see a small gift left behind for you by the children. Thank the Maiden of spring and Pan.

It is time to leave. Turn and find your way back to your inner home.

BELTANE/MAY DAY

Beltane is one of the four sacred fire festivals of the Celtic year. Of the four, Beltane, the celebration of fertility, and its opposite, Samhain, ritual of remembrance, are the two most important on the Celtic calendar.

Beltane is the renewal of growth and regeneration of life. Seeds burst beneath the ground; flowers open, inviting the bee to land; and animals call out looking for mates. While it's a celebration of spring, it also heralds in the nascent summer.

King and Queen of May Dancing around the May Pole, a form of phallic symbol, and activities to help wake the Earth into full fruitfulness have been a part of May Day celebrations in Europe for centuries, and carried over to the United States. Although the Puritans, uncomfortable with the sexual connotations of the rite, tried to outlaw the dance in seventeenth century, it has remained a popular tradition in many areas, practiced by Pagans and non-Pagans alike.

Ribbons are blowing free in the wind—long colorful strips of color against the blue sky. They are fluttering from the tree branches as you make your way into your clearing. The hawthorn and other flowering bushes are in full bloom. Their small, beautiful blossoms fill the air with a warm, sweet scent. A honeybee flies by you, heavy with pollen. It greedily drops down to explore the flowers on the ground. Finished with its survey, it flies off toward its hive, leaving behind a dusting of yellow.

The stream is full, flowing swiftly between green banks. You remember this place and are comfortable here. You hear the sheep calling to each other in the meadow across the water. You shade your eyes and look toward the sound. The field is green and brown. You realize that a section of the pasture has been cordoned off and plowed. The dark, rich earth, laid open to the sky, awaits the seed.

From the woods behind you, you hear voices raised in song and laughter. You can barely make out the words, but it sounds like ". . . Hurray . . . hurray . . . the lusty month of May . . ."

The ribbons rise and fall in the breeze. Their motion points toward a path between an oak and a hawthorn tree that you hadn't noticed before. The music is coming from that direction.

You walk toward the path. While passing under the large branches of the hawthorn, you stop to remove one of the ribbons. There are many colors to choose from. Select the color that represents something in your life that you would like to watch grow in the coming season.

The cloth ribbon unties easily. You wrap it in your hand and enter the woods. The dirt path is easy to follow. The sounds of laughter and merriment guide you. The forest smells lush—of old growth that is decaying, and of sweet flowers and fresh new leaves. You see a dark, moss-covered log, a tree long fallen. On the other side of it, you notice a small vernal pool. The tree frogs in the pool are singing in their own way, calling to mates.

You continue on. The path begins to slope upward, and the trees start to thin. The voices are getting louder. You emerge from the woods into an apple orchard on the top of a gentle hill. The apple trees are all in full bloom. The petals of the delicate pink flowers sprinkle down on you as you walk beneath them.

In the center of the grove is a group of people, milling around, talking, and laughing. They smile and greet you as you approach. In the center of the crowd, you see a group digging a hole in the ground about nine inches wide. The grassy sod has been carefully placed on either side of the hole. They dig into the earth, pulling the soil out to deepen the cavity. The soil is placed on either side of the sod.

A great cheering arises from the crowd. Coming through the grove is a group of people carrying a long, thick pole. With much laughter the pole is brought to the center of the grove near where you stand. Then the assembly grows very quiet. From out of the woods emerges a young couple. She has flowers tied in Her long flowing hair and a crown of flowers upon Her head. Her features are as delicate as the flowers, more beautiful than a thousand paintings. She holds the hand of a young man. His body is muscular and strong. His step is light. His eyes twinkle with youth and merriment. He wears a crown of leaves and woodland flowers. You recognize that they are the King and Queen of May.

The gathering makes way for Them as they enter and approach the pole. The Lady strokes it lightly with her fingers, then goes to stand by the hole and waits. The Lord helps raise the rod and plant it deep into the ground. As the shaft settles into place and is secured, another cheer rises from the crowd. The May Pole stands, connecting Earth and sky. Those holding the pole let go, releasing the ribbons secured to its top. The bright ribbons flutter high in the breeze. People rush forward, jumping up to capture one of the streamers.

As you watch, you sadly realize that your ribbon is still in your hand. You look down at the ground in disappointment, and rub the cloth between your fingers, feeling its potential. When you look up again, the Lady is standing before you smiling. She reaches forward and takes your ribbon, allowing it to slide its length through your fingers before claiming it as Her own. People make way for Her as she approaches the May Pole with your ribbon in Her hands. The Lord of May lets out a full-bodied laugh as the Lady lets Him know that She would like His help. He kneels before Her, offering His body as a platform to reach the top of the tall rod. He raises her up on His broad shoulders "piggyback." She grabs hold of the shaft of the pole, wrapping Her arms tightly around it and hugging it between Her breasts. So perched, She takes your ribbon and fastens it to the tip with the rest. She then removes the wreath from Her head and places it on the top of the pole. She smiles down at the God, then slowly and sensuously slides down His body to the ground. He turns around to face Her; They merge into each other's arms in a sensual embrace.

Your ribbon is now fluttering on the breeze. You thank the God and Goddess of the new summer *(pause)* and leap to catch its end, feeling light, strong, and joyous! *(pause)*

As the celebrants stand in a circle around the pole, the bright ribbons form a cone of many colors. You join them. The music starts. The dance begins. You weave your ribbons in and out, around the pole.

As dancers pass by you, they give you a wink and a smile. Perhaps there is one whose glance suggests more than flirtation. You joyfully return the gesture. Each turn about the pole brings you closer to the center. As you weave, you can feel the energy being pulled down from the sky to the fertile Earth below and up from the Earth to the shining sky, forming the double helix of life. The hopes each of you placed in the ribbons awaken like spring flowers. You become dizzy with excitement as the dance moves faster and faster, the energy swelling until it is finally released. All the ribbons are secured to the May Pole, now bright with braided color.

The dance ended, you notice that the sun is starting to set. Couples are pairing off and strolling into the woods together. They wave good-bye to you as they disappear into the green shadows. You walk through the apple grove back toward the path that led you here. Standing under the boughs of the apple trees, the person from the dance is waiting for you. If you would like, spend some time together enjoying the May eve. *(Pause long enough for personal interaction.)*

When you're ready, wander back down the gentle slope and

into the woods. You pass by the log with its pool and head toward your clearing.

As you reach the opening, you hear soft whispers. Peering into the woods, you see the divine couple lying together on the damp earth beneath a new canopy of green buds. Their laughter and joy fill the air around Them. It is their union that stirs to life the plants and animals. You quietly leave Them to Their pleasures.

You emerge from the forest. A full moon has risen. You notice movement in the plowed field and hear laughter. The fields will bear a good bounty in the fall.

It's time to leave. Take one more look at the May eve, and find your way back to your inner home.

Seeds of Growth   The Green Man, or Jack-in-the-Green, is the new spring growth and the fertility of spring. Covered in green leaves from his head to his toe, He is the European agricultural God of unbound growth, fertility, and change. He is the seed of potential that bursts open with the warming rays of the sun.

You find yourself in an overgrown, green garden filled with lush vegetation. Colorful flowers are in bloom. The sun is shining above you, and a gentle breeze touches your checks. The wind brings the scent of spring—a damp, clean smell of wet earth and new growth. The ground is soft beneath your feet. You can hear birds singing and playing in the branches of the trees and in the thick foliage around you.

You have been to this garden before. It feels safe and familiar. You pass by thick foliage and flower beds. You cannot see anyone in the garden, but you sense that you're not alone. You pass beneath a large tree and notice movement. A pair of eyes peers at you from the branches above. With a flurry of leaves and a giggle, the Green Man drops out of the tree. He dances about you merrily, pleased with Himself for surprising you. The green leaves make up His mantle rustle and bounce with His movement.

The Green Man extends a closed hand to you, and you realize that He is offering you a gift. Will you accept it? *(a presumed
yes)* You open your hand, and he drops something into it—a
seed. You look at it for a moment. It is a seed of opportunity. He
invites you to come sit upon His back. You climb up the vines
and perch on what you assume are His shoulders. He then begins to grow . . . and grow . . . and grow . . . until you are up as
high as the tops of the trees. From there you can see every aspect of the garden. You realize that you can also see beyond the
garden, to the untended ground outside, which is also full of
life and potential.

Around you are the various aspects of your life. You can see
your home. Your work. Your friends, family, and relationships.
You see your creative and educational pursuits. All the various
parts of your life. As you look carefully, you also notice those interests that you once put aside so you could concentrate on
what seemed most important at the time. These areas all hold
the possibility of growth.

The seed in your hand begins to grow very warm. Soon you
can't hold on to it any longer. You open your hand, and the
seed jumps out, flying as fast as it can go . . . out of the garden.
You watch it as it flies. Notice carefully where the seed is headed
and where it lands. That is the neglected area of your life that
you long to tend, carefully weed, and fertilize with growth-giving
nutrients. The seed is indicating and offering you potential
growth, if you so desire.

Jack begins to shrink again. Smaller and smaller, until He is
back to the size of a healthy bush. He smiles broadly at you
again.

"Knowledge," He says to you, "is the first step; action is the
second. How do you plan on helping it grow?"

He does not wait for an answer. With a laugh and twinkling
eyes, He dances away into the foliage, leaving you to contemplate its meaning. Call out a good-bye and a thank-you to the

Green Man. Find the path that brought you here and return to your inner home.

LITHA/MIDSUMMER/SUMMER SOLSTICE

Just as there is the longest night, so is there the longest day. At the height of summer's heat, the sun reaches its full zenith—and then the days begin to shorten, bringing the other half of the cycle.

Height of Summer You're in the heat of June. You find yourself walking down the gentle slope of a green field. You've been here before. You are comfortable and familiar with your surroundings.

In your hands is a picnic basket and a blanket. As you take a deep breath, you can smell the mingled scents of cool running water and freshly mowed grass. The sun is high in the sky. Its warmth bakes into your bones.

The edges of the field are dotted with dandelions, buttercups, and daisies. The sheep pasture is empty today. You notice the garden as you walk by. The crop is doing well. The corn has grown almost to waist-height. Before you is the stream. The forest is on the other side of the water.

You put down your basket, spread your blanket, and flop to the ground. Stretching out and relaxing, you savor the warmth of the season and being outside on a beautiful summer's day.

You are here to celebrate the solstice. The day is perfect. The sky is bright blue overhead, dotted with a few white, fluffy clouds. You feel an afternoon breeze blow through your hair. You open your basket and take out your picnic lunch. You feast on tomato sandwiches and salads of lettuce, cucumbers, green peppers, and onions. You drink iced tea and enjoy fresh-picked strawberries dipped in chocolate. You find yourself wishing that the light would never end. That night and winter would stay away forever.

The heat of the afternoon sun beats on you. You begin to feel hot. The gently flowing stream invites you. You decide to take a dip.

It's too shallow at the crossing stones to swim, so you walk a short way down to where the stream curves. There you find the sandbar of a swimming hole where the dark green water looks deep enough to cover and cool your body. You remove your clothes, leaving them draped on a bush, and enter the stream. You feel the flowing water slide past your hot skin. You dive beneath the surface. Cool and refreshing, it envelops you. When you reemerge and stand waist-deep in the shallow, you notice the contrast between the heat and brightness of the sun above and the cool darkness of the water below. It fills you with the energy that is life.

As you finish your swim, something in the woods catches your eye. Something seems to be calling you from the shadows near a tall oak tree. You put your clothes back on and go to investigate.

Using the stepping-stones, you cross the stream to the clearing before the forest. You pass by the path to the apple orchard and the perching rock, cross the small field, and enter the cool, green shade of the forest by a tall oak tree. Hidden in the shadows, you see a beautiful moon-colored moth. Her large white wings vibrate with emotion as you approach. When you reach her, she alights from the oak and flies into the forest to land on the bark of another tree. Carefully stepping over the vegetation, you follow her into the dark shade of the forest. Its coolness surrounds you.

As you reach her, she again flies off. She is so beautiful. Her iridescent wings glow. You just have to see her, perhaps even touch her feathery wings. You follow as she leads you deeper and deeper into the dark, cool woods. Finally, she ends her flight, landing on the bark of a tall pine. You creep quietly up to her. She is even more beautiful than you first thought.

You admire the moth for a few minutes, turn to go, then suddenly realize where you are. Your moon moth has taken you far from the clearing and the stream into the darkness of the woods.

"If the days kept getting longer and longer," you hear a man's voice behind you say, "soon there will be no more night. Not all creatures can survive under the hot light of day."

You turn and find a young man. His dark eyes, sad and kind, penetrate into you. You know you've seen them before, on a field of battle. The moon moth flutters over to land on His dark cape, her wings gently beating, caressing the fabric.

"Day is balanced with night . . . heat with cold . . . summer with winter," continues the young Holly King, "in the eternal cycle of death and rebirth." You look around the forest. In the heat of the summer and the brightness of the long days, you had forgotten how wonderful the cooling dark could be. A group of fireflies hovers around your moth. Overhead you hear the call of an owl, as if it were expressing a longing for the longer nights. You remember the beauty of the moon's glow on fresh snow.

Give homage to the Holly King, king of nights. Speak to Him, if you wish. He may have something to tell you. *(Pause to allow for personal interaction.)* When you're done, the moth flutters off His cape, and the King turns and leaves. The sun will soon set, and He must meet His brother.

It's time for you to go. The moth leads you back through the woods and to the edge of your clearing. You thank her before stepping once more into the light. You walk through the clearing and cross back over the stream to the field and your blanket. You notice that along the edges of the woods, lights are blinking here and there. The fireflies will soon come out to play, and the moth will fly out to greet the moon.

After a moment, you pick up your basket and blanket and head home.

A View to Tomorrow   You find yourself entering into a traveling carnival. Brightly colored posters and vendor stands line the makeshift amusement park. The scents of popcorn and cotton candy, wood chips and oil, are all around you. People are talking, laughing, and enjoying the sights and sounds of the carnival. Carousel music fills the air. Amusement rides clang and clunk. You hear the joyful screams of children enjoying the thrill of the Turn-About, the cars of the ride spinning at dizzying pace around and around. Food and toy vendors encourage you to buy their merchandise. Barkers call out to you come "step right up" and play their games, promising easy success. Plush teddy bears and stuffed animals fill their stalls for the potential winners. You wander among the colors and scents, enjoying the scenery.

In the center of the carnival, you find a large Ferris wheel. The round metal structure slowly turns, lifting the cars high up to the blue sky and Earthward again. You approach the ticket booth in front of the ride and buy a ticket. The woman behind the counter smiles at you as she hands you the small piece of stamped paper. You walk to the line for the Ferris wheel and wait your turn. Soon you are stepping up on the platform. The attendant opens the restraining bar on the front of the car and invites you to take a seat. The car rocks slightly back and forth as you step in and sit down. The attendant closes the bar and steps back. The metal seat is smooth and warm from the heat of the sun. You hold on to the bar as the ride begins.

The ground begins to move away from you as the wheel slowly carries you upward. A quarter of the way up, the ride stops to allow other passengers into the cars below. You see the inner workings of the wheel before you. Peering over the side, you can see the ground below. The ride begins moving again, slowly bringing you up . . . and up . . . toward the sky.

When you reach the top, the ride stops again. The sun shines warmly down on you. The wind blows lightly through your hair, and you feel completely free. You look around. You are high above the trees now, at the pinnacle of the wheel. The ground is far below; people and objects down there look very, very small.

You can see the world stretch out before you in all directions. Perhaps you can see something you never noticed before, something that carries an important meaning or message for you. *(pause)*

The wheel begins again, moving you a quarter of the way back down to the Earth before stopping. You are at eye level with the trees now. A robin perched on a branch looks at you inquisitively. The ride turns and you find the solid ground rushing up to meet you . . . then around and back up . . . and up . . . and up . . . moving upward, becoming part of the sky, and then that moment when down . . . down . . . down . . . to the Earth below . . . returning again to the top, for one fleeting moment the highest point in the cycle . . . and then back to the lowest point on the wheel.

The circle turns, just as the seasons turn. The height of a summer's sun leads to the bittersweet moment when, just as the harvest ripens, the year begins to wane, bringing you closer to the dark, cold winter's days. The ride slows and stops with you once again at the summit. Take a moment to enjoy the sun, the day, and the height of summer. *(pause)*

You return to the Earth. The ride slows and comes to a stop. The attendant opens the restraining bar and helps you out of the car. He smiles and waves good-bye as you step down from the platform. Spend a few more minutes enjoying the sounds, sights, and smells of the carnival. If there is someone you would like to speak with, a vendor, attendant, barker, or any other rider of the wheel, take a moment for that now. *(Pause for personal interaction.)*

It's time to leave. Find your way back through the carnival to the entrance and find your way back to your inner home.

LAMMAS/LUGHNASADH

Lammas or Lughnasadh is the first of the three harvest festivals celebrating the ripening and harvesting of the grain. Demeter,

Ceres, and other goddesses of the harvest bestow their bounty on the people at this time of year.

Lughnasadh is named for Lugh, the Celtic God of many talents. The festival actually commemorates funeral games held by Lugh in honor of his foster mother, Tailtu. She died from exhaustion while attempting to clear a forest to create farmland, another example of sacrifice for the good of the tribe.

Slicing Bread—The Grain Harvest This is the season of John Barleycorn, the European God of the grain. Grain is a staple of life in many cultures, and their religions reflect this reality. Rites that celebrate the transformations of the grain, from planting to harvest, are at the heart of many festival cycles. One recurring theme in such rites portrays the essence of the God being absorbed into the grain. He is then cut down, a harvest sacrifice for the good of the tribe. In His rebirth each spring, we see the continuity of the cycle and the renewal of life.

The heat hangs heavy in the air as you enter into the clearing. It is accented by the loud humming of June beetles and the buzz of bees. There is hardly any breeze. A brook is beside you. The flowing waters of the brook look appealing. You think about removing your clothes and jumping in, but then you hear the sound of pipes in the fields on the other side of the brook. You're curious about what's happening, and go to find out.

You cross the brook using stepping-stones and make your way up the gentle slope. There is a fence around the pasture. You find the gate, open it, and enter the field. The hay smells sweet and strong. The crickets are chirping. They hop out of your way as you walk through the tall grass. The grass tickles your hands and rubs against your legs as you make your way through it. A hare scampers and hides, camouflaged among the browns and greens.

You reach the garden that was planted last spring. You remember the planting rites and notice that the vegetables are full and lush. You reach out and part the large, rough leaves of a zucchini plant to see the shiny green fruit hidden beneath them. The cornstalks are tall—almost as tall as you. Nubs of young ears line their surface. The tomatoes are not quite ripe, but the peas and beans can be picked. You snap off one of the pea pods and break it in half. The fresh green scent is released. You place the peas in your mouth and savor their sweet taste.

You walk through the garden admiring the growth. The musical sound that beckoned to you is coming from the other side of the hill. With the excitement of discovery, you walk on.

As you reach the top of the hill and look down, you see stretched out before you an ocean of yellow grain. A gentle breeze comes through. The shafts sway lightly in the wind, creating a wave of wheat. Below you is a couple sitting by a hedgerow. They both appear to be of early middle age. She has the wide hips and breasts of motherhood; He, a thick yellow growth of beard on His chin. He is playing His pipes for Her, a wistful, plaintive lament. You watch as He finishes His song. They stand and embrace. It does not appear to be a sad scene, yet you feel a sense of sweet parting.

They release their lovers' embrace. She gently smiles, touching His fuzzy cheek. You hear Her call Him "John." He throws His head back and laughs at some private joke shared between them. The sound echoes through the field. He then kisses Her good-bye and walks into the field of grain. His fingers lightly play along the tops of the sheaves as He makes His way deeper and deeper into the tall growth. He wades until He stands in the center of the field. He is completely surrounded by grain. His outstretched palms lie lightly on the heads of the seeds. He looks over to where the Lady stands. As She waves to Him, he smiles and slowly starts to expand, become translucent, and fade from sight. His essence is pouring into the grain all around Him until all that is left is the grain. A breeze ripples the wheat, reflecting the sun in a wave of golden hues. When you look back to the Lady, She too has gone.

The silence is soon replaced with excited, happy voices.

People—men, women, and children—are coming over the hill, carrying baskets and harvesting equipment. They begin the harvest, singing joyful songs. You can smell the fresh hay as it lands on the ground to be raked into mounds. You are handed a tool, a rake or a scythe. The wooden surface is smooth from years of use. You take it and help with the harvest. *(Pause long enough for the task.)*

It takes time for all of the sheaves to be cut and bound, but finally, you stand up and stretch. Your muscles may be sore, but you feel satisfied with the work you've accomplished. You look around the field. It appears that the grain has all been cut. Then you notice one spot. One small sheaf still stands, waving in the wind. A young girl emerges from the crowd, carrying a small sickle. Calls of encouragement follow her into the field. She approaches the sheaf and shyly cuts it. A cheer rings out. She gathers the fallen grain and returns to her mother. Together, they quickly fashion a small doll from it, holding it up to the crowd, which responds with more cheers and song.

While the merriment continues, the young girl uncovers a basket filled with freshly baked bread. Its rich scent makes your mouth water. A keg of cold ale is brought up from the stream and opened. Each person walks past the mother and daughter, taking a piece of cut bread from the basket and a glass of cold brewed and fermented grain. Both are symbols of the Earth's and John Barleycorn's sacrifice for the good of the people.

The young girl smiles up at you as she hands you your piece of bread. It feels warm in your hands. You realize the bread contains the essence of the Earth and sun and of the God. You give thanks as you bite into it, tasting the love that it holds. Enjoy your glass of ale and your bread, the fruits of your work and gifts from the Gods. *(pause)*

The sun is beginning to set. The harvesters are getting ready to leave for the day. They wave good-bye to you as they, and you, begin to make your way home. You walk up the slope, through the green garden, and back into the pasture. Find the gate and close it tight behind you. Before you is the stream with its crossing stones. You lightly jump from one to the other, back into the clearing, and return to your inner home.

The Wheat From the Chaff The concept of natural cycles doesn't just apply to a farmer's ongoing round of sowing and reaping. Many other kinds of work and reward can be understood by using the cyclical model. Consider your own labors this year. How close are you to realizing your goals? How well have you separated the chaff, those bits that are hampering your success, from your own wheat, the harvest that can nourish and sustain you?

You stand outside on the top of a hill open to the air. The sun is shining down, warming you. You can see the green valley below you. A gentle breeze is blowing, carrying with it the sweet scent of hay. The ground before you has been cleared to make a large, flat area. Stones form a hard threshing floor with a lip of threshold all around you.

All around you are bundles of wheat. A thick layer of wheat is scattered on the floor. You are surrounded with sheaves of wheat. Leaning against the threshold is a large flail. It looks like a long stick with a short stick attached to it by a short chain Once the grain has been harvested, this is the tool used to thresh the grain, breaking the chaff, the nonedible husks, away from the nourishing seeds.

You pick up the flail. The short stick swings back and forth by the chain. It feels heavy in your hands, the wood smooth from years of use. You look down at the layer of wheat on the hard stone floor. It reminds you of a bundle of rune sticks, tossed onto a tabletop and scattered, forming a pattern you may be able to read. Stand and ponder that pattern for a moment. *(pause)* You may see the outlines of something that you meant to accomplish this season, but were unable to bring to fruition.

You can see the chaff that obstructs you from reaching the nourishing grain, the harvest for which you have labored in the summer heat.

You feel the weight of the flail in your hands. The beater is swinging from side to side. You heft the flail and swing your arm, striking the grain with the beater. It lands with a satisfying thud. You strike the grain again, feeling the vibration in your hands as it hits the hard rock surface. And again. You set up a rhythm . . . thump . . . thump . . . thump . . . like a drumbeat. Continue until the chaff has been loosened and separated from your grain. *(pause)*

You're sweating hard and panting a bit when you stand back to survey your work. The wind picks up, cooling you some. But although the chaff is now separated, it still lies on top of your seed, covering it. You turn to get a drink of water. Near the water bottle, you see another tool waiting for you. The winnow looks much like a curved wooden pitchfork with wide, thick teeth. You take the winnow and scoop up a shovelful of wheat and castings. As the wind blows, you throw the load up into the air. The wind catches the chaff, separating it from the wheat and blowing it away from you. The heavier seed drops back to the stone threshing floor, where you can easily retrieve it. And again you pick up another scoop and throw it upward, allowing that which has hindered you to blow away with the breeze. Continue until you have cast out all that has been in your way, leaving behind only that which will nourish and sustain you. *(Pause to accomplish the task.)*

When you are finished, you have a mound of seed. This is your harvest . . . your sustenance and your potential. Nearby there is a miller who can grind your seed into flour. Think about the ways that you can now fulfill your plans. What can help you? What steps can you take to bring your projects to sweet fruition? When you are ready, find your way back to your inner home.

MABON/FALL EQUINOX

Fall equinox, also known as Mabon, occurs on the 21st or 22nd of September. It's the main harvest festival of the Wiccan calendar and marks the beginning of Autumn. The Goddess manifests as the bountiful Mother as the fruits of summer are harvested to be eaten or stored for the winter.

Within the celebration, there is also a touch of trepidation. The days are shortening, and winter with its cold chill will soon be approaching.

Judging the Harvest The smell of burning and decaying leaves is all around you as you find yourself entering into the clearing. The air holds a slight chill. The trees of the forest have taken on bright colors. Vibrant reds and oranges mix among greens and yellows. A brook flows gently by. Along its edges are clusters of colorful leaves, carried there by the flowing water. On the other side of the waters you can see the gentle slope of a pasture and the remnants of a vegetable garden.

The sounds of music and laughter touch your ears. They come from the forest. You realize that this is the harvest feast. Eagerly, you follow the sound. It leads you to a path. You pass under the large branches of a hawthorn and an oak tree and enter the forest. The sounds of laughter and merriment guide you. The woods smell dark and rich, of old growth that is decaying. You see a dark, moss-covered log, a tree long fallen. On the other side of it, you notice what must have been a small vernal pool in spring. The waters receded during the heat of summer, leaving just wet mud and fallen leaves. The frogs have moved on.

You continue on. The path begins to climb, and the trees start to thin. The voices are getting louder. You emerge from the woods into an apple orchard on the top of a gentle hill. The apple trees are filled with red fruit. Overripe apples, fallen from the trees, are scattered on the ground. Their sweet scent fills the air. Bees buzz by you, to land on the decaying fruit, collecting the sugar held within the apples. Old wooden ladders stand under the trees, and baskets filled with apples rest on the ground. You reach up to the branches of a tree and pick a red apple. Its shiny skin feels smooth and warm in your hand. You realize that if you cut the apple in half, you will find the star that is hidden within it. Take a bite of the fruit and savor the gift of the Earth and the Goddess. Feel its sweetness on your tongue. *(pause)*

You allow the laughter and the music to draw you to the far end of the apple grove. As you approach, you see the harvest fair. You can see many happy people, gathered around a small group of musicians. Perhaps some of the young folk are dancing. You may want to join them later on.

Makeshift tables and canopies have been set up in rows. The tables and floors of some booths are filled with colorful fruits and vegetables: red peppers, green zucchini, yellow corn, orange pumpkins, and a wide assortment of squash. Others display golden-crusted pies, jars of honey, and fruit preserves. A long board on cinder blocks offers glasses of fresh apple cider and ale. A basket of apples sits on the ground before it. Some tables proudly display blue ribbons in front of their wares. The smells of apple and pumpkin pie, fragrant with sweet spices, make your mouth water.

People are walking up and down the row, admiring the harvest. You join them, slowly wandering from table to table.

At the end of the row, you find animal pens filled with fresh hay. Sheep, goats, and cows, their coats all freshly washed, stand chewing on the straw. In a field on the other side of the pens, you can see a horse pulling contest in progress. The large beasts are pulling heavy cement objects across a space in a trial of speed, strength, and stamina.

You stop before the sheep pen. There are eight in the stall. They come up to the fence to greet you, allowing you to scratch them behind their ears and feel their soft woolly bodies. You notice that across from the sheep is a booth with a woman spinning. She has baskets of wool next to her spinning wheel. On her table are baskets of yarn and wool sweaters. She smiles at you as you watch her nimble fingers transform the fiber into strong thread. The large wheel spins around and around. You watch in fascination, calmed by the rhythmic motion.

After a little while, the sound of cheering attracts you. You realize that at the end of the fairgrounds, beneath a large canopy, a crowd of people has formed. Curious, you go and join them. Under the shade of the tarp, you see a small stage. On either side of the stage are baskets. Each has a sign nearby with the word SEED printed on it in big black letters.

A woman stands on the stage, reviewing a group of zucchini presented to Her by their growers. She has the full hips and breasts of motherhood. Her hair is pulled back in a matronly fashion. A crown of grain and fall flowers sits upon Her head. She has a regal air of ancient wisdom about Her. You recognize this is Demeter, the harvest Mother.

She views the offerings before Her. Then She points to the two largest and best of the fruits. A cheer rises from the crowd. The winning farmers, with grins on their faces, thank the Goddess. They walk to the baskets and put the winning fruit in. More vegetables are brought before Her. She surveys them, and again chooses the best of each kind. The winners are added to the seed baskets while the people cheer. The vegetables that are not chosen will soon be cooked and eaten or made into preserves for the winter. The best of this year's crop is saved to improve the breed.

During a break, the Lady approaches you. She slowly looks you over, from your toes up to the top of your head. You know that She is quietly judging you. Think about those parts of yourself that you would like to continue to develop for future use, those that will sustain you, and that which should be enjoyed today. Perhaps you think of your body and your mind. Today your body may be flexible and strong, but it will fail with age. Your mind can expand with time, retaining the memories that can be planted in future generations. She looks straight into your eyes with the question unspoken. Allow your own answer to fill you. *(pause)*

She smiles, nods with satisfaction, and returns to the competition. Stay, if you will, watching the separation of the harvest, or return to the festivities of the fairgrounds. Spend a few more minutes enjoying the sounds, sights, and smells of the harvest festival. If there is someone you would like to speak with, a vendor, harvester, spinner, or any other celebrant, take a moment for that now. *(Pause for personal interaction.)*

It's time to return. Wander back through the fairgrounds. People wave good-bye to you as you leave and enter the apple grove. The baskets of fruit have been collected. If you wish, you may pick another apple and eat it as you make your way down the gentle slope and into the woods. You pass by the log, under the branches of the oak and hawthorn, and return to the clearing. Take a last look around and find your way back to your inner home.

Teetering on the Edge Mabon is a time of equal balance between day and night—a brief moment before the turning of the wheel tips the balance temporarily toward the darkness. There's a gentle rhythm that occurs. At the winter solstice, the night is at its peak of strength. It then begins to recede as the days grow longer, until we once more return to equilibrium.

You find yourself walking into a city park. You can hear the sound of people talking and children laughing. The sun is shining overheard. The gravel path is soft beneath your feet. Ahead of you is a large tree. Sitting beneath it, your friends are waiting for you. You greet each other with hugs and hellos.

A friend's child grabs you by the hand and asks if you would please take her to the playground. You look to her parents and they give their approval. She pulls you in the direction of the sound of children's laugher. You can hear the swings squeaking and children playing.

She runs over to a swing and gets on, asking for a push. You get behind her. Grabbing the sides of the swing, you pull her and the swing up into the air and release it. The momentum swings her forward and back. You continue to gently push her to her screams of "Higher! Higher!" She swings back and forth, pumping her legs, keeping her own sense of time and rhythm like a pendulum.

After a few minutes she puts her feet down, dragging them along the ground, slowing herself until she comes to a stop. She jumps off the swing and points to a seesaw. Excitedly, she asks if you'll ride with her. Without waiting for an answer, she runs to the end that's on the ground and hops on. You walk over to the seesaw and push the elevated end down low enough for you to swing your leg over. You can feel the child's weight through your legs but you can easily hold her up in the air.

Slowly you bend your legs, lowering yourself to the ground while raising her higher in the air. Then you straighten your legs again, allowing her weight to bring her back to the ground. She pushes off with her feet and again you bend your legs, raising her high up in the air. She squeals with delight as you lower her back to the ground. With the great imbalance of weight, you are in control of the seesaw.

She continues for several more minutes before hopping off to run toward the slide. As you lower the seesaw back to a level position, you hear a friend behind you say, "It's my turn!" He walks over and pushes down on the elevated end, throws his leg over, and sits. You find yourself suddenly rising upward while his heavier weight brings his end of the seesaw down to ground. You let out a gasp of surprise. He chuckles playfully at you. He says, "Ready," and pushes up off the ground, lifting himself into the air as you move back down toward the Earth. You do not stay down long, as gravity pulls his larger frame back to Earth. He straightens his legs and stands, keeping control of the movement and bringing you to a level point. Your friend then bends his legs slightly, just as you had when you played with the child.

Slowly he moves you back up as his end of the seesaw goes down, only this time more gently. He then pushes up, so that your feet touch the ground.

Another friend comes over and jokingly pushes him from the seesaw, saying, "It's my turn!" You hear your first friend's daughter calling out, "Daddy, Daddy, watch me slide!" He wanders off with her.

Standing back at the balance point, your new friend climbs easily on. Your weights match much more evenly. You share the balance of the plank between you. You push up and gently rise in the air as your friend moves to the ground. And now it's her turn to push herself up and rise into the sky as you return to the Earth. You move evenly and slowly back and forth, up and down . . . much like the rhythm of the child and the swing you watched just a little while before. The world is in balance, moving in time and rhythm to your shared experience.

After a minute, you hear a familiar strain of music and the ringing of a bell. You hear your friend's daughter scream, "Ice cream!" You get off the seesaw and join her as she races for the truck, walking on the Earth.

When you finish you ice cream, it's time to leave. You say good-bye to your friends, turn, and find your way back to your inner home.

SAMHAIN

With the harvest in and the birds taking flight to warmer lands, the year ends. The empty branches of the trees loom like thin skeleton bones against the backdrop of a darkened sky. In an agricultural cycle, this is the time of year when the cattle are slaughtered. With the smell of blood and smoke on the air, it is no surprise that people's minds turned to thoughts of death and to those loved ones who went before them.

At Samhain we honor the completeness of the cycle. We give thanks for the fullness of year, from the return of the sun to the reaping of the harvest. We look toward the future and hope that what we have received will be enough to sustain us in the dark season ahead. In my community, many of us come together to remember those who have left us, giving thanks to them for the wisdom and love that they shared with us. We also acknowledge and celebrate the new lives that were birthed during the past year. In this way, we embrace the fullness of the wheel.

Through the Veil ⌂

From the moment we're born, we begin to die. Death is a natural part of the cycle of life. Most Wiccans do not believe that death is the end of existence. We see the cycle of rebirth around us in the plants and trees. Those whom we love are never completely gone. They live on in our hearts and minds.

Even with solid beliefs in a form of life after death, it's still difficult for those who remain in the physical world. Speaking to the spirits of those who have passed can be emotionally challenging. Still, doing this can help us find closure for our immediate grief. Later, we may receive wisdom, guidance, and love from those beyond the veil.

This pathworking begins in a location that's familiar to you and your departed loved one. It should be a place where you created happy memories, or a place that you strongly associate with her. I've included both human and animal spirits, for the loss of a pet can be just as painful as losing any other close companion. Although the example below has been written in the feminine, it can, of course, be changed to correspond to either sex.

Look around you. You know this place well. It's a place where you have shared many happy memories with someone whom you loved. Here, you are safe. Here you can allow your loved one to visit because you know that it's safe. See your space around you. Relax into it.

This journey is a special journey. Tonight is a time of remembrance. Tonight a loved one will visit you, to talk and remember with you, to give counsel, to mourn with you. Whatever emotions this visit brings, you are not afraid. You know you're safe. You can cry with your loved one, laugh with your loved one, talk with your loved one. You know that it will be a good visit. Take a deep breath . . . and we begin.

Turn your mind to the west, to the home of the ancestors. The Veil between the living and the dead is at its thinnest right now. On the other side, your loved one waits. See this Veil—a wall of wispy gray smoke, a living fog—standing outside the space you're in. Just as you remember your friends and family who have passed before you, they, too, remember you. They stand on the other side hoping that you'll reach out to them and allow them to be with you, if just for one moment. The Veil stands in the west. Behind it, you can make out movement. But to your eyes, the movers are only shapeless forms.

They are ready. If you would allow them that moment, now is the time to invite them to join you in this circle. In your heart and mind, bring up her image—and call out her name.

There is movement behind the Veil as your call is heard. Speak her name again. And a third time. Slowly, the Veil parts . . . and your loved one steps out from the smoke. She is slowly making her way toward you . . . answering your call. She comes closer . . . Can you feel her? She approaches the western boundary of your space. It is the spirit of the loved one you have called forth. Will you allow her to enter?

(Allow the participants time to respond. If they don't want the spirit to enter, indicate that they can have their visit at the boundary.)

She is here. Can you feel her? She stands before you . . . now.

Can you smell her? The musty smell of sweet desire . . . the pungent odor of damp earth . . . wood shavings . . . or oil and rust. Is it lavender, peaches, and sunlight? Perhaps it's the smell of animal fur . . . or fresh and clean as spring. Musky and rich. Breathe in and remember how she smelled. *(pause)*

Is there a taste on your tongue that she has placed there to remind you of her? Her taste on your tongue as you kissed her check . . . her mouth . . . salty tears of joy . . . of sorrow . . . of sweat upon skin. Perhaps the taste of a favorite food shared. Savor it . . . drink it in and stir it with your mind. *(pause)*

Do you remember the sound of her voice? Deep and full . . . light and airy . . . full-bodied laughter . . . or a high-pitched giggle? A deep purr within your ear at night . . . a sharp bark to warn you of danger? Soft and filled with compassion . . . rough and raspy? Listen for her voice.

Do you remember her touch? Warm lips upon your skin . . . [*masculine examples:* the rough stubble of a beard upon your cheek . . . the tickle of whiskers . . .] the sweet caress of smooth, warm flesh . . . coarse, cracked hands callused with work . . . a touch that is weak and dry, wrinkled with age . . . a gentle caress . . . a rough but playful pat. She reaches for you now and touches you with that memory. *(pause)*

Do you remember how she looked when her eyes met yours? Blue . . . brown . . . black as the night or gray as the seas? Her smile . . . was it broad or thin . . . lips full or cracked with age? The tilt of a chin. The shake of a head. Face soft-skinned or covered with whiskers. Hair, brown as chestnuts, blond, black, or full white? Thinning on top or a cascading mane? Do you remember how she looked? *(pause)*

Allow yourself to remember her. It's your memory that gives her strength . . . gives her form on this plane. Share with her now your favorite memory of her. Let her know that she is not forgotten. If you harbor pain, unresolved issues and words . . . now is the time to express this to her. Open yourself to her so that she may share a message.

(Allow time for personal interaction.)

It's time for her to leave . . . It's time for you to bid her goodbye. *(pause)* Say farewell . . . and let her return to her realm. *(pause)* She is now slowly returning. Watch her as she makes her way westward, back toward the hazy Veil that separates our worlds. Before she returns to the mists, she turns to look back at you . . . now she turns again and passes through the Veil. Know that if you remember her, she will always be with you.

She has returned to her world, and you must now return to yours. Turn and see the way that you entered, and return now to your inner home.

The Lord and Lady of Winter ♤

⌘ A drum or a CD or tape of a drumbeat.

Samhain is the time of endings and the time of beginnings. All things eventually die and decompose. Compost nurtures new growth, fulfilling the cycle of death and rebirth.

You find yourself stepping into your clearing. It's night, and the moon is rising above the horizon. You can hear the familiar sound of the stream. Across the waters, you can see the harvested field, lit by the moon. The empty cornstalks, gathered into bundles, show as dark shadows against the night sky. The air is chilled. The scents of burning leaves and decay ride on the wind. The forest is beside you. The trees are bare, their leaves scattered on the forest floor. They remind you of a skeleton's bones. Sticks and leaves crack under your feet as you step forward.

The forest is filled with a thick mist. Something inside the forest calls to you. You walk past the path that leads to the apple orchard and then by your rock. You lightly touch its rough surface for reassurance before you continue along the edge of the woods. You are drawn to a small trail that leads into the woods. You pause a moment before entering the mist. Some inner sense leads you along through the dark. You see that there is an opening in the trees ahead and make your way toward it.

You step out into an ancient graveyard framed by the thick forest growth. The stone markers of various sizes and shapes form crooked lines. Some are cracked with age. A few are broken. It's difficult to read the time-worn names on the stones. You notice willow trees carved on the surface of many of the markers. You walk by them, slowly moving toward the center of the graveyard . . . and to the figure that stands there waiting for you.

She slowly turns and looks directly at you. You recognize the Crone, Goddess of the crossroads between life and death. Pay homage to the Lady. *(pause)*

She looks at you and speaks. "The cycle has turned to the dead of the year. It is now my time and my domain. I am the giver of life and of death. I am the Crone, grown wise with age, and I bring with me knowledge—I also bring with me the darkness. It is Samhain, the time of endings. Fields lie bare, their bounty stripped from the vines. Empty cornstalks stand against a gray sky. Brown leaves swirl in chilling winds. The cold creeps in—it surrounds you—and reminds you of death. The Veil between the worlds of the living and the underworld is so very thin right now. Can you not feel it? Can you not feel my presence? I walk with you at this time of year. Does this frighten you? Does the thought of death frighten you?

"Ah, but is it really the parting—or is it the sorrow, pain, and grief that come with the loss that that you truly fear? All that is created dies. This is part of the cycle, a part of the dance that you call life. As you were born into this world, you will all someday die. All those whom you know, all those whom you love, will come to me behind the Veil. At the time of endings, know that I held the hands of those who parted the Veil before you, guiding them and giving them peace. I am also there to hold and comfort you in your pain as you miss and grieve for those who have gone. For the living, the dance of sorrow is not an easy one. But just as you all enjoy the dance of life, you must all experience the dance of sorrow.

"I, too, know sorrow. Every year in spring my beloved Green Man rises. I am young then . . . and beautiful. We dance under the full moon and lie together on the damp earth beneath a new canopy of green buds. Our laughter and joy fill the air, and the flowers, plants, and animals respond with the quickening of life. He grows tall and strong . . . until Lammas, when he is cut down. But when something dies, it decomposes and recomposes into another form."

A bird screeches in the distance. There is movement in the mist behind the Crone. A tall, muscular figure with antlers emerges from the fog to stand by Her side. His face is in shadow, but you recognize the Horned God, leader of the hunt, Lord of the shadows, protector of the tribe, the Lord of death. Fear touches you. Pay homage to the Horned One. *(pause)*

He speaks to you: "We are the ones who wait in the dead of the year, in the last dark hours where there is only silence. Be fearless and look upon us. I have other faces and other names. Yet do not fear me . . . remember you trusted me in the lush spring green . . . finding enchantment with me, you found me merry in summer dance; fear not to meet me in the autumn forest hunt, nor in the winter's snows. The Earth will again move from barren to green; so shall you flower and bear the fruits of life again. I am the great Lord of death who waits for you. Have faith in life and trust in me, as the wheel of the year brings forth the time of my domain, take me into your heart as I have always taken you into mine."

The year passes before you. You remember the Holly and the Oak of solstice, the swelling of the Lady's belly at Imbolc, the sound of Kore's laughter, the King and Queen of May, the Green Man of summer, the Lady of harvest and John Barleycorn's sacrifice. You realize that they stand before you. If you will, open your heart and embrace the fullness of the cycle.

(Begin a soft, slow heartbeat rhythm on the drum.)

You hear the sound of a drumbeat. It's steady, like the beating of your own heart. You find your feet beginning to move of their own accord, dancing in rhythm with the beating of the drum. *(Slowly begin to speed up the rhythm of the drum.)*

You feel the Earth beneath your feet, soft yet strong. The heat within your body as you move to the beat of the drum. You dance within the graveyard. An expression of life among the symbols of death. You dance around the Crone and the Horned

One. *(Speed up the rhythm of the drum to a pace suitable for dancing. Pause to allow for the experience.)*

Feel the energy swirling and surging within you with each step . . . with each beat. Your mouth opens and you take in life-giving breath . . . and let out noises and sounds of sorrow and joy. Release the old year as you dance, and raise energy for blessings for the new year.

(Allow the drum to reach a crescendo, then slow the rhythm . . . returning it to a slow heartbeat drum . . . while also quieting the sound.)

The energy begins to dissipate. Your heartbeat slows and returns to normal. The drum quiets until the sound disappears into the night. (*Stop the drum.*)

The Old Ones smile. Thank Them. They slowly fade, disappearing into the mist. You know that they are always with you, and that you will see them again. Turn and find the path that led you to this site. You have no trouble seeing it. Follow it back to the clearing. You pass your rock and find your way back to your inner home.

Spirits of Place: The Ancestors and Spirits of the Land

The cycles of time turn against a stable backdrop of place. Many spirits are anchored to particular localities. The tree spirits exist rooted in the land. Animal spirits forage for food or play in the meadows or forests or the waters of the lake. Spirits of the Earth dwell in the stolid boulders. And the spirits of people who once lived in a place create atmospheres that touch the lives of those who live there now, often in ways unseen. All these and more are members of what we call the ancients, the ancestors, or the Old Ones.

SPIRITS OF THE LAND

The spirits of nature exist everywhere, in the farmlands and wild places and in the city, surrounded by concrete and steel. If you live in a city, just look around you. Life creeps up through sidewalk cracks, fills open lots, and sings from the cultivated parks.

This exercise, created by Anluan, asks you to pick one location in order to connect with the spirits that exist within and around it. This location should be just a short walk from your home or your workplace so you can visit it often throughout the year. You don't actually have to be in your place while you do this exercise, but you do have to be familiar with what your place is like at any season. Repeat this exercise at intervals throughout the year and notice the changes the seasons bring to the spirits of this place.

You find yourself standing under a tree near where you live. It might be part of a forest, on the edge of a field, overlooking the water, in a park, or simply growing at the curbside of your block.

You sit at the tree's base and become aware of the Earth under you. As you take a breath in, feel the tree's strength cradle and support you. You relax your mind and feel the day slip away. You remember a time when you were held safe and the world seemed new. For the world is new. As you breathe in and out, you feel yourself slip back to a time before structure, before knowing, a time before words and language when everything was possible. Looking out into your environment, you see the world refreshed and aglow with wonder.

As you breathe in, hear first the beating of your own heart. Breathe in again and you extend beyond yourself. You feel and hear the spirit of the tree before you. You sit where spirit and matter share a place and can communicate without language. You breathe in and hear the voice of the tree sing to you and the green world come alive.

You realize there are others who share this place. You become aware of the spirits that surround you in your everyday world. You can hear them in a new way. You see their brightness. They have been hiding behind or perhaps within some of the plants that surround you.

You watch quietly as they come out. You are surprised at their abundance. You delight in watching them interact with the world, unseen by any other who may happen by. You hide, protected by your tree, as you sit and watch for a while. (*Pause to allow for personal experience.*)

Shhhhhhhhhh. (*a quiet noise to accustom and bring back your travelers to the speaking world of your voice*)

After some time of exploring, you hear the song of your tree change, calling you back. It's time to return to your own world. The world of language. The world of knowing.

You smile at the spirits as they vanish. You watch as the plants and animals return to daily routines. You hear the tree whisper its good-byes. As you open your eyes again, the structure of your workaday world comes back into focus . . . and you are home. You remember that you never really left and that you share that home with others—and can return to visit with them again.

Next time you visit your tree in the physical world, leave an offering of thanks.

SPIRITS OF PLACE—ANCESTORS

Our ancestors are not just those whose genes and names we carry. They are not only those whose thoughts and deeds inspire us. They are also the unknown people who have touched us in ways unseen. Prior to this exercise, if you don't know already, find out something about your building, neighborhood, and town. When was the building built? By whom? Immigrants who may not have been able to afford living in what they created? Farmers who gathered together their family, friends, and neighbors to help raise the roof? A contractor nailing together pieces of a prefabricated house? How has the ethnic diversity in your neighborhood changed over time? The use of the land? Spend some time getting to know those who had an effect on the place where you live and therefore on you, too.

It's late afternoon. You find yourself walking out the front door of your current home. Look around for a moment. You can see the front of your building, the street, and all that is familiar to you. Find someplace to sit, on a stoop, step, or porch, and enjoy the sunshine. As you relax, you watch the people on the street before you. You might see workers fixing a pothole, a neighbor sweeping his sidewalk or watering his gardens, children playing while their parents chat and watch. These are people whom you might see every day, or only for this moment.

Think about the people who live and work around you every day. The lives they lead and the relationships they maintain. As the sun begins to sink in the sky, turn your thoughts to those who have lived and worked in this place before you. Where did they come from? What did they do? Where did they go?

Allow your eyes to lose focus as you think about people who lived here a generation before you arrived. See the area as it looked when they were young. How have things changed? See them as they went about their day, working the land, perhaps building or living in the structures that still stand here. Watch their lives and the relationships they shared. You breathe deep again and you can see them going about their daily tasks.

You sit and you watch a while . . . looking over your neighborhood and imagining those who lived here in earlier times. Slowly you reach back farther, now two generations back. See the world through their eyes.

Continue stepping back through the past generations that lived in this place until you come to only Earth, trees, water, and sky. *(Pause to allow for personal experience.)*

Shhhhhhhhhh. *(a quiet noise to accustom and bring back your travelers to the speaking world of your voice)*

You feel the afternoon wind blow against your face. The sun

goes in behind the clouds, and you feel the air begin to cool. You open your eyes and look about and see your neighbors as they head home. And it's time you did the same. You stand, stretch your legs, and return to your inner home.

SPIRITS OF PLACE—SUMMER PASTURES OF NEW YORK

I'm offering this as an example of how to integrate the spirits of place, the ancestors, and the Mighty Ones of the seasonal cycles all into one working. Judy Harrow, who was living in New York City at the time, crafted a journey within familiar local scenes. After you have explored this pathworking, create your own based on the spirits of your immediate environment. What spirits walk your land? What deities make themselves known to you, and in what manner? What ancestors have touched your life, and in what ways?

Come with me, if you will, to the green and living heart of the city. You have been working hard all day, and now you deserve rest and play.

We get there by a journey through the underground. You hold a coin that was created only to give people entry here. Place it in the turnstile now and enter. Stand on the platform among the heat and the crowd. Many different kinds of people are here—the wealthy and the homeless, men and women, immigrants and those who grew up here, all races, all cultures. Far beyond those broad differences, there are many different personal stories, laughter and tears, fulfillment and frustration. Some say the city holds nine million stories.

In a roar of noise and light, the train comes. Step in. Do you find a seat? As the train moves off, you feel the vibration and the motion; the noise of it fills your ear. In this brighter light, you can look around. Notice the differences of clothing, of faces. Notice the many different things people are doing: sleeping, reading, listening to music, eating. Some are working, briefcases open on their laps; some are caring for children. Most of them are too busy about their own concerns to notice you watching them.

But there, in the corner, an old, old woman looks at you, and Her attention draws your eye. Her clothing is soiled and shabby. Her face is all wrinkled, Her hair gray and tangled. That over-loaded shopping cart might hold everything She owns in this world. Still, Her stone-gray eyes are clear, deep, timeless. Your eyes meet Hers and seem to lock into engagement with them. You cannot evade Her steady gaze. She seems to look deep into you, to see all that you hide, even from yourself. It's as though She is weighing your soul. The moment stretches. No word can be said across the crowd, over the noise of the train. But at length She nods, smiles very slightly, and falls asleep as the train pulls in to Eighty-first Street.

Climb the stairs from one kind of heat to another. Here the sun has been beating down, heating the pavement all day. See the dark, looming mass of the museum . . . then, as the traffic light changes, put the streets behind you and walk into the green park.

It's instantly cooler in the shade of the trees, and somehow easier. Still crowded, but a different feeling to it here. Most of this crowd is here by choice. They must have just mowed some grass; the fragrance is pervasive. As you move farther into the park, the sound of wind in the trees replaces the sound of traffic. Not all white noise is the same. And in your muscles you can feel the gentle slope as the path rises and falls.

Carefully cross the bicycle path, and head up one more rise, and now the Delacorte Theater is to your right, a large, round mass. Behind it, the vertical thrust of the Belvedere Tower, look-ing like the reconstructed Norman castle that it is. Your fan-tasies of jousting knights are dispelled by the instruments of the weather station, visible high in the tower.

People are selling food from pushcarts near the theater.

Some of it looks or smells good to you. If you like, you can buy some for yourself. It's hours still to show time, but already people are beginning to line up. Go past the theater to find your place on line.

On your right, beyond the theater, under the tower, is the pond. Take a few minutes to enjoy the scene: ducks, dogs, and children playing in and around the water, quacking, barking, splashing, and laughing, parents calling for caution.

And right here, to the left of the curving path, is the start of the line. It's not a normal queue. It's more like a string of picnic blankets under the trees beside the path. The path, and the line of trees, curves to your left around the edge of the lawn. It's full of people today, all enjoying the summer afternoon. Some are flying kites, some playing Frisbee, and there's a softball game off to the far side. Others are relaxing on their blankets in the shade. Some brought picnics from home; others, like you, bought food from the pushcarts. Some have stretched out comfortably on their blankets for a pretheater snooze. Some are eating, reading, or playing cards or board games with each other. Some are sketching or working on handcrafts like spinning or embroidery. Some are embracing, in all possible combinations—this is New York. Some are engaged in intense discussions. Many are listening to music, most from boom boxes—but a few are playing instruments themselves. Somehow the many different styles of music don't seem to clash. This is Central Park in summer.

You've reached the end of the line without finding your friends. No surprise; you expected to be the first here, to hold the place for the others. You spread your blanket under a tree and just enjoy the scene. Your snack tastes good and contents you. The summer warmth here is relaxing. You lie back. Your muscles relax into the Earth. The last bit of stress is gone. You let yourself drift, as people walk past you, lengthening the line along the path around the field.

In time, something draws your attention to the next tree down the line. There is a woman sitting on a blanket much like yours. She is young, or is She ageless? A long skirt and peasant blouse that would have gone equally without notice in the 1960s or the 1860s. Long hair that reminds you of the color of day-lilies. She is crocheting an elaborate lacy pattern. Her hand-work fascinates you. It may seem to glow, or to hum, or to vibrate. You are curious. She notices you, smiles an invitation. You come closer to get a better look at the work, and at the woman.

Her summer-green eyes are clear, deep, and timeless. Your eyes meet and join. You know it's rude to stare, but somehow you have no will to pull your gaze away from those eyes. Nor does your gaze annoy Her. Rather, it seems that She lets you look deep inside, to see secrets long hidden or ignored.

And a story unfolds. Once, long ago and far away, the young people would take the good flocks to the high country for the summer. They would make themselves little huts for sleep, but their days were spent outdoors with the wildflowers and the blue sky, and the Lady of summer. Away from the cautious elders, the summer was a time of freedom, of playfulness, and of loving. Sometimes lasting bonds were formed of that loving; sometimes babies came.

Then the land and the people were conquered, and then came the terrible time of the hunger. The foreign landlords sold every crop but the potatoes, and the potatoes rotted in the bins. Many died. Most who lived had to leave. Some came here, to this very ground. They called it Nanny Goat Hill. This was their place of new beginning, a slum, a shantytown little more substantial than those ancient shelters in the summer hills. The Lady of summer came here with them, in an old fiddle that they played to ease the seasickness and the homesickness.

The people took root here. Many adapted, learned the ways of Greyface, became proper and prosperous, moved to better neighborhoods. The Lady of summer stayed in the shanties. Eventually the city cleared away the village and made this park where people dance, sing, feast, make music, and love, all in Her presence, as Her people always have, whether or not they knew Her name.

She asks you to look around at the people who enjoy the summer here. Their ancestors lived all over the Earth. They come from every continent, every culture. Some even had great-great-grandparents who lived right here, when this place was called Nanny Goat Hill. But ancestry does not matter. What matters is celebration, the spirit of the summer pasture, and that can move within any child of Earth.

Does She touch your hand? Does She kiss you gently on the forehead? Do you have a question for Her? Does She answer? Does She leave you with a picture or a word? Can you recall Her scent? Know that She lives in the heart of the city, in the heart of the summer, in the fiddles and the boom boxes. She lives wherever people come together in love and pleasure in a grassy field under the sky. And Her warm and playful heart is open to you, always.

And now, your friends have come, calling you back to your own blanket and to their welcome and happy company. The evening is warm and pleasant. The park is green. Will you tell them what you have seen and done? The choice is yours.

Take some time now to enjoy the company of your friends and an evening in the park. When the evening is over, you will return to your own bed and sleep soundly. In the morning, you will be fresh, rested, and alert. And for now, return when you are ready to this time and place.

ᛒ

Trance journey allows us to receive a deeper understanding of the myths and spiritual beliefs of our religion. With deeper understanding we can embrace the lessons, integrating them into our own being, our hearts and minds. With trance we become a part of the cycle, experiencing and balancing ourselves with the rhythms and patterns of the Earth, bringing us together as a tribe, a people, a community.

CHAPTER SIX

☙❧

Coven Work, Coven Play

Sharing altered states with committed and trusted friends helps us learn more about trance, about each other, about ourselves, and about the Gods and Goddesses of our faith. When groups enter trance together, members strengthen their psychic and emotional connections to one another. These strong and solid connections support a healthy group mind which, in turn, nurtures each member's personal development. The growth of each member further enriches the group mind. Shared trance releases a vibrant spiral of growth. The creative energy of many well-functioning groups contributes to the ongoing development of our traditions and our community.

As with any group exercise, dialogue is important. Describing your visions to each other while they are occurring helps to keep everyone together in their experience, creating trust and familiarity. Even more important, sharing trance work as it happens creates deeper links among members as they build on each other's perceptions. Chapter 2 includes suggestions on developing or strengthening this skill.

The following guided meditations are only a few examples of journeys that can be used to develop your group mind. Most are bare outlines for facilitator use, because the real work is creative and interactive. The facilitator should be aware of each action as it happens and give directions or suggestions based on the participants' responses.

Shared trance journeys work best when all participants have a common understanding of core beliefs and ethics. Make sure you take the opportunity to discuss this as a group prior to wandering down the path together. Remember—your inner world is a very personal, intimate space. Share it only with those you trust.

I recommend that group members keep their trance journals nearby. When you return from a trance adventure, first take a few quiet moments for members to record their individual perceptions and reactions in their journals. Once that's done, the group can discuss what they experienced. Sharing these insights will influence each person's understanding of the journey. They may learn still more by reflecting on how group discussion augmented or changed their personal reactions.

Most important, have fun! This is work, but it is also play. Enjoy your time together in the inner realms. Laugh together, dance together, explore together, and grow together.

Revealing Our Inner Selves

This exercise is based on one found in the book *Mind Games,* by Masters and Houston.[*] It is meant to deepen and strengthen mutual understanding within a group.

I've separated the exercise into three pieces. You can proceed directly from one to the next, or take breaks for reflection, discussion, and recording. If you choose to take breaks between the sections, remember to begin each segment with the trance induction.

For this exercise, you will work with a partner whose face will be your visual focus for an open-eyed trance experience. I suggest that you use the same partner for all three exercises, then change partners. Repeat the exercises until each member has

---

[*]Robert Masters and Jean Houston. *Mind Games: The Guide to Inner Space* (New York: Dell Publishing, 1972; 1993) pp.32–34.

had an opportunity to work with everyone else in the group. Remember to record your experiences with each partner. Later, you may choose to share these notes and your experiences with the group.

If you are practicing alone, the first two parts of this exercise can be done while gazing at your own image in a mirror. For section one, focus on the question, "Who am I?" For section two, ask either "Who have I been?" or "Who will I become?"

I'm assuming that you have already completed the pretrance steps (stretching, grounding, relaxation, and induction) and are in a relaxed state of consciousness.

TRANCE SETUP

Pick a partner. It doesn't matter how well you know this person. Sit facing each other. Make comfortable eye contact. Look deep into your partner's eyes. Focus completely on the sound of my voice and the sight of your partner's face. Listen closely; look closely.

Breathe gently in . . . and out. Feel the beat of your heart, the rising and falling of your chest. As you breathe, you can feel your muscles start to relax. As you relax, your focus holds steady. You keep looking at your partner, as your body continues to slide into peaceful relaxation. You've been here before. You know that it's a wonderful and comfortable place that you are entering, so you allow your muscles to relax further . . . and further.

As your body relaxes, your perceptions begin to shift. You feel yourself gently moving into trance, going deeper and deeper. You relax even more as your consciousness moves deeper . . . and deeper . . . entering into an alternative state of being, into an alternative state of consciousness. Your focus is completely on your partner before you and the sound of my voice as you continue to move deeper . . . and deeper . . . and deeper . . . into relaxation . . . into trance.

Part I—Seeing Behind the Masks
Your focus is completely on your partner's face and the sound of my voice as you continue to move deeper . . . and deeper . . . and deeper . . . into relaxation . . . into trance.

As you continue to focus on your partner's face you begin to notice changes occurring. They may begin as subtle shifts . . . gradually . . . they become more pronounced. Watch as the face before you softens and changes. It is not the same face that it was a moment ago. We all have different masks that we show to the world—different identities that reflect various aspects of our personalities. Watch, as many masks move across your partner's face . . . until it stabilizes, revealing his true face. Relax deep into his eyes.

Realize that while you have been watching your partner's metamorphoses, you have been changing too. You are relaxed and open to your partner, revealing your inner self to him, as he is revealing himself to you, as you become more fully aware of each other.

Now slowly begin moving your consciousness back to yourself and your body. Become conscious of your breathing. Your perceptions are returning to the everyday while you retain all that you have learned. Awareness starts returning to the world around you, then to your body, your muscles, yourself . . . until you return completely.

Questions for Contemplation and Discussion Record and then discuss your experiences with your partner. How closely did your perceptions match with your partner's self-image? How close did his vision of you come to the way you perceive yourself? Did you learn something new about your partner? About yourself? Do you believe that this exercise helps you understand your covenmates more deeply?

Part II—Another Time, Another Place
Look closely at your partner. Look deep into your partner's eyes so that all is tuned out except the sound of my voice and her face. Keep looking closely at your partner while listening to the sound of my voice.

Breathe gently in . . . and out. Feel the beat of your heart, the rising and falling of your chest. As you breathe, you feel your muscles start to relax. As you relax, your focus steadies and deepens. You keep looking at your partner as your body continues to slide into peaceful relaxation. You've been here before. You know that is it a wonderful and comfortable place that you are entering, so you allow your muscles to relax further . . . and further.

As your body relaxes, your perceptions begin to shift. You begin to feel yourself gently moving into trance, going deeper and deeper. You relax even more as your consciousness moves deeper . . . and deeper . . . entering into an alternate state of being, into an alternate state of consciousness. Your focus is completely on your partner's face and the sound of my voice as you continue to move deeper . . . and deeper . . . and deeper . . . into relaxation . . . into trance.

Become aware of time. Feel time as it moves around you in its circular motion. Each breath you take . . . the swirls of time . . . moves you forward, one day, one hour, one minute, one second. As you become aware of the passage of time, feel time begin to slow down. One hour slows to one day . . . one minute to one hour . . . one minute, one second. Time slows down . . . still slower . . . until it stops.

Now feel a pull as time begins to move backward . . . taking you backward into time. Observe as your partner's face begins to soften and change. Time continues moving into the past. As you watch you see the years fall away. She appears younger with each passing moment. Until the familiar face wavers completely, to be replaced by another. The face you now see is from a previous existence. It is someone else . . . another identify . . . another life . . . in another time. It continues to slowly shift and change as time continues moving you back . . . back . . . back . . . Watch as your partner's face reveals to you other lives lived . . . until time stops and begins to move forward again. Like an elastic band pulled taut and released, your partner's face quickly shifts and changes as you move closer and closer, back to the present. Your partner's face returns to the one that is familiar as time returns to the present. Relax deep into her eyes.

Realize that while you have been watching you partner's metamorphoses, you too have been changing. You are relaxed and open to your partner, revealing your previous selves to her, as she is revealing her selves to you. You are becoming more fully aware of each other.

Now slowly begin moving your consciousness back to your self and your body. Become conscious of your breathing. Your perceptions returning to the everyday, and yet retaining all you have learned. Awareness returning to here and now, to the world around you. Your body, your muscles, yourself. Until you completely return.

Questions for Contemplation and Discussion Record and then discuss your experiences with your partner. Record the faces you saw, their age, sex, race, hair color, clothing or jewelry (if seen), nationality, personal hygiene, or anything else you noticed while in trance. Did hearing of your perceptions bring up any past memories or associations for your partner? Did you learn something new about your partner? About yourself? Do you think this exercise helps you understand your covenmates more deeply?

Part III—Becoming Another
Your focus is completely on your partner before you and the sound of my voice as you continue to move deeper . . . and deeper . . . and deeper . . . into relaxation . . . into trance.

Keep looking at your partner's face. You are very familiar with that face. You have seen it undergo many changes. You have observed it as the masks of time were peeled away, seen the different identities that are hidden behind the eyes that you gaze into right now, and witnessed the different possibilities that are held within that face. Look very, very closely at your partner and allow yourself to go deeper, still listening to my voice, and deeper.

Do you wonder what it would be like to be your partner? To be inside his shell and see the world through his eyes? Go deeper and wonder what it would be like to be that person who sits before you. Feel yourself start to slip out of your body . . . and move beyond your physical form. Feel your partner as your identities move past each other in the space between you . . . and enter into the body of your partner.

Sense what it is like to be in this body. Notice the difference in the shape, size, weight, and feel. Experience how this body responds as you touch something around you. Become aware of the world as seen through this body. How does this body feel? Are you more or less happy? Anxious? Calm? Depressed? Do you have more or less energy? Know the world through this body. *(pause)* Then focus on your partner and see yourself through the eyes of another.

Now slowly begin to move your identity back to your own body. Feel your partner's essence as you pass each other in the space between you. Your consciousness returns back firmly into your own body, along with the knowledge that you have gained.

Now slowly begin moving your consciousness back to yourself and your body. Become conscious of your breathing. Your perceptions return to the everyday, while retaining all that you have learned. Awareness returns to the world around you. You become aware of your body, your muscles, yourself . . . until you return completely.

Questions for Contemplation and Discussion Record and then discuss your experiences with your partner. How is the world different when experienced through another body? Did you learn something new about your partner? About yourself? Do you believe this exercise helps you understand your covenmate more deeply?

A Visitor Comes a-Calling

The first time I did this exercise, I found it frightening, intimidating, and amazing all at the same time. The idea of allowing someone, even someone I knew, into my safe space was terrifying. Never mind the thought of his bringing a guest! And then there was the notion that I had to describe this stranger. My stomach went into knots just thinking about it.

To help ease into the situation, I created as my safe space a walled garden with an ornate metal gate. This way I could start by seeing my guests with a barrier between us. The gate gave me more control over the situation. I could open the gate and invite them in when I felt comfortable and ready.

Still, I had doubts that when the time came I would see anyone other than my friend on the other side of the gate. Yet, when my friend came forward and introduced his guest, I could clearly see a gentleman with curly red hair standing beside him. The guest was tall and long-legged, with bright blue eyes and a big smile. I also noticed he had a white cast on his right arm.

When I returned to the physical plane, I recorded my experience then discussed it with my trance partner. To my complete amazement, my description was correct all the way down to the broken arm! Others in my group had similar results. This simple exercise proved to me that trance states are not just exercises of imagination. They open a new world of possibilities.

Reminder: As with any group exercise, dialogue is important. Describing your visions to each other while they are occurring helps to keep people together in their experience, creating trust and familiarity while creating deeper links between members as they build on each other's perceptions.

Do this exercise twice with the same partner, so that each of you can experience both roles. At the completion of each exercise, record your experiences, reactions, and reflections in your trance journal. When you've done it from both sides, discuss your experiences and impressions with your trance partner. Compare your trance perceptions.

THE BASICS

Choose a partner. One must then agree to be the visitor and the other the host or hostess. An alternative is to pick one to three people from the group to act as visitor(s). The visitor must decide who he will bring as a guest before entering trance. This guest should be someone who is not known to their trance partner or to the group. The visitor should fix this person clearly in his mind.

You should agree in advance on the Otherworld location where you will meet. For me this was a walled garden, but it could easily be your inner home, the coven space, or any place where you feel safe and comfortable.

The facilitator (or tape) guides everyone into a relaxed state, then brings them to the previously agreed upon location. The visitor should remain on the edge or just outside of this location while his trance partner or the other participants enter. While those inside the space become acquainted with the environment, the visitor should focus on the essence of the guest he has brought along.

When all is ready, the first visitor and his guest are invited to come forward to be introduced. After a suitable time, the facilitator (or tape) will indicate an ending to the exercise and guide all present back to waking reality.

THE ACTION

I'm assuming that you have already completed the pretrance steps (stretching, grounding, relaxation, and induction) and are in an altered state.

You find yourself in a familiar place. You feel comfortable here. You see/smell/hear the *(add in details about the environment and encourage exploration)*. You feel very relaxed and open to any new experiences that may occur here.

As you relax even more into your environment, you sense someone approaching. *(How he approaches will depend on the location. If it is a wall, can the top of his head be seen? Is he wandering between the trees or down a dirt path? Is there knock on a door?)*

You realize that it is someone you know, someone you trust. Greet your friend as he comes forward to meet you. *(pause)*

You also realize that he has brought someone with him. Your friend introduces his guest to you. *(This is a general introduction of name and perhaps a bit of information. Example: This is my friend Adam. We've known each other since college.)*

Greet your guest. Take a good look at her. Notice her body. Is it big or small? Large or thin? What color is her skin? Eyes? Hair? Do you notice any particular scents? Is the sound of her voice soft or loud? High or low? What feelings does this person stir in you? Allow her to tell you something about herself. Does she have any message for you or anyone else?

It is time for your guests to depart. Thank them for coming to visit. *(pause)* Watch them as they depart. It is now time for you to return. Take a last look around and find the door that leads you home.

Questions for Contemplation and Discussion   Record what you experienced. Note the face, body, age, sex, race, hair color, clothing or jewelry (if seen), scent, voice, or anything else that you may have noticed. Where did you choose to meet your visitor and his guest? How did you feel about bringing them into this space? Discuss with you partner how close your vision or feeling about the individual came to the reality. Were you able to identify the guest? Did she share any message? Did you receive any feelings (for example, was she sad or happy?) from her. What, if any, use might this exercise have? What is it developing?

The Box in the Corner

⌘ Crayons and paper

I assume that your group has already created a group inner sanctuary. If not, please go back to chapter 3.

During this exercise, you are asked to experience a variety of objects within four different scenarios. Each scenario increases in difficulty. I suggest doing them over different trance journeys, allowing time in between for the experience to settle. Unless your coven is already well developed, you will find skipping the lower to begin with upper levels very frustrating, so I suggest doing them in order.

This exercise asks people to draw while in trance. By picture and symbol, we can sometimes express ideas that are still too deep, too new, or too subtle to form into words.

People in trance are not necessarily careful or physically well-coordinated. If you'll be working indoors, prepare by spreading a drop cloth or some newspapers to protect your floor. Do not use any sharp instruments, not even pens or pencils. Crayons, pastels, or soft markers are best. Give each participant some sheets of paper, and ask them to initial and number the sheets in advance. Also have some crayons or markers within easy reach of each participant. They may even want to enter trance with a crayon in their hand. The facilitator should gather the sheets as they are filled, then return them at the end of the exercise.

The easiest method is to instruct the group to first see the object clearly in their minds. Then tell them to open their eyes and see that object superimposed on the blank paper. Using their crayon, they can draw the outline of what they are seeing. They may want to add some other colors. Be careful to allow only a few minutes for the drawing, or those who finish first may lose focus. Once each drawing is completed, if they choose, they can once again close their eyes.

Each scenario begins with the same general introduction.

INTRODUCTION

The participants are brought into trance and led to their coven space. This can be the shared inner temple or collective hangout previously created and explored by the coven.

You find yourself in a familiar place. You feel comfortable here and you relax into the familiarity of the space. You see/smell/hear the *(add in details about the environment and encourage exploration)*. You feel very, very relaxed and open to any new experiences that may occur here. Take a moment to look around you, explore, rediscover your coven's inner circle and each other. *(pause for personal interaction)*

You notice a large wooden box, the size of a child's toy box, sitting to one side of the space.

"Who would like to open the box and see what is inside?" *(pause to allow response)*

"I will."

"(Name) will open the box. (Name), go to the box . . . lift the cover . . . and look inside. Pick one of the objects inside the box and, while focusing on the object as intently as you can, show it to those who are there with you."

Scenario 1 Prior to entering trance a small set of symbols and colors are decided upon by the members of the group. Each should have its own shape, texture, and scent. For example: Green circle. It has a soft, springy texture as if covered with grass, and a deep earthy scent. Blue triangle. It has a cold, smooth surface, like a sheet of glass, and the scent of salt water.

One at a time, each participant reaches into the box and removes a symbol. He announces what it is to the coven. As it is passed around the circle, the coven verbally describes the object. Each member is encouraged to elaborate on previous descriptions or feelings about the object. The symbols are then returned to the box.

Scenario 2 The setup is exactly the same except that when a participant chooses a symbol, she does not tell the coven which one. After the object is taken from the box, the individual members of the coven describe the object as it is passed around the circle. Each member is encouraged to either elaborate on previous descriptions and feelings about the object or, if he believes the object is different from the previous descriptions, describe what he believes he is holding.

Using paper (one per object) and crayons, the participants can be instructed to draw each object as it is removed from the box and passed around the circle.

When the exercise is over, compare your lists.

Scenario 3 The setup is exactly the same as scenarios 1 and 2 except that no words are spoken. One member removes an object from the box and passes it around the circle. People acknowledge the movement of the object ["I have it. I'm now giving it to (Name)."] but do not name or describe it.

Using paper (one per object) and crayons, the participants can be instructed to draw each object as it is removed from the box and passed around the circle. When the coven returns from trance, have them compare the lists.

Scenario 4 The setup is exactly the same as Scenario 1 but instead of symbols, three-dimensional objects are removed. These can be actual items that are known to the participants, such as tools on the altar; or imaginary, such as a snowflake. What the objects are may, or may not, be discussed prior to the exercise. Either way, use items that are familiar to all participants. Repeat scenarios 1, 2, and 3 using the three-dimensional objects. Again, crayons and paper can be used while in trance to record each object.

Questions for Contemplation and Discussion What differences, if any, did you notice between the symbols and the three-dimensional objects? Were some objects easier to identify than others? If yes, for what reasons do you think it was easier? How can you change this exercise to better suit your coven?

If the objects are not discussed prior to the exercise, Scenario 3 is extremely difficult. Do not get discouraged if some members were unable to sense the objects without a clue. If you find that you are unable to accomplish this exercise, do not think that you are a failure or a poor witch. Not all people can develop the strong psychic abilities that this type of exercise demands. But please, keep trying! With perseverance, you might unlock the door.

The Group Picnic

If your group created a coven sanctuary (see chapter 3), you will already be familiar with seeing and responding to each other in trance. The following exercise builds on this experience. Having the ability to actively interact with the members of your group while in trance is imperative for the rest of this chapter.

The trance facilitator will lead the group into a deep trance either separately (down their individual staircases, elevators, etc.) or together (train station, etc.). Either method, all mem-

bers of the group should find themselves at an old boat dock.*
The participants are taken on a boat ride to an open meadow.
When they arrive, they will have a picnic. During the entire exercise, participants are highly encouraged to speak and interact
with each other.

I am including a generalization for facilitator use. The facilitator should be aware of the action as it happens and give directions or suggestions based on the participants' responses.
Because this exercise is interactive, no two trips to the meadow
will ever be the same. The exercise can and should be repeated
as often as the group likes. As the participants become comfortable with the exercise, they will find it easier to talk and interact. With each visit to the meadow, the group will fill in more
details, creating a more vivid inner image. As the image becomes more detailed and more familiar, each trip will be easier,
and more rewarding, than the last.

My home is surrounded by woods, rivers, and meadows.
The inner meadow is very similar to this familiar landscape,
easily visualized and adapted by the members of my coven. But
the meadow might not be as easy to work with if you live in a
city or by the ocean. Use whatever environment is suitable for
your group. Whether you stand under a massive oak or a swaying palm tree, in a pasture or a park, the principles are the
same.

You find yourself standing on the wide wooden planks of an old
boat dock. Before you a deep green river gently flows by. The
waves lap at the moorings of the dock and the edges of the
shore. A gentle breeze caresses your body. Across the river you
can see woods and a range of tree-covered hills rising behind
them. The sun is shining down, warming your body and the

---

*This is very loosely based on an exercise in *Mind Games*.

river's waters. The heat heightens the river's scent of moss and mud. You feel completely relaxed and content.

As you stand admiring the view, you realize that you are not alone. The other members of your group are also standing here, enjoying the day. You have come together on this lovely day to go on a picnic. Who is at the boat dock? *(allow time for response and until all are present)*

You noticed that there is a boat tied to the dock. Inside the boat is a big blanket. You remember that you brought a picnic lunch with you. You can see that everyone else has also brought along a picnic lunch. Together, you walk down the dock to the boat. Help each other into the boat and make yourselves comfortable. *(allow time for interaction)* Who will untie the boat? *(allow time for response)*

The boat is set adrift on the waves. It drifts downstream, following the slow current. The waves gently rock the boat as it moves down the stream. You can hear the waters lapping at the sides of the boat. The sun warms you. You become one with the movements as the boat continues to drift downriver. You watch the scenery as you slowly pass by. What do you see along the shores? *(allow time for response)*

The boat continues to float downstream, gently rocking. You feel calm and relaxed, even a little sleepy, as your boat takes you farther and farther down the river. Finally your boat drifts to the edge of shore and up onto the banks. You have arrived at your destination—a large green meadow. Help each other out of the boat *(allow time for interaction)* and pull the boat safely onto the shore. Don't forget your picnic lunch.

You walk through the tall, green grasses, which tickle your ankles. Flowers are scattered around you. Their sweet scent, mixed with the green grass, fills the air. Above you swallows are flying in an acrobatic dance, their song carried on the breeze. There are many choices where to have your picnic. In the center of the field is an old oak. On the edges of the field is a forest.

Or you can choose to stay by the shore of the river to take a swim in the cooling waters. Where would you like to have your picnic? *(allow time for response)*

(The trance facilitator should encourage the participants to explore their surroundings and suggest scenarios that will cause them to interact with each other. A few suggestion are: show and share their picnic lunches; play Frisbee in the field; catch butterflies. Give the participants plenty of pauses to allow for personal interactions. After a suitable time, bring all the participants back to the boat.)

You help each other climb back into the boat. *(allow time for response)* As you make yourself comfortable, a wave picks up the boat, sending it back into the water. You find that the currents have changed, and the boat is now drifting back. You watch the shore pass by as you travel farther and farther up. The boat gently rocks back and forth. You can hear the waters lapping against the hull as the boat continues floating upstream and you move closer and closer to the dock where you began your journey.

When you reach the dock the boat stops alongside it. Who will tie up the boat? *(allow time for response)* Leaving the picnic basket and the blanket behind, you help each other out of the boat and back onto the dock. *(allow time for interaction)*

The trance facilitator should finish by leading the participants back to the physical world in the same manner they were brought into trance.

Questions for Contemplation and Discussion Record and discuss your experiences. What emotions did this exercise create for you? Were you uncomfortable? Shy? Excited? Why?

Discuss the environment. What did you notice? In what ways did your observations differ? How were they the same? Did you notice anything that you would like to go back and investigate further? In what ways did the dialogue between the participants help or hinder you in the journey?

Peering Over the Balcony—The Elements

I assume that your group has already created a group inner sanctuary. If not, please go back to chapter 3.

Again, I am including only a generalization for facilitator use. During the entire exercise, participants are highly encouraged to speak and interact with each other. The facilitator should be aware of the action as it happens and give directions or suggestions based on the participants' responses.

You find yourself in a familiar place. You feel comfortable here and you relax into the familiarity of the space. You see/smell/hear the *(add in details about the environment and encourage exploration)*. You feel very, very relaxed and open to any new experiences that may occur. Take a moment to look around you, greet each other, explore, rediscover your coven's inner-plane temple. *(pause for personal interaction)*

It is time to begin. Without a word, you come together in the center of your space and join hands to form a circle. Together, you breathe in . . . and out . . . and in again. As you continue to breathe together, open up to the energy as it flows through you and each member, connecting each to all the others. See this warm circle of light that surrounds you. Feel the energy as it travels from one to another . . . to another . . . and around the circle. This bond will continue to join you as you travel together into other worlds.

You notice that, as you have been focusing on your circle, four doors have become visible in the four cardinal directions of your space. A pale yellow door in the East, a bright red door in the South, a dark blue door in the West and a dark green door to the North.

Together, you walk to the yellow door. As you approach, you notice that the door is not solid but made of a gauzy material. The bottom of the material rises and falls, shifts and rolls, carried on a gentle breeze flowing from the other side. Each flutter carries with it the scent of spring flowers and wet earth. Who will open the curtain? *(pause response)* The curtain is pulled aside and you cross the threshold. You find yourself standing on a balcony. Before you is the realm of Air. Describe what you observe of the airy realm. *(pause for personal interaction)*

Turn around and, leaving the realm of Air, step back over the threshold, returning to your inner space. Together you walk toward the red door. As you get closer, you notice that it is wavering. With each movement the door sparkles and glows like a thousand small flames combined to form a shimmering wall of light. When you reach your hand toward the door, you can feel warmth emenating from it. How will you open and pass through the door? *(Pause for personal response. Use a method suggested by the group to open or move through the door.)* Before you is the realm of Fire. Describe what you observe of the fiery realm. *(pause for personal interaction)*

Turn around and, leaving the realm of Fire, step over the threshold, returning to your inner space. Together you walk toward the dark blue door. As you get closer, you notice that it is moving. The door is actually a cascading waterfall. The mist from the waters swirls up and around you, dampening your face. How will you open and pass through the door? *(Pause for personal response. Use a method suggested by the group to open or move through the door.)* You find yourself standing on a balcony. Before you is the realm of Water. Describe what you observe of the watery realm. *(pause for personal interaction)*

Turn around and, leaving the realm of Water, step over the threshold, returning to your inner space. Together you walk toward the dark green door. As you get closer, you notice that the door is a door. Made of rough-hewn, heavy wood, the door stands large and solid before you. You reach forward and feel the bark of the tree from which it was made. Your hand comes back slightly sticky, smelling of pine. How will you open and pass through the door? *(Pause for personal response. Use a method suggested by the group to open or move through the door.)* You find yourself standing on a balcony. Before you is the realm of Earth. Describe what you observe of the earthly realm. *(pause for personal interaction)*

Turn around and, leaving the realm of Earth, step over the threshold, returning to your inner space. Together you walk toward the center of your space and join hands to form a circle. You can feel the doors around you and the Elements observing you from the portals of their realms. You experience a movement before you. As you look up you notice that there is doorway forming inside the center of your circle. From behind a misty glow, something beckons for you to enter. Will you pass through the door? *(pause for personal response)* You find yourself standing on a flat platform. All around you is the place of Spirit. Describe what you observe. *(pause for personal interaction)*

Turn around and, leaving the realm of Spirit, step over the threshold, returning to your inner space. Together you again join hands to form a circle. You can feel the energies moving around you, moving through you. Feel the connection that exists between each other and between your group and all that is. As you open to these energies, the doors disappear. Enjoy the feelings for another moment, and then prepare to return to the everyday waking world.

The trance facilitator should finish by leading the participants back to the physical world in the same manner they were brought into trance.

Questions for Contemplation and Discussion   Record and discuss your experiences. What emotions did this exercise create for you? How were they different for each Element? Discuss each environment. What did you notice? In what ways did your observations differ? How were they the same? Did you notice anything that you would like to go back to and investigate further? Consider for future trips returning to the Elemental doorways and stepping off of the balconies to explore each of the realms.

Dead Ends and Corners—Finding Each Other

This exercise will further develop the connections between participants, helping members to locate each other during trance adventures. This allows participants to travel together to the same environment, separate once there to allow individual experience, then regroup to return together. Learning to locate each other while in trance is also a safety measure. If a member of your group experiences trouble during a trance journey, it's most helpful for the other participants to locate and then help guide that person back to their safe space.

The facilitator or trance tape should lead the participants through their individual or group trance inductions to arrive before the gates of an old English garden.

A very tall, ornately crafted metal gate marks the entrance to the walled garden. On the other side of the gate, you can see a well-tended garden with vibrant colors dispersed among rich greens. The sweet scent of roses, cedar mulch, and freshly cut grass permeates the air. You can hear birds singing and the faint sound of water splashing from an unseen fountain.

In silent agreement you step forward, join hands, and form a circle. You close your eyes, and together you take a deep breath in . . . and out . . . and in again. As you continue to breathe together, open to the energy as it flows through each member, connecting each to all the others. See the warm circle of light that surrounds you. Feel the energy as it travels from one to another . . . to another . . . and around the circle. This bond will continue to join you as you travel together. It remains even as you release hands and collectively turn again to face the gate.

You reach forward to grasp the gate's metal bars. Having absorbed the heat of the day, they feel warm to the touch. Together, you take a breath and push. With a squeak, the gate slides open. Together, you pass through the opening and into the garden.

A path leads from the gate into the garden. You follow it as it winds its way past the many carefully tended flower beds and bushes. Squirrels run across the grass looking for hidden nuts. An occasional garden statue catches your eye. You feel peaceful and content.

The path leads you to a hedge wall. You look at the hedges before you. They stand so high that, even if you stand on tiptoe, you are unable to see over them. Colorful, flowering vines are entwined with the leaves of the hedge, rising up and over the top of the wall. They give off a light scent that mixes with the earthy smell of grasses, branches, and leaves. You reach forward and touch the barrier. The tangled mass of thick branches forms an impenetrable wall that will not allow even a hand to pass through. A small sign in front of the hedge states, Welcome to the Magical Maze. You decide to split up. Each will walk along the outside of the maze, until the maze reveals to him or her an opening. Let us know when you have found your personal doorway to the maze. *(Pause until all have indicated they have found an opening.)*

As you stand viewing the opening, you know that your covenmates are at this moment standing before other openings into this maze. At the center of this living puzzle, you will find each other. Without fear, you step into the shady path.

The walls rise up to either side of you and the path is in front of you. Before you go deeper within the maze, stop, close your eyes, and take a deep breath. Recall your covenmates, as they prepare to explore other entries to this same maze. Although you can't see them, you can feel the energy that moves among all of you. It is feels like an invisible string, drawing you toward the others. Allow your inner sense that connects you to guide you to each other as you walk farther into the maze.

You begin walking. Walls rise around you. Sharp and unexpected corners greet you. The path twists . . . and turns. Each corner looks like the turn before it. You soon lose your sense of direction. You come to a fork in the path. Open yourself and, sensing the presense of the others, let this connection guide you like a homing beacon toward the center of the maze. Continue making your way through the maze. Allow your inner sense to guide you. *(pause for personal interaction)*

As you get closer to the center, the presence of your coven-mates grows stronger. With each turn, you feel them nearer. You take a corner and suddenly you find yourself in the center of the maze. You can see the other members of your coven as they also enter the center.

You walk to the center of the space and greet each other. You join hands to form a circle. You can feel the energies moving around you, moving through you. Feel the connection that exists between each other and among your group and all that is. Enjoy the feelings of connectedness for a moment. When you are ready, you can take some time to explore the center of the maze. What do you observe around you? *(pause for personal interaction)*

It is time to prepare to return to the everyday waking world. You notice a door in one of the hedges. You walk to the door and open it. Behind the door is a corridor that leads straight to the outside of the maze. Together you walk down the passageway.

The trance facilitator should finish by leading the participants back to the physical world in the same manner they were brought into trance.

Questions for Contemplation and Discussion   Record and discuss your experiences. What emotions did this exercise create for you? What other methods could you use to help you locate members of your coven while in trance? Describe the garden gate and the garden. What garden statues, if any, did you notice? How might they relate to your experience in the garden maze? Describe your personal opening to the maze. What might it represent? Describe what you saw in the center of the maze. What did you notice? In what ways did your observations differ? How were they the same? What do you believe this represents?

The Wind Beneath My Wings—Helping Each Other

When Canadian geese migrate, they fly for long periods of time, traveling great distances. The secret for their stamina can be seen in their easily identifiable V-shaped flight pattern. This formation is a cooperative, aerodynamic, energy efficient way of flight. The geese in front break the air with their bodies, creating a tailwind for those in the back to ride on. As the leaders tire, they fall back, allowing those who were in back to move forward to take their place. The previous leaders then have the opportunity to rest and regain their strength, bolstered by the tailwinds of others. This cooperation and sharing of tasks allows all the members of the flock to travel farther, faster, and longer.

When a well-functioning coven works magic or enters trance together, the members draw their strength from themselves and each other in a reciprocal relationship. Some individuals, however, may have difficulties in accepting their personal limitations, relinquishing control, or asking for help from their covenmates. Using the model of the geese, the following is an exercise in mutual cooperation and support.

The trance facilitator will lead the group into a deep trance either separately (down their individual staircases, elevators, etc.) or together (train station, etc.).

You find yourself standing on green and yellow grass before an open pond. The trees around the pond are vibrant in fall colored splendor. There is a chill to the air. You can smell the scent of leaves burning and the decay of plants. A flock of Canadian geese rests on the pond's waters. Suddenly, something startles them. The sounds of their splashing water and honking fill the air. Sensing no immediate danger, they settle back down and begin to feed, dunking their long black necks into the deep waters to grab at the shoots of water plants that float beneath the surface.

As you watch them, you find that you want to go and join the flock. As you step forward you realize that your body feels strange. You look down at yourself and discover a broad, gray chest covered with feathers. Your feet are flat and webbed, and although they hold your weight, walking feels strangely awkward. You stretch your arms open wide and see the large wings of a goose. You feel the familiar sense of your covenmates around you. Looking around you, you see the other members of your coven also stretching their wings and discovering their new goose selves. Spend a few moments observing the changes in each other. *(pause for personal interaction)*

The pond beckons. Together, you waddle over to the water's edge and enter the green pond. Your body floats easily on the surface. Your thick down of feathers keeps you dry and warm. You instinctively use your webbed feet to keep your balance as you bob gently up and down on the waves. A pond plant moving gently on the currents catches your eye. You plunge your long neck down below the surface and snatch the tasty morsel. Around you is your flock, enjoying the pond and the moment. *(pause)*

A brisk wind blows across the water. You notice that the other wild geese are taking flight. It stirs something inside you. You can see that your covenmates have felt it too. There is another place that calls you now—a place you need to be, now that the sky grows dark early and the air is chilled.

A need builds to join the wild geese up in the sky. Your feet push hard on the water, propelling your body forward. You feel your wings open and move of their own accord . . . flapping, scooping the air . . . moving faster and faster . . . until you feel your body lift from the surface of the water and up into the air. Together you climb higher and higher until you soar above the trees. You look down at the Earth below you.

Instinctively, your group forms a V shape with your bodies. Who is at the apex leading the flock? Who is flying on the sides, carried by the tailwind of the leaders? *(allow time for responses)*

It is difficult being the leader. Your head and long neck extend straight out from your body, cutting and breaking the resistance of the wind as you move forward. It is hard work. In time, you feel yourself tire. Your breathing becomes hard and labored from the effort. Your wings slow and you feel yourself start to fall back from your group. Who will take your place? *(allow time for response)*

As (name) moves forward, you move to the back of the flock where you do not have the hard job of cutting the wind. Instead, you are carried along on the tailwind. Aided by the strength of the others, you catch your breath and regain your energy.

Spend time allowing everyone to take the role of leader. Experience the feel of the resistant push of the air as you move forward until you tire from the strain. When you tire, allow yourself to ask the members of your group for help. Then permit yourself to let go, to relinquish the role of leader and fall back onto the collective strength of your group. Allow them to help aid and support you and trust that another will continue in your place. *(Allow enough time for personal interaction. The facilitator should encourage dialogue.)*

As the sun begins to set, you notice something on the Earth below you. Together, you make your way down toward a pond. You spiral down through the air until, with a splash, you all land on the surface of the water. The trees and grass around you are green and lush, and the air and water are warm. The pond is filled with good things to eat. Through cooperation, by trading off leadership roles and accepting the support of the others, you have reached your collective goal. Explore and enjoy your winter spot in the warm south. *(pause for personal interaction)*

You realize that it is also time to return to the physical world. Together, you make your way to the edge of the pond and out of the water. As you shake the last drops from your body, you feel it begin to alter and change, moving back to your human form.

The trance facilitator should finish by leading the participants back to the physical world in the same manner they were brought into trance.

Questions for Contemplation and Discussion Record and discuss your experiences. What did you notice about being a goose? In what ways did your senses change? Did you notice any correlation between your animal and human selves? When you took to the skies, what did you notice about the Earth below you? What was forest? Meadow? Mountain? Desert?

How did it feel leading your group in flight? How did it feel allowing yourself to relinquish this control? Can you think of other exercises that would help in developing trust and cooperation among your participants?

Running With the Herd—Protecting a Member

This is another example that utilizes animal instincts for coven development. The American bison, like many other herd animals, instinctually surround and protect their young when threatened. The stronger members of the group place their bodies between a perceived danger and those who are the most vulnerable of their herd, even physically fighting off a predator if the need arises.

Within a well-functioning coven, members trust that the others of their group will come to their aid if they should fall into a vulnerable state while in the trance realms (or at any other time). For example, creating a protective circle around a member who is seriously ill or who, while in trance, feels threatened by a vision. Using the model of the American bison, this exercise is meant to strengthen the group's instinct to work as a whole to protect one another.

The trance facilitator will lead the group into a deep trance either separately (down their individual staircases, elevators, etc.) or together (train station, etc.).

You find yourself standing on an open, grassy plain. The sun shines down, warming your body. Tall yellow grasses surround you, gently swaying in a light breeze. You breathe in deeply and realize that your sense of smell has sharpened. With each inhalation, you can smell the rich scents of animal musk, dry earth, and grass. The grass smells so tantalizing. Just the thought of it makes your mouth water with hunger. You want to taste it on your tongue, feel the grains grind between your massive teeth. You hear the heavy sound of hooves hitting the ground and large bodies moving. Looking around, you see you are a part of a herd of bison who are grazing on the tall prairie grass. Their massive heads, covered with shaggy fur, sit atop large-muscled, dark brown bodies. You feel the weight of your own hide on your massive shoulders. You move your large head to look at your new bison body. As you do so, you realize that your covenmates are around you, also exploring their new shape. Take a few minutes to taste the sweet grasses and enjoy being a member of the herd.

You smell danger on the wind. Predators have come to feast upon the weakest members of your herd. Someone lets out a bellow of warning. You feel the ground moving as the herd draws tightly together. The young are forced to the center and surrounded by the stronger adults. You can sense that the danger is moving quickly toward your group.

Suddenly, you notice a young calf that has been separated from the herd. You look up and see that the other members of your group have realized the same thing. Without a word, you quickly come together to form a circle around the calf. Together, you breathe in . . . and out . . . and in again. As you continue to breathe together, you open to the energy as it flows through each member, connecting each one to all the others. See this warm circle of light that surrounds you. Feel the energy as it travels from one to another . . . to another . . . and around the circle. You can feel your massive bodies and the energies of your circle forming a wall around the calf.

The danger makes itself known. You can see a small pack of coyotes slinking through the grasses. They make their way over to the main herd. A bull charges, thrusting its heavy horns in the direction of the intruders. The pack scatters. They again creep up on the other side of the herd to be met with a wall of bison. The coyotes dance about, trying to avoid the sharp and heavy hooves.

The calf cries out for his mother. Its calls catch the attention of the pack. They start making their way toward your circle. They crouch low to the ground, looking for a break in your circle that would let them get at your vulnerable charge. You pull your circle in tight and wait. Suddenly a lone coyote charges toward you. You meet the predator before it reaches your circle. Using your massive head and horns, you knock it away into the grass. Another coyote charges but it can't get through your kicking hooves. The coyotes try again to break through your circle to reach the calf within and again you easily fend them off. Finally, discouraged, the pack slinks back into the grass to go hunt easier game.

As the scent of danger dissipates, the herd begins to move apart and graze again. You open your protective circle. The bellowing calf rushes out to go find his mother.

Spend time practicing creating a protective circles around each other. Take turns allowing each member of your group to experience the energy and safety found within the center of the circle. Enjoy the flow of energy as it connects each member, forming the circle. *(pause for interaction)*

It is time to return to the physical world. Take one more look around at the grazing herd. Together, you make your way to the edge of the field. The grasses stroke your body as you make your way through them. With each tickle, you feel your body begin to alter and change, moving back to its normal form.

The trance facilitator should finish by leading the participants back to the physical world in the same manner they were brought into trance.

Questions for Contemplation and Discussion Record and discuss your experiences. What did you notice about being a bison? In what ways did your senses change? How did it feel being a member of a herd? Did you notice any correlation between your animal and human selves? What emotions did the attacking coyotes create for you? How did it feel protecting a vulnerable member of your herd? How would you describe your protective circle? How did it feel when you took your turn inside the center of it? Understanding that not all participants want to be protected from difficult situations, under what circumstances would you want to create a group protective circle during a trance state? Can you think of other exercises that would help in developing a sense of group protection among your participants?

You're Not Alone

The previous exercises can be combined to help an individual work through difficult, but perhaps necessary, pathworking. For example, a covener whose childhood contained an abusive father (who had since passed on) participated in a journey to confront the painful memory in order to move beyond it. The entire coven journeyed with their covenmate to provide support. Their presence gave her the courage to do what she needed to do in order to make closure with her father and find inner peace.

Beyond providing encouragement and support, there are

other advantages of working as a group for the betterment of one member. One is that each individual brings back to the waking world his own insights to the situation. This can add dimensions that may not have been previously considered during the pathworking. Another is the safety factor. If the experience becomes threatening or too intense for the participant, the members of her group can either form a protective circle around her or help lead her back to her safe space and the waking world.

Careful planning should go into creating this form of pathworking. Some things to be considered are:

- What is the goal of the pathworking and how will you accomplish it?
- Where are you going and in what environment is it to occur?
- Are their any particular deities that you plan on meeting and, if yes, what will you be requesting of them?

What does the participant expect from his covenmates? Under what circumstances should they intervene? You should decide in advance on an easily remembered symbol or "safe word" (such as the word or color "red") that a person can use if he finds himself overwhelmed and in need of assistance.

Go back and look through previous journeys in this book to see how they may be adapted for group work. As you read, notice how a trance journey is constructed. A standard guided meditation consists of the setting and exploration of the environment, introduction of the issue, opportunity for transformation or growth (revealing of the mystery, communication with the gods, facing a fear, etc.), integration of the transformation or resolution, and return.

The Strings That Bind—Past Life Connections

It is not unusual for members of a coven to become immediately and deeply connected with each other. As many Wiccans believe in some form of reincarnation, they may feel a sense of destiny among the members of a coven, a perception that relationships begun in past lives have drawn them together here and now. Some Witches believe that our present life is in part a playing out of past karma.

The following exercise is a past-life trance regression but it differs from most. One individual volunteers to explore a possible past life. As this person travels to her past, the coven accompanies her. The purpose is to explore any possible past-life connections and see how they relate to current situations.

The pathworking will be addressing the group as a whole but the focus will be on one member. This person will be pulled back to a particular time. The group will follow along. It might be helpful to tie a string connecting each group member to the focus person before you begin this exercise. Remember that once you reach the past-life destination, expressing what you are experiencing as it occurs is important. Describing your visions to each other while they are taking place helps to build on each other's perceptions and creates deeper links among members. It also helps to keep people together in their experience.

I'm assuming that you have already completed the pretrance steps (stretching, grounding, relaxation, and induction) and are in a relaxed state. As you should now be familiar with how to enter and leave your inner coven home, these workings begin from there.

Lie down and relax in your space. (pause) As you breathe, you feel your muscles start to relax, and your body moves into peaceful relaxation. Allow the question, Who have I been? to form in your mind. Your muscles relax more . . . and more.

As your body relaxes, your perceptions begin to shift. You

begin to feel yourself moving deeper into trance . . . going deeper, and deeper . . . relaxing even more as your consciousness moves deeper . . . and deeper. Your focus is completely on the sound of my voice as you continue to move deeper . . . and deeper . . . and deeper . . . into relaxation . . . into trance as you listen to the sound of my voice.

You continue to breathe. With each breath you feel yourself becoming lighter, and lighter, until you start to float. With each breath you rise higher. A door forms above you. You float upward, weightless, without concern or effort. You move through the door, and find yourself in the sky up above the trees. You can sense the other members of your group around you. Together, you continue to rise, moving over the mountains, rising even higher as you move through the atmosphere over the Earth. Rising higher, the Earth first fills your field of vision and then shrinks beneath you.

As you pull away from the Earth, the moon comes into view . . . and you float by it. Soon they are pinpoints of light. You are drifting through space, among the stars. You can see the sun at the center of our solar system. You can see the planets moving through their orbits in rhythm.

As you watch, you notice the movement of the planets begins to slow . . . and slow . . . until they stop . . . and then the planets begin to reverse direction. At first they move slowly. Soon they take on more and more speed. Time moves backward and the years begin to reverse. As the years fall away, you begin to feel the stirring of a memory of a life once lived. The planets once again slow . . . and come to a stop at the point in time to which you have been drawn. As the planets start to slowly move forward, you feel a tug as you are pulled back to Earth by the force of this previous life. As you approach the now enlarged Earth with the moon shining over your shoulder, you feel yourself slip into that life you once lived. You are not alone. You can feel the presence of the others around you. Together, you are ready to explore as you need.

[Now the facilitator asks the focal person, "What is around you?" and guides him as he explores and describes his situation. This will help other group members gather in the same inner time and space. When it feels appropriate, encourage other group members to describe their own perceptions of this adventure.]

Once established, other directions for the participants can include:

- What do you notice about yourself? How do you feel? What is your age? Race? Sex? What are you wearing?
- Look at each other and describe your impressions.
- Do you see any connections between the trance leader and members of the group? If yes, what?

When it feels like the group has completed their work for this session, guide their return.

You feel yourself becoming lighter and lighter . . . slipping out from this earlier life and floating back up to the sky, through the clouds, the atmosphere, and back into space.

As you pull away from the Earth, the moon comes into view . . . and you float by it. Soon Earth and moon are pinpoints of light. You are again drifting among the stars. You can see the sun at the center of the celestial clock. You can see the planets in their orbits moving in time.

As you watch, you notice the movement of the planets becomes faster and faster as they take on more and more speed. Time moves forward and the years begin to go by. As the years pass, you begin to feel the stirring of the memory of your current life. The planets once again slow. You feel a tug as you are pulled back to Earth by the force of this life. You pass the moon and move toward the Earth. You feel yourself floating downward, moving through the Earth's atmosphere . . . through the clouds . . . over the mountains. The trees come closer . . . until you see the door to your coven's sanctuary. You pass through the door without effort and return. You can feel the other members of your group around you.

The trance facilitator should make sure that all people have returned to this time before bringing the participants back to physical reality.

Questions for Contemplation and Discussion Record and then discuss your experiences within the group. Were there any past-life connections between participants? How are these past relationships reflected in your current life? What insights has this exercise provided on the current dynamics within your group? Did you learn something new about any of the members of your group? About yourself?

Coven Working by Sacred Space

The use of visual cues as a means for induction is one of the many methods for entering and participating in shared trance working. The following is an exercise created and used by Rev. Joanna L. Mlynarski and Sacred Space. They have graciously allowed me to include it with this collection as a demonstration of how their coven works with trance. It is one in a series that their coven traditionally uses to help develop and strengthen their group mind. The coven space they refer to at the beginning of this exercise can either be an actual, physical temple space or a coven inner-plane temple.

This pathworking can be done alone or shared with a small group. It's best to work in a safe and familiar place. This could be a temple room or secluded campfire.

Choose your key symbols in advance. Each group member

can research and meditate on these symbols. Then pool your discoveries to establish a common vocabulary and begin to build a group mind.

Our group works in a temple room. We place a low circular table in the center, large enough to accommodate all participants. This table is covered with a black cloth. We have a blue lamp at the center of the table. A votive candle in a blue glass would work equally well.

We then place square cards on the table facedown, one card for each member. These cards are four inches by four inches in size and made of simple poster board. On one side they are totally black, and the other side white. The white side has a black symbol on it, previously agreed upon by the group.

The west wall of the temple room is totally draped in deep purple cloth or curtain; this will establish our place of departure.

After all is set, each member of the group, wearing dark or black robes, will enter the room one at a time, silently, sitting at one of the places at the table. Once they choose where they sit they must always sit in the same spot.

One of the cards is then turned over (each week a different person will expose their card in turn). The card is then silently handed clockwise around the table. Each member will hold the card and gaze at the symbol on the card. They will close their eyes then open them to view the card, three times. This repetition impresses the card's symbol on their minds. After all the members have completed this, we ring a bell three times, letting it resound after each ring. This is the beginning.

The chosen leader guides the group in deep breathing and relaxation. When the group is ready, the leader asks them to, in their mind's eye, turn to face the west wall, and to imaginatively project the symbol onto the purple curtain. After a time, the curtain parts, allowing each member to pass through it to the inner realms.

An example of a structured journey follows . . .

The symbol used is a flame. The pathworking is designed to enhance the knowledge of inner desires and passions or drives of the self. All is set up as usual. A card is handed around with a single flame painted upon it. A bell is rung.

We become aware of the curtain on the west wall. It still covers the entire wall but now there is a picture upon it. This picture is one of a large flame. At its centermost point, the flame is a brilliant white color. As this color radiates out toward the edges of the flame it changes from white to deep blue to lighter blue to green, from the green to yellow, from yellow to orange, and from orange to vibrant red. Running from the top of the curtain to the bottom, directly in the center, is a slit. This is the opening portal.

We rise from our bodies and one by one we step through the curtain. Slowly our eyes become accustomed to our surroundings. It is night and we are standing on a dirt path within a forest. The forest is rather strange and unfamiliar to us. The foliage is very tropical looking, almost alien and otherworldly, with strange looking trees and vines. It is very tangled and thick, almost claustrophobic to us. And all is dripping wet. It is very humid here. We decide to remove our robes and discover that underneath we are wearing silky, sheer, blood-red robes. These are comfortable and protect us from the elements.

We begin to walk the path. We can smell the odor of rotting vegetation—somewhat like a swamp, yet not totally unpleasant. There is very little sound here. The earth is very claylike beneath our feet, yet it is warm and solid. As we walk we notice that it seems to be getting lighter. It is not the dawn. The junglelike forest is getting less and less dense. The air becomes slightly cooler. We become aware of sounds that arise from within the forest; perhaps these are birds of the night, perhaps insects or frogs. We cannot distinguish these sounds yet, but we are a little frightened of them or what might be making them. We continue on.

New sounds begin to occur. These sounds are much more ominous and much closer to us. As our fear increases, we gather a little closer and travel a little faster, hurrying through this dark place.

We are amazed by the familiar smell of a campfire. We continue toward it. Up ahead on our path we see a glow. As we draw nearer we reach a small clearing. In the center is a small stone circle with a most welcoming fire within. It is not the comfort of warmth that we feel, but a comfort of light and safety. As we enter the clearing we see a small group of people. They are not aware of us.

This is a small family or clan. There are two females. One looks about thirteen or fourteen. The other seems much older. Her breasts are heavy and her skin hangs somewhat. She sqats near a flat stone placed directly on the ground, holding a more rounded stone in her hand. She seems to be crushing some green leaves between the stones.

The younger woman is also in a squatting position. We now see that she is very pregnant and about to give birth.

Now we notice the other two people. A man who appears about forty is standing to the other side of the fire. He appears to be anxious and is busy with a long sharp pole. He wears nothing but what seems to be a twined vine about his waist. The fourth person is a young boy, a toddler. He sits quietly by himself and gazes at the older woman as she works her stones.

Within moments the younger woman begins to moan quietly. Her breathing becomes rapid and she begins to undulate her hips. Still in her squatting position, she sweats heavily and her moans become louder. The older woman begins to make clicking sounds as she starts rubbing the crushed, mucousy leaves on the young woman's swollen belly. The man now begins to sing or something like singing. As he does little jumping steps, he raises his spearlike pole and stabs the sky. Then in all directions, it appears as if he is fighting hidden enemies.

The pregnant woman weeps and strains at her womb and we are all humbled to her, as all is done quietly without screams, without doctors or nurses, alone with only perhaps her mother to help. She reaches down to guide the head of the child that is beginning to emerge from her. The older woman begins to chant and throws a handful of pebbles to the earth; she is reading the meaning of the stones.

Now the mother begins to grunt loudly. The older woman's hands, thickly covered with the slimly vegetation that she has been grinding, reach under the laboring woman. She continues to chant her clicking sounds while massaging. The man continues his protective actions and pays no attention to the drama unfolding before us.

We all, too, begin to push for the mother, as we feel the intensity of this birth. Suddenly, the young girl cries out as a gush of movement takes place from beneath her and the older woman helps pull the infant from her body. The baby seems lifeless at first. Both women busy themselves by cleaning, rubbing, and moving the baby. Then a small cry emerges from its body and life has begun again.

The older woman, still clicking her sounds, reapplies the vegetation mash to the infant and to the mother's vaginal area. It seems to us she is preparing for a second birth. The older woman then guides the new mother to lay flat. As she does, the new mother puts the baby to her breast. The child suckles easily, and a look of peace comes over the mother's face.

The older woman begins to attend to the mother's vagina, rubbing it and her still swollen belly at the same time. She also makes symbols in the blood of the mother on the mother's thighs. Very shortly the afterbirth emerges. The mother bites the umbilical cord free.

We now witness a strange event as the old woman raises the

afterbirth in her hands up high and then places it in a shallow, scooped-out hole. She lays leaves on top and then scoops dirt over it as if it were a grave. Stones and more leaves are placed carefully over it.

We realize the mother and infant have fallen into a peaceful sleep. So too has the toddler who has crept over to the new mother. The three have nestled together in sleep. The older woman sleeps now, too.

The man, now quiet, remains by the fire, throwing small pieces of wood into the flame. He will stay vigilant and will not rest until sometime later in the day.

We realize that it is getting light out. We have spent the entire night witnessing this wonderful scene. Our fears have vanished and a new sense of being has come to us. It is getting very light out, but the fire still continues, and we see the path continues. But this is better left for another journey, at another time.

We thank the small group for allowing us to be here. They cannot hear us, but we thank them and wish all of them good luck.

We turn and begin back on the path. This time our path seems different. We can see the forest of vines and vegetation clearly in the daylight. We hear the ominous sounds again, yet this time we see that which created it: a large furry animal, much like a tree sloth, seems to be trying to bed down for the day. It sees us and quickly moves out of our sight. We continue on as the forest gets denser about us and we see other creatures: tree toads and birds. These, also, have produced the sounds that frightened us on our journey in. We smile as we realize that it was our own fear of the unknown that frightened us. The unknown is to be understood and not feared.

We now come to our portal, finding our robes that we discarded at the beginning. Mysteriously they have been hung neatly for us—another mystery to our journey. We rerobe and hug each other as one by one we file through the curtain and back to our temple room and the blue flame at the center of our table. Looking back at our curtain, we see that it has changed. It is now white with a clear symbol of a flame outlined in black, a very pleasant sight. We return to our places at the table, and back to the here and now. Our journey is done for now.

Trance journeys, when shared by a group or coven, can provide participants with insights both into themselves and each other. Each time the coven travels together, the participants will become more comfortable with the trance realms. They will find it easier to talk and interact. As each experience builds on the one before, the trips become easier and more rewarding, and the group is able to create more vivid images and finer details.

Shared trance opens doors for psychic and emotional connection between members. These shared inner visions naturally transform something within each participant. Such changes will also be reflected in the outer world as the group continues to grow and develop magically.

CONCLUSION

ଓଃୡୈ

When I was a child, my friends and I used to have lawn-chair campouts in my backyard. We'd pull out the old chairs, stretch them out under the stars, throw our sleeping bags on them and tell stories to each other. Sometimes the stories were of mythic heros battling and fairies dancing, but most often it was the creation of fantasies and the young dreams of childhood.

Lying on my back, peering straight up into the darkness of the sky and watching a lazy star flicker, the stories took on deeper meanings and textures. The tapestry of possibilities was woven among the stars, almost as though we could reach up and touch it. At times, it even seemed like the tales were being enacted above me.

Sometimes we would awake the next morning covered with morning dew, and wonder was it a dream or did we fly last night to some magical place beyond the backyard of home?

What we were doing, without realizing it, was entering into a light form of trance and allowing our shared imaginings to take us into the deeper realms of possibility. These trips were unplanned and unstructured, yet filled with wonder, mystery, and magic.

In guided meditation, we enter trance intentionally and with a clear purpose. This purpose may be to open ourselves to self-discovery, create personal transformation, develop or strengthen group bonding, receive a deeper understanding of the myths and symbols of our religion, or communicate with the Gods and Goddesses.

Try the pathworkings in this book. Keep the ones that seem to work well for you or your group. Adapt others to suit your needs. Best of all, take these as a model and create your own pathworkings, built from your own needs, environment, and metaphors. Each person or group has their own life experiences, and these are your unique entries into the sacred inner realms.

Be honest about what does and does not work for you and your group. Don't think you've failed if some of the exercises here just don't work for you. The learning process is based on trial and error. Often we find what works best for us by a process of elimination. The best way to learn from a "failed" experiment is to take it apart. Figure out what parts were useful, what parts were not, and why. Keep only what works. Flesh it out with your own creativity. Try it again. Keep critiquing. Keep learning. Keep creating, and share your discoveries with others. Together we can keep our traditions alive and growing.

Always remember that the core purpose of trance work is to go inside ourselves, to find something there that cannot be found anywhere else. This is the mystery, the adventure, and the joyous surprise of the path. Wonders are still woven among the stars. Enjoy!

ABOUT THE AUTHOR

Laura Wildman is a Gardnerian Witch trained in the Protean tradition. Along with organizing and participating in hundreds of rituals and workshops since 1985, she has lectured and taught classes on Wicca for more than fifteen years. Through the Covenant of the Goddess, she is a legally recognized Wicca clergy in her home state of Massachusetts and has performed over a hundred handfasting and wedding ceremonies. Laura is also a faculty member and chair of the Interfaith Development and Community Rites of Passage Department at Cherry Hill Seminary, a Pagan seminary located in Vermont, through which she teaches classes on wedding officiation.

Laura is the cofounder of the original New Moon, a nonprofit Pagan networking organization in the Boston area. It serves those whose religious focus is polytheistic or nature-centered. New Moon acts as an interfaith group, bringing together any and all on spiritually life-affirming paths for the purpose of sharing knowledge and making social connections. She is also one of the founders of New Moon New York and New Moon in the Valley.

Laura Wildman lives in western Massachusetts with her husband, Tom, and assorted critters. She is the high priestess of the Apple and Oak Coven, and is active in the Covenant of the Goddess local chapter, Weavers CoG.

Theory
and
Practice
of
REGRESSIVE
EDUCATION

Educational Heretics Press exists to question
the dogmas of education in general,
and of schooling in particular.

Theory
and
Practice
of
REGRESSIVE
EDUCATION

Roland
Meighan

with contributions by
Professor Sir Hermann Bondi
Martin Coles
Professor Philip Gammage
Janet Meighan

Educational Heretics Press

Published 1993 by Educational Heretics Press
113 Arundel Drive, Bramcote Hills, Nottingham NG9 3FQ

Copyright © 1993 Educational Heretics Press

British Cataloguing in Publication Data

A catalogue record for this book is available from the British Library

Meighan, Roland

Theory and Practice of Regressive Education

ISBN   0-9518022-3-2

Design and production: Educational Heretics Press

Printed by Mastaprint, Stapleford, Nottinghamshire

CONTENTS

Introduction: the nature of regressive education

In the UK and the USA, there has been a sustained attack, for about twenty years, on something labelled 'progessive education'. The attack was, at first, tentative, then more confident, and then strident. In the 1988 Education Act and the various subsequent revisions, the attackers claimed victory. Yet the obscurity of the target makes the claim difficult to evaluate. There are two immediate problems. The first is what is meant by progressive education, and the second, what is replacing it that is so superior.

The first problem is not easy to resolve and it is not the purpose of this book to do so. But a few comments would seem to be necessary before moving on. In his book *Assessing Radical Education*, Nigel Wright identified multiple uses of the term 'progressive' as applied to education. In another book, *No Master High or Low*, John Shotton also notes the ambiguity of the term 'progressive' and distinguishes all uses of it from the concept of libertarian education. Despite this demonstrable ambiguity, simple souls have continued to use the term as if it had some clear and coherent meaning as well as confusing it with the ideas of libertarian education. In contrast, the virtues of something hailed as traditional education, or even real education, have been extolled. Sadly, for those who like a simple world, neither of these terms is clear or coherent.

In the case of 'traditional', this is often taken to mean formal class teaching with authoritarian control methods. Yet there is a long-standing tradition regarding the ideas of Socrates and Quintilian both advocating a form of autonomous education. Socrates was noted for the approach advocating that a teacher enter into an individual dialogue with each pupil. Quintilian held that Roman education should follow rather similar principles:

"The skilled teacher, when a pupil is entrusted to his care, will first of all seek to discover his ability and natural disposition and will next observe how the mind of his pupil is to be handled.......for in this respect, there is an unbelievable variety, and types of mind are no less numerous than types of body."

This raises the question of which of these two rivals, formal class teaching or individual dialogue, is the true traditional approach. The problem is not resolved by talking instead about 'real' education. Before an actual Campaign for Real Education set itself up in the UK, I was engaged, rather whimsically, in some conversations about designing such a campaign. We soon ran into the problem that no agreed definition of 'real' was possible. Only rival 'real' educations could be identified, so several 'real' education campaigns would be necessary to do justice to the reality. There would need to be a real **autonomous** education campaign, and a real **democratic** education campaign and a real **authoritarian** education campaign at the very least. The campaign that did set itself up adopted the last position, so its title perhaps should be corrected to read: The Campaign for Real Authoritarian Education.

There is, therefore, a serious linguistic problem here. Even if we could agree on the definition of the true traditional approach, its opposite is modern or some synonym rather than the term progressive, and we cannot find a clear, coherent definition of progressive, in any case. The opposite of progressive is regressive. **So the mystery investigated in this book is that of the nature of regressive education and schooling and the basis for its claim to be the superior approach we must adopt in the UK.**

The next problem is concerned with the term **education.** In common discourse, education has come to be regarded as, more or less, synonymous with schooling. Mark Twain disagreed in his remark that he never allowed schooling to interfere with his education. The grandmother of Margaret Mead, the celebrated anthropologist, proclaimed that she wanted Margaret to have an education, so she kept her out of school. Winston Churchill goes into more detail on the matter in a letter to his Minister of Education, R.A. Butler, in 1944:

"Dear Rab,
You are taking your task on education altogether too seriously. Schools have not necessarily much to do with education; I know you will say my Harrovian experience has caused me to generalise, but I can assure you that they are mainly institutions of control where certain basic habits must be inculcated in the young. Education is quite different and has little place in school.

I am impressed in this not only by my own life but by that of those on the Labour benches. Observe them well. Where the schools failed to do their job the sons of the poor fastened themselves to the Workers Educational Associations and the Night Institutes and educated themselves.

It is little wonder that you should mistake schools with education. I suggest Rab that you give less attention to schools and more to the Institutes in your bill when it is ready.

Yours ever,

Winston

Winston Churchill gives us a possible start in identifying the characteristics of regressive schooling, but I propose that we try to distance ourselves from the problem a little by looking at the debate in the USA about these matters. In passing, however, it might be worth noting that, in the light of Churchill's remarks, the campaign I mentioned might be renamed the Campaign for Real Authoritarian Schooling, in the cause of accuracy.

When Regressive America Began to Recapture Schooling

In his book *Teach Your Own*, John Holt explains how a limited and rather weak kind of educational reform known as progressive schooling was fashionable in the USA for a time but that it was short-lived. Regressive America, he notes, began to re-assert itself and to try to recapture schooling. He concluded that this had always been the position of the majority anyway, but that their confidence had been temporarily shaken by the analyses of the so-called deschooling writers such as Goodman, Reimer, Illich and also by Holt himself. Holt was not a deschooler but a reschooler, for he wanted to make schools into places where children would be encouraged and helped to explore and make sense of the world around them, in the ways that most interested them, without the interference of uninvited teaching.

Reluctantly, he came to the conclusion that very few people in the USA, inside the schools or out, were willing to support giving more choice and self-direction to children. He began to explore the uncomfortable idea that most adults in the USA actively distrust and rather dislike most children, sometimes even their own. He concluded that people whose lives are boring, painful or meaningless tend to resent those who seem to suffer less than they do. They think they must oppress their children 'for their own good'. Therefore, the great majority of boring, regimented schools were doing exactly what most people thought was needed: i.e. teach them that 'Life Is No Picnic' and teach them to 'Shut Up And Do As You Are Told'.

John Holt was opposed to such schools and said of them that they demonstrated that a school based on such a view was not a good idea gone wrong, but a bad idea from the start.

As regards the 'Back To The Basics' rhetoric, Holt observed that this was really code for 'No More Fun And Games In School'. Most adults in the USA do not care all that much about reading; they read very little themselves, for like most Americans, they spend much of their leisure time watching T.V. They want their children, when their time comes, to be able and willing, to hold down full-time painful jobs like their parents. To get them ready for this you need to make school as much like a full-time painful job as possible.

A middle class couple who had transferred their son to the school where Holt was teaching, were pleased that there had been a great improvement in both their son's studies and his behaviour, but 'worried about how much fun he is having in school. After all, he is going to have to spend the rest of his life doing things he doesn't like, and he may as well get used to it now.'

The reason for this bleak outlook was **fatalism**, not cruelty or mean-spiritedness per se, although by force of habit they could soon change into that. This was how the world seemed to them and it was not going to change for the better. Until such attitudes changed, John Holt concluded, any general movement for school reform was doomed.

John Holt's analysis was supported by other USA writers. Dr. M. W. Sullivan, was asked to respond to the statement that 'eventually, the child probably will have to face unpleasant working situations and narrow competition. There will be unreasonable deadlines, hasty instructions that will have to be understood and heeded - all sorts of hardships.' Sullivan stated that the old idea that if you want your children to get along in life, you put them in unpleasant situations as soon as possible, was seriously flawed. The old idea was that if they are going to be in lousy situations where they feel inadequate and frustrated later, it was best to put them in lousy situations where they feel inadequate and frustrated now, so that they can get used to it .

Yet, Sullivan noted, studies of the behaviour of USA Marines in World War Two and in Vietnam, who went through the worst experiences, showed that the ones who cracked were the ones who had had a tough upbringing. The ones who coped best with the intolerable conditions were the ones who had had 'fortunate' childhoods where they had had encouragement, success and sustained confidence-building experiences.

Other voices in the USA spoke out against regressive ideas for schooling. One was that of Dr. H. G. McCurdey of the University of North Carolina. He reported his studies into the backgrounds of those very high achievers often referred to as geniuses. His analysis identified three major factors:
1. a high degree of individual attention focused upon the child by parents and other adults, expressed in educational activities accompanied by abundant affection.
2. Only limited contact with other children but plenty of contact with a variety of supportive adults.
3. An environment rich in, and supportive of, imagination and fantasy.
McCurdy goes on to conclude that the mass education system in the USA is a vast experiment in reducing these three factors to the absolute minimum and inevitably suppresses the occurrence of genius as a result. It follows that the more regressive the schooling philosophy, the more the suppression of originality, independence of thought and imagination, associated with the high achievement we call genius.

In his book *Education and Ecstasy*, George B. Leonard contributed some ideas about the nature and consequences of regressive education. He proposed that schools and colleges have served an economy that needed reliable, predictable human components by ironing out those human impulses and capabilities that got in the way. Half of all learning capability was systematically reduced in the early years of compulsory schooling, and instead, children were required to learn both that there exist pre-determined right answers for almost everything, and that the whole business of learning is mostly dull and painful. With the bulk of learning ability wiped out, later schooling could proceed to slow down and cool out what was left of each human component's capacity to learn and change. By the age of six or seven, children were thus measurably slowed as free-ranging learners and by sixteen they were finished.

Regressive Schooling in Poland

Support for Leonard's proposition comes from Poland. The latest UK fashion in schooling, the National Curriculum approach, has, of course, been running in the former Yugoslavia, the former USSR, the former East Germany, and Poland for over forty years. The principal of Kielce College in Poland states why they are rather anxious to get away from such an approach:

"Years of uniformity have submerged parts of our personalities."

In May 1993, when Philip Toogood asked the Assistant Dean of the Faculty of Education at the University of Poznan, Professor Eugenia Potulicka, how she could account for the uncritical acceptance of the National Curriculum concept in the UK on the basis of her studies of the 1988 Education Act, she replied that it was because we lacked experience of the long term stultifying effects of such an approach. (Ironically, the ideas for education in the future being debated in Poland are the Flexischooling and Flexicollege models developed in the UK, but like all good British inventions, ignored by officialdom here. Thus, the Polish translation of *Flexischooling* sold out within months.)

Potulicka was seconded to spend time in England studying the 1988 Education Reform Act. I asked her what she would report to her University, the Solidarity Education Committee and ultimately, the Government. She replied without hesitation, "Oh, I shall tell them that it is totalitarian." Her directness took me a little by surprise, so she explained that she knew all the tell-tale signs of such a system, having lived under one all her life. With the 400 extra powers given to the Secretary for State for Education, she added, he or she was now able to act like a Russian Commissar and liable to act on whims, in defiance of evidence or reason, and without consultation. You must judge for yourselves the accuracy of her prophecy.

From these excursions into the analyses of people in other countries, we can begin to construct a profile of regressive schooling ideas:

> It favours tightly controlled learning rather than eclectic and spontaneous enquiry - 'Shut up and learn to do as you are told', as John Holt puts it.
> A set curriculum imposed by adults is preferable to a curriculum fostering self-direction or any kind of free-ranging learning.
> The key lessons are that 'Life is no picnic, so school should be no picnic' and that learning is hard, difficult and painful.
> Regimentation and boredom are necessary, perhaps essential, to schooling.
> Teaching means formal instruction and authoritarian control - 'constipated teachers and constipated teaching' as one pupil portrayed it.

Learning to work without pleasure in school is a necessary pre-requisite to coping with the pain, frustration and dullness of employment - that is if you are lucky enough to be offered any.
This is the Reality of Society and nothing can change for the better, so be fatalistic and endure it by getting toughened up.

Spiritually, it all seems to be a modified re-run of John Wesley's philosophy:

"Break their wills betimes: begin this great work before they can run alone, before they can speak plain, or perhaps speak at all. Let him have nothing he cries for, absolutely nothing, great or small. Make him do as he is bid, if you whip him ten times running to effect it. Break his will now and his soul will live, and he will bless you to all eternity."

The Secretary of State for Education in the UK, John Patten, endorsed the Wesley line, although coming from the Roman Catholic tradition himself, and in 1993 called for a return to traditional religious values including ideas of sin, hell and punishment. I mention this just in case you think the analysis is too severe.

The educational press in the UK has given considerable support to the ideas of regressive schooling. The Times Educational Supplement quoted this letter somewhat approvingly in 1984:

"So it is refreshing to discover a letter to the headmaster of Langley private school in Norwich from a father imploring the headmaster thus: 'You need to take James by the scruff of the neck, ram his nose into a book and kick his arse every time he gazes out of the window.' The parent in question runs his own advertising and marketing agency. And marketing men have a way with words."

Advocates of regressive schooling have resorted to labelling anyone who agreed with them as a sensible person and anyone who disagreed with them in insulting terms. In one book alone, *What Is Wrong With Our Schools,* anyone who took an opposing view to that being offered was described as crazy, or brainwashed, or flashy, or new-style, or faceless facilitators, or Politically Motivated Intruders, or progressives, or child-centred activists, or wets, or hotheads, or loonies, or nihilists. The writers contributing to this book were liable to contradict each other on fundamental issues and so run the risk of having to insult each other. One writer defended the idea of a National Curriculum, another advocated a teacher-defined curriculum since a 'National Curriculum is far too powerful an instrument to entrust to central government.' One writer defended the idea of compulsory schooling whereas another wanted voluntary schooling. One believed that schooling in the UK is compulsory, but another was better informed because she had elected to exercise her right in law to operate home-based education.

A common error in analysis is the assumption that education is a relatively simple problem and that a simple solution, recognised by all sensible people, exists. These can be expressed as a series of 'salvations'. For one writer in the book noted above, it is salvation by phonics, for another by formal instruction, for yet another by teaching subjects. Another favours salvation by testing, someone else by compulsory religious instruction based on the King James version of the Bible, and a third by Nationalism. One favoured a National Curriculum, another a secular curriculum.

Subjects as Ancestor Worship?

One feature of the return of more regressive schooling has been the emphasis on subjects and the imposition of these on younger and younger children. As I have indicated elsewhere (e.g. in *A Sociology of Educating*) subjects represent a kind of ancestor worship and do not match the knowledge characteristics of a society in a state of knowledge explosion and in the situations of a communications and technological revolution. It follows that they have only a modest part to play in the scheme of things; they are only part of the tool kit of knowledge and declining in importance year by year. It may be that subject teachers have little or no future in education because all they know can be readily made available in books, interactive videos, computer programmes and distance-teaching materials. A place for the 'learning coaches' type of teacher looks more secure. A plea from Robert W. Cole, the editor of Phi Delta Kappan, in November 1987 makes the point:

"As we plunge towards the 21st century, why can't we recognise that all courses are one course? ....Let us acknowledge in school what we know is true outside of school: real life rarely recognises the tidy pigeonholes into which students are forced in most classrooms. ......

A truly valuable education helps children make sense of their world. Dividing schools into disciplines fails to prepare kids for the untidiness of life. Flexibility and breadth will better equip young people to deal with a world of dazzling change and complexity. ....

Consider, for instance, the dangerously short-sighted zeal that leads a state to mandate the number of minutes that teachers must devote to each subject. This is not forward-looking education. It promotes a rule-bound, lock-step mindless teaching. It makes robots out of teachers - and ultimately out of children too.

Educating for the 21st century is not a list; it's not a set of guidelines; it's not a curriculum. It's a way of thinking. In the years that lie ahead, beware the rule-bound; they live by lists and would have others live by them. Beware the categorisers who divide children and curricula and loyalties into neat little domains over which they can rule in myopic comfort; there are no divisions in education worth taking seriously. Beware the frightened; they cannot allow themselves to accept change. Beware the angry; their bitterness can kill desire - and children too.

Education is not merely the transmission of information. If you're in education just to make kids memorise so that you can make things easier for yourself, get out. We need instead to construct for ourselves (and for the children in our charge) patterns with which to make sense of the world. We must sell understanding, not information. We must be wise, not just smart."

Cole's wife, Robin, was expecting their baby at the time, thus sharpening his concerns about schools and the future.

Perhaps at this point I should state my own position. I am not kindly disposed towards the kind of schooling that was going on in the 1960's and 1970's, and said so at the time, although it was a bit less harmful than the regressive schooling which appears to have replaced it. The change appears to be one of degree, however, rather than kind. Thus, the schooling system throughout my lifetime has been moribund. The system provided me with a schooling in a prestigious grammar school for boys that was an insult to the intelligence. I was surprised that few of my peer group seemed to notice. A locally 'well regarded' comprehensive school did the same for my son. After the 1988 Education Act the system will do the same for the next generation. Most of the recent changes are cosmetic: fundamentally, the 1988 Education Act merely reaffirms adult coercion and an outdated model of schooling as before, but more centralised and more severe. Toffler observes:

"Much of the change (in education systems) is no more than an attempt to refine the existing machinery, making it more efficient in the pursuit of obsolete goals."

Nor am I in favour of a sole diet of libertarian schooling, although it could easily do less harm than either of the other two.

My position is beyond this debate, the *Age of Unreason* debate as Charles Handy describes it in his book, into the theory and practice of flexischooling and flexi-education and the need to regenerate both schooling and society simultaneously. *Flexischooling* produces a synthesis out of the futile debates concerning which of the three main ideologies of education is the right one, by incorporating all three.

It was Paul Goodman in his book *Compulsory Mis-education* who proposed that there is no right education except growing up into a worthwhile world and that when there is excessive concern with 'the problem of education' it simply means that the grown-ups do not have such a world and do not really know how to set about constructing one.

Twenty-one ways to discourage fluent reading

by Martin Coles
University of Nottingham

Debates about the classroom methodologies that should be used to teach reading, and about the kind of texts to offer young children learning to read are not new. As long ago as 1908 E.B. Huey in *The Psychology and Pedagogy of Reading* said this of reading primers:

"No trouble has been taken to write what the child would naturally say about the subject in hand, nor indeed to say anything connectedly or continuously, as even an adult would naturally talk about the subject."

And in 1975 the government report *A Language for Life* ('The Bullock Report') welcomed the initiative of schools which provided 'real books' for young children and praised those teachers who adapted reading methodologies to individual children rather than the other way round. But despite the great attention given to this subject, if we believe the press and politicians, reading standards are falling, just as they were in 1912 when a head teacher wrote in The Times that "Reading standards are falling because parents no longer read to their children and too much time is spent listening to the gramophone".

Never mind, now that reforming school education has become a national hobby the politicians will put it all right. "If we go back to the basics all will be well," a Minister for Education tells us. So we have the National Curriculum with 'benchmark' attainment targets for children at the ages of 7, 9, 11 and 14 which, the documents explain, are there to raise expectations of pupils who frequently are not challenged enough. Lists of objectives for 'most' children at specific chronological ages are, we are told, a proven and essential way towards raising standards of achievement. The government has spoken, who are we to disagree? After all, children in school these days do have life far too easy. So, in this spirit of providing ideas and encouraging practices that will mean children putting their noses to the grindstone, knuckling down, and pulling their socks up, I make the following proposals with regard to reading.

1. Ensure that children learn the rules of reading. Learning to read is like learning to ride a bike. Just as learning about the laws of gravity and the mechanics of balance help when learning to ride a bicycle, so mastering the rules of reading, i.e. learning the rules of grammar, knowing such things as consonant blends and vowel digraphs, will help with reading.

2. Ignore those who insist on the primacy of practice. I have heard ridiculous slogans like 'children learn to read by reading'. Ignore such siren voices. Lots of non-reading activity will speed the development of reading. Follow the advice of a writer to *Language and Literacy News* (Autumn 1992): "I prevent my strugglers from reading so they will learn phonics". If being drilled in phonics and learning words on flash cards is a struggle for children so much the better. Struggle is good for the soul.

3. Some teachers hold reading conferences, spending five or ten minutes with a child and her/his book once a week and then suggest that the child read to herself/himself or a parent (see rule 9) or another child in the class or school between times. What an unprofessional practice! Real professionals make it clear that reading is only to be done when a teacher is listening.

4. It is essential to hear a child read every day. If this means hearing two children at once, one on either side, or handing out spellings while children read to you, so be it. It is not important that you show an interest or listen attentively. It is only important that the child gets a daily dose of that mystical experience - reading to teacher.

5. Never let a child read a passage to you that he or she has chosen. Remember you are trying to make reading difficult, not easy. Pick a passage at random, the more complex the better. Remember about that grindstone. And when hearing a child read, do correct all decoding errors. No point at all in engaging the child in some discussion to do with the meaning of text (see rule 16).

6. Very early on children must learn the sound of letter clusters which make up words. Get children to think of individual separate words as problems to be solved. I know solving these word problems is a difficult skill to learn, especially since there are over 300 spelling-to-sound correspondences in English, but so much the better. Learning these makes reading really difficult.

7. It has been pointed out to me that knowing how to pronouce 'ho' at the beginning of a word depends on what follows: ...ot; ...ok;...pe; ...use; ...rse; ...ney; ...ur; ...nest; ...ist. Of course this suggests that phonics must be applied from right to left. It is also true that one sound has many spellings, as in ice, lie, signs, height, high, island, guide, buy, dye; and that one spelling has many sounds, as in want, wall, village, majestic, fate, fat, father, and this without taking into account accent. I'm afraid these are just more problems that have to be overcome, but look on the bright side. They do mean more noses to the grindstone.

8. Do ensure that a child knows all the words in one book before allowing her/him to take another one. Excellent teachers insist on this even if it means re-reading a book six or seven times. These teachers know what it means to make reading difficult.

9. Never involve parents in helping their child to read. Avoid nonsense like paired reading and home-school reading link schemes. Anyone would think that schools are in the business of educating parents about reading. How can parents ever know the 300 spelling-to-sound correspondences needed to teach children to read? And involving parents might suggest that they are the most influential people in children's lives when the world knows that role properly belongs to teachers.

10. Records are there to spur children on. There really is no need to make notes about a child's progress, interests, problems. A simple tick in a column when a child has finished one book and can move onto the next is all that is required. Any child seeing this tick is bound to be spurred on to put their nose to the grindstone in order to reach the next higher book. They really will be racing to read.

11. Never allow children to choose their own reading material. Children are, like lunatics, incapable of making sensible choices. They must be guided through a structured and graded scheme regardless of their interests. Allow a child to choose a book outside the scheme once and they may start to read books that take their fancy as a habit and then you won't know where you are. They will never finish the scheme. Nor should you offer suggestions about reading material outside the scheme. You may, accidentally, hit on a book that the child really enjoys reading and that won't help make reading difficult, will it?

12. Ensure that children are required to write a report on everything they read. This requirement must be religiously enforced or certain children may start to consider reading merely as a pleasurable experience and not a school subject.

13. Do not at any cost allow children to see you reading. If you cannot avoid the temptation to read, then ensure that your reading material is related to your job - school reports, memos, records and such like. For some children you may be the only adult role model of a reader they encounter. So important, then, that you are never caught reading for pleasure by any of these children lest they be led into thinking that reading is intended to be an enjoyable experience instead of a mere functional skill.

14. Do not bother to read to children once they are past Year Two. Only really young children enjoy listening to stories and older children will become fidgety and fractious if you attempt to read fiction to them. Moreover, if by some strange quirk one or two children did enjoy listening to stories then they may begin to see reading in a favourable light and that would make reading dangerously easy.

15. Make sure that you don't allow children to read to each other. There are scandalous situations in some classrooms where small groups of children read short stories to each other by taking it in turns to read. How are these children ever going to realise that reading is only important when the teacher is listening (see rule 3).

16. Ideas about developing worthwhile reading strategies with notions about context and prediction, and asking children to look for meaning in the text are typically dangerous radical extravagances, certainly not intended to encourage children to knuckle down to real reading. Real reading, remember, is simply building words from letter sounds.

17. There is only one reason why children should use language in schools - the instructional one. They are there to read and write, and learn to read and write they will, whether they like it or not. Never mind all this absurdity about the end point of language being genuine communication, that print is about meaning and communicating meaning. The end point of language in school is the last book in the reading scheme and, as politicians are so right in reminding us, success in spelling. Fix children's minds firmly on those two goals and you are sure to make reading difficult.

18. Reading and writing are not complementary. Do not confuse children by encouraging them to read their own writing. After all their own writing will only contain language they are familiar with, so how can they learn to tackle passages

with difficult unknown words if they read only what they have written themselves? The practice will simply engender false confidence.

19. Phrases like 'an authentic literary environment', 'a print-rich environment' and 'a rich language environment' are merely current vogue. The suggestion is that children's reading can be improved by having lots of notice-boards and labels and messages and pamphlets and magazines and notebooks and instructions around the classroom. I have even heard it suggested that children's writing be placed on walls for others to read. These strange ideas are based on the odd notion that children who are successful in learning to read are aware of the significance of written language, that children need to know that reading is *for* something, even enjoyment! Of course the truth is that children who are successful in learning to read are those who work hard to learn their letter-sound correspondences and put their noses to the grindstone to get through the reading scheme. They know what reading is for. It's for getting on to the next level.

20. Remember to focus on methods and materials. If you want to make reading really difficult, ignore the child's point of view. Concentrate entirely on what you, the teacher, ought to be doing and not what the child might be trying to do.

And finally:

21. Ignore those who suggest that children who are reading well have learnt to do so despite you, that many millions of children have learnt to read in the past with abysmal materials and negligible teaching. If you have competent readers in the class, they are demonstrating fluency solely as a result of your good teaching methods. And if you don't have competent readers in your class then it is almost certainly not your fault, but that of the teacher who had them before you, or the school that had them before you, or their parents who had them in the first place.

The weeding out of 'candidate twenty-two'

Regressive education requires the establishment of an 'objective' scheme for the appraisal of teachers to weed out the 'undesirables'.

Rating Scale: Appraisal of Teacher Behaviour

Candidate :   number 22

Rating Scale: 1 = excellent, 2 = good, 3 = average, 4 = below average, 5 = poor

Personal Qualities

Personal appearance	score: 4	Dresses casually in a monastic-style garment
Self-confidence	5	Lacking in confidence - always asking questions
Use of English	4	Has a foreign or regional accent

Classroom Techniques

Organisation	score: 5	Has no seating plan
Room appearance	4	Lacks eye-catching displays
Use of supplies	1	Very economical: does not use any teaching aids

Instructional Techniques

Preparation	score: 5	No sign of any
Course design	3	Over-flexible in allowing students to wander to different topics
Subject knowledge	4	Does not display authority in content - has to question pupils to verify points
Clarity of aims	4	Wanders from question to question exploring issues rather than teaching them

Relational Techniques

Tact and consideration	5	Constantly embarrasses pupils by asking them questions
Response of class	2	Class is friendly and good humoured

Professional Attitudes

Professional commitment	5	Does not belong to any association
Professional development	5	Does not attend any courses
Parental relations	5	Room for improvement - parents are anxious to get rid of him
Adaptability	5	Prone to suicide by poison when under duress

Appraisal

He does not have much to offer in education and he should be encouraged to seek other employment

Name of teacher: Socrates

(Adapted from J. Gauss in *Phi Delta Kappan*, January 1962)

When regressive America began to recapture schooling

John Holt (1923-85) established himself as a writer, educator, and lecturer of significance with the publication of his first book *How Children Fail.*   He wrote ten books including other world best sellers such as *How Children Learn* and *The Underachieving School.* He visited England in April 1982 for the last time.   Soon afterwards he developed cancer and he died in September 1985 aged 63.

The vision John Holt had of a school is contained in these words:
"Why not then make schools into places in which children would be allowed, encouraged, and (if and when they asked) helped to explore and make sense of the world around them ....in the ways that most interested them?"

In the 1960's, he spent his time trying to further this vision of schools in the USA and elsewhere through his teaching, writing and lecturing.   By 1968, however, John Holt had begun to confront the issue of compulsion:
"But by 1968 or so I had come to feel strongly that the kinds of changes I wanted to see in schools, above all the ways teachers related to students, could not happen as long as schools were compulsory. ....Since compulsory school attendance laws force teachers to do police work and so prevent them from doing real teaching, it would be in their best interests, as well as those of parents and children, to have these laws repealed, or at least greatly modified."

Yet, even as he and others lobbied for reforms along these lines in the USA. the situation began to change.   For a while, he noted, school reform was in fashion, but then it went out of fashion.   Regressive America began to re-assert itself. Indeed, he concluded that regressive attitudes to education might even make up the majority view.
"Very few people, inside the schools or out, were willing to support or even tolerate giving more freedom, choice and self-direction to children."

Thus, in his books *Escape From Childhood* and *Instead of Education* he explored the uncomfortable idea that most adults in the USA have come actively to distrust and rather dislike most children, sometimes even their own.   He proposed that people whose lives are hard or boring or painful or meaningless - people who suffer - tend to resent those who seem to suffer less than they do, and will make them suffer if they can. People in chains, with no apparent hope of losing them, want to put chains on others.

"In short, it was becoming clear to me that the great majority of boring, regimented schools were doing exactly what most people wanted them to do. Teach children about Reality. Teach them that Life Is No Picnic. Teach them to Shut Up And Do What You're Told."

John Holt was not impressed by such schools. He said of them that they demonstrated that a school based on such a view was not just a good idea gone wrong, but a bad idea from the start.

"Back To The Basics", he concluded, was really code for "No More Fun And Games In School", for most adults in the USA do not care all that much about reading as such, since they read little themselves, for like most Americans, they spend much of their leisure time watching T.V.

"What they want their children to learn is how to work. By that they don't mean to do good and skilful work they can be proud of. They don't have that kind of work themselves, and never expect to. They don't even call that "work". They want their children, when their time comes, to be able and willing, to hold down full-time painful jobs of their own. The best way to get them ready to do this is to make school as much like a full-time painful job as possible."

This was not just a working class attitude, he noted. A middle class couple who had transferred their son to the school Holt was teaching in were pleased that there had been a great improvement in both their son's studies and his behaviour, but expressed their anxieties thus:

"You know, his father and I worry a little about how much fun he is having in school. After all, he is going to have to spend the rest of his life doing things he doesn't like, and he may as well get used to it now."

The reasons for these bleak attitudes were not cruelty or mean-spiritedness per se, but fatalism. In their view, this was how the world was and it was not going to change for the better. Whilst such parents were in a majority, John Holt concluded, any general movement for school reform was doomed.

At this point, he decided to work with the minority of more optimistic parents who wanted something different and who were active in setting up small alternative schools. These usually struggled because of the problems of finance. But some of these parents had begun to educate their children at home and needed support. Therefore, John Holt established a service organisation called **Growing Without**

Schooling. Home-based education became the focus of his writing and activity. His last two books, *Teach Your Own,* which outlined the experience of families in the USA educating at home, and *Learning All the Time,* emphasises and reviews the role of parents as educators, especially in early childhood.

At first, John Holt had expected change to come from within schools. Some has, and more may well do so. But at the end, he had decided that the example, success and influence of parents educating at home could well be more decisive:
"Our chief educational problem is not to find a way to make homes more like schools. If anything, it is to make schools less like schools."

Children don't get taller by being measured

by Philip Gammage
University of Nottingham

Even a modest acquaintance with educational systems in developed countries in the 1990s makes one aware that many of them, notably the English-speaking ones, have, for the most part, been through a long period of utilitarianism and 'back to basics' approaches and are now emerging into a somewhat different climate of ideas. I say 'for the most part', because I believe that Britain has misread the signs and is now seriously out of step.

As we in Britain move into a period of centrally defined curricula and a truly massive apparatus for testing the child at four 'key' stages, other developed countries are rediscovering the importance of personalised (or moderately personalised) education, and are noting the importance of different outcomes for different children. As we begin to assemble a curriculum not dissimilar from that laid down in 1940 for Grammar Schools, as we begin to assume that testing lies at the heart of education, other societies are beginning to note that process and creativity, change and readaption are at least as important as Dewey ever proposed. Moreover, they may be at least as important, even when conceived in utilitarian terms, as any mere list of competencies in the 'old' basics or the 'new' technologies.

Put at its simplest, the 1988 Education Reform Act was a mess. As an essay in education and its purposes, it would fail dismally if marked at even first year undergraduate level! Its child, the National Curriculum, was conceived in such haste as to be ill-made; and some of us have doubts whether its life will be very long or very fruitful. For, without its Schools Examinations & Assessment Council (SEAC) splints, it cannot move. With them, it is exceedingly cumbersome and likely to destroy much that its older siblings strove hard to achieve.

No one would pretend that the British educational system was in good heart before the 1988 Education Reform Act. But I contend that the ERA has actually weakened some of those principle elements in British education that were good.

Nice places to be in

Despite the fulminations and recriminations of the Black Paper writers, British primary education has been in fairly good heart since the late 1960s. True, it is perhaps unfair to generalise concerning a system of some 23,000 small schools (England and Wales). True, large numbers of the buildings were old and possibly inadequate. True, there were noted and well documented weaknesses in certain curriculum areas, notably maths and science. But for the most part the British primary school had a strong reputation with its parents and children (NOT "clients") and it certainly enjoyed a powerful reputation for good practice (not always deserved) abroad. Whether one sees it as resulting from the dominant characteristic of adult-orientation in the prepubertal child, or whether one attributes it to the essentially tolerant and happy atmosphere of most primary schools the fact is that British primary schools have been nice places to be in, as visitor, parent, teacher, or child.

During the last ten years, I suppose I have visited well over a hundred primary schools. In only one have I felt any sense of repression. In almost all I have observed busy children and staff, felt a strong pulse of creativity, been impressed by the variety of occupations and interests. Above all, I have seen mixtures of work which seems to contain both developmentally desirable matching to interests and levels of cognition, along with judicious awareness of basic skills and the needs of society. I have not seen sloppiness, nor hotbeds of anarchy. I have rarely seen unoccupied children. I have usually seen very interested children, though I have very occasionally observed poor record-keeping. I have often been amazed at the skill displayed in organising classrooms. I have once or twice thought that perhaps the most able were insufficiently stretched. But, above all, my abiding impression is one of satisfaction with the obvious pleasure registered by the children in their own learning.

Visiting primary schools more recently, however, I have been struck by the sense of gloom and foreboding which seems ever present in the staffroom. Whilst I can honestly say that this does not, as yet, seem to have pervaded the actual classroom, it is clear that primary teachers feel let down, unrecognised and misunderstood. Above all they feel weighed down by the National Curriculum and its SEAC lineaments (in terms of testing for key stages one and two).

I am not anti-assessment, though I do not think the reasons for assessment are sufficiently debated or understood. I do not believe it is satisfactory simply to draw up the map of experience after the event, as it were. I believe that teachers need to make clear and regular use of diagnostic assessment so that they can better match and monitor learning processes. Like those who wrote the TGAT Report (DES 1988), I share the belief that schools function best when they plan, do and review. Unlike TGAT, however, I do not believe that assessment lies at the heart of learning. No, I am unreformed and of Plowden hue in that I still reckon the *child* to lie at the heart of learning. I believe in what Elkind has called "developmentally based practice". This phrase of Elkind's can be summed up very simply as meaning that, above all, the curriculum cannot be imposed from outside but must take into account the entering characteristics of the learners. This latter is not just a nod in the direction of children's passing interests; it is fundamental to sensitive match and to real ownership of the learning experiences by the child.

Whilst it is difficult to overestimate the importance of diagnostic assessment (and let us not leave out awareness of affective components here), all other forms are as grass. Comparability between individuals is massively difficult. Comparability between schools and systems is wellnigh impossible. So why is the English system so determined to impose such a massive bureaucracy of testing upon its teachers and children? Are we aware that other countries have tried them and found them inadequate? Is it simply that politicians have been unable to learn some of the fundamental lessons of comparative education and have misguidedly followed the wrong or inappropriate indicators? Is it more sinister? Is it that the language and metaphors of the market place have become so pervasive that politicians (and even some educators who should know better) think that curricula are 'delivered', like parcels? Is it that some see schools as mini-factories and children as products to be matched, graded and quality controlled, or, worse, cloned and homogenised, so that the 'product' is always the same?

I think part of the problem lies in the nature of theory and of ideology in education. The two are not easily separated; and, in early childhood education, are often thoroughly confused. Added to which, the teachers are inclined to want to focus on the job in hand and are, by and large, unused to clearly articulating a defence of practice; still less to building esoteric and pretentious descriptions of their professional practice (as some might consider law or medicine do). In short, the somewhat 'cosy' and certainly often encapsulated role of the teacher is itself inimical to the building of an articulate outward wall of defensive language. Indeed, it might also prevent much which is truly described as reflection on practice, or at least of the codification of that practice in any intelligible and presentable form. The latter is left to 'academics', a term used by real teachers as one of near contempt. This dislike, or rather denial, of theory is a great weakness in the teachers' defences. It is not helped, either, by the dislike of anything which seems theoretical, or even mildly professional, by politicians or those concerned to administer education quickly, cheaply and directly!

Those working with young children of roughly ages three to nine years, are dealing with human beings whose whole being usually seems oriented to learning, doing, finding out, owning, joining, and so on. Whilst this may be no more that the crudest of caricatures, it is clearly what one sees and experiences when among a class of thirty or so children. To be with children of this age is undeniably exciting; it is also totally consuming and emotionally draining. It can also be surprisingly intellectually demanding, with questions of the 'why' sort which would tax a first-class philosopher. To be among such a group for any reasonable length of time makes one very aware of the danger in seeing curricula as somehow fashioned outside of the children. It is not, I would aver, that primary teachers are perverse, that they like to be thought of as modestly child-centred, or characterised as 'Dewey-eyed'; rather it is the undeniable pressure that forces one to acknowledge the vastly different perceptions which greet, process, internalise and make anew ideas which are 'provided' by the teacher. Again, this means that they often need to be able to link, to follow apparent 'red-herrings', to abandon certain threads of exposition and to search for others. Moreover, because of the wide developmental range usually found in such classrooms (I have known four year olds just starting to speak coherently and others already reading well), the notion of some uniform presentation and assimilation is usually far from reality.

The extreme variability in development is, of course, important, however inconvenient it is for politicians or those desiring certain uniform behaviours and competencies. As Elkind says, variety in early and middle childhood may have something to do with the biological concept of redundancy. "The display of variation in early childhood may be a form of redundancy, a precursor to variational displays of adolescent, which could serve as a kind of preselection even before adolescence." (1989, p.48) Elkind goes on to argue that an appropriate curriculum is one that can be tuned-in to at different levels and have different outcomes which are internally consistent with that particular child's needs and levels of cognition.

Since the middle to late 1980s there has been an increasing number of educational writers and researchers (mainly now in North America) making it very clear that curricula for young children are best designed from a clearly developmental perspective. They have pointed out that what teachers of young children know, and perhaps feel, rather than articulate, is that self-initiated learning is often the key to thorough capitalisation on the child's potential. They have emphasised that challenge and variation are key features, that growth is holistic and involves a mix of cognitive, social, physical and emotional in ways that do not easily reflect well in externally conceived packages of testable skills. (vide, Bloom, 1988, Bredekamnp, 1987, Weikart, 1987)

None of the above would be likely to surprise the majority of infant and junior school teachers in Britain. Indeed, the older ones would point to the Plowden Report (CACE, 1987) and no doubt remark that much of their initial training, subsequent in-service courses and their own experiences would lead inevitably to such a conclusion, even if they could not spell it out in acceptable 'academic' ways. Why then is the 1988 Education Reform Act so seemingly 'out of step' with professional knowledge? There seem to be three main reasons for this.

Firstly, there is an undoubted residue of something akin to socially deprived (or class) attitudes to education lying deep within large sections of the British populace. Whether this surfaces in a fear/dislike of teachers and things to do with school (an attitude still all too often stereotypically displayed by certain blue-collar groups), or whether it is evident in the exemption of independent schools (the private schools of the upper/middle classes) from the National Curriculum, I am not too sure. Certainly one can still discern the bones of our social class structure in state schooling, since the very buildings themselves are often such that, if the Factory Acts applied, they would be condemned as unsuitable and rebuilt.

Secondly, there is a crudely commercial view of education which dominates much of the discussion of its aims and purposes. Schooling, we are told, is to get you somewhere, preferably profitable. It is about the good society (i.e. the competitive, economically stable one where workers are flexible, well-matched to changing demands, and so on.) Whilst all societies have to recognise that they socialise their young into some sort of 'goodness and fit' with the political and economic direction believed desirable, many have been at pains to place the quality of the culture and its aesthetic and social concerns firmly on the agenda too. This latter aspect of education's purposes is rarely heard in Britain. Indeed, I have heard it expressed elsewhere (in Northern Alberta) as "We are not just about getting our kids jobs, we are about the whole value of our culture". Such a view is regarded as rather odd in England. We are exhorted to pay attention to the world of work (both in the National Curriculum and in the documents concerned with Initial Teacher Training (DES Circular 24/89)). Rarely are we asked to devote more time to aesthetic awareness, music, philosophy, and sociology. The core of the curriculum is short-term. The assumption is that content is what matters; and a content of (usually) mind-boggling utilitarianism!

Thirdly, a deep distrust of 'experts' in education, particularly the views of the so-called 'establishment' (lecturers in education, inspectors, teacher-trainers, and so on) led to a deliberate disenfranchising of their opinions by many of the politicians concerned. Unlike the recent thorough and careful consultation going on in the wake of the Sullivan Commission (1988) in British Columbia, those of us involved in the consultations in England have frequently been dismayed by the disregard of the profession's views. It is hard to think of comparable situations. Would the medical profession be allowed virtually no input into the discussions on In-Vitro Fertilisation (IVF)? Such a thought is preposterous. Yet the views of teachers and their trainers are often dismissed in Britain as though they constituted some particularly obnoxious form of special pleading. Even the debate about history in the National Curriculum seems (1991) to have been resolved by an arbitrary and unargued assertion as to 'where history stops' by a single politician. The dislike of teacher-trainers is certainly a characteristic of those on what is sometimes regarded as the right of the Conservative Party. But it is not confined to single party politics. Politicians of different political complexions seem to view the whole business of training teachers as of doubtful value. Surely, they argue, teaching is best learned by apprenticeship, by following the advice of experienced teachers. The strange thing about such a view is that it is often preceded by a downright and vigorous condemnation of existing teachers and their practices. If logic were followed, they would thus be proposing that teachers are poor, but are sufficiently good to train new ones! Much of this complex arena simply reduces to one major feature; a belief that teaching is a semi-skilled operation at best and that, as operatives, teachers can 'deliver' what they are instructed to do!

It may be that the old-style incrementalism and local variation (partly dependent on the whim, and sometimes the extreme far-sightedness of Local Education Authorities) was not good enough. Few would argue that Britain at the end of the twentieth century had an adequate staying rate or participation rate in further and higher education. In current European league tables we appear to rank way behind most European Community partners. Many have been concerned with the inability of industry and commerce to commit themselves effectively and wholeheartedly to supporting education. Certainly our record, compared with that of Germany or France, has been poor. Thus, there was and is much that needs doing to improve our secondary education and our access to further and higher education. But was the 1988 Education Reform Act (reminiscent of the Newcastle Commission Report of 1863) really the way to go about it; and will it, in reality, simply damage much that has been good about British education? I cannot think that we needed the Schools Examinations and Assessment Council at all, even though it has been at pains collectively to point out that simple testing procedures of the sort advocated by Mrs. Thatcher when she was Prime Minister (and still advocated by a right wing Think Tank), are likely to lead to little real information and much distortion. I cannot see any advantage in increasing the burden of assessment, beneath the age of 16 or so. The GCSE was a liberalising, if rushed, advance in the procedure of measuring school achievement. Why test at 7, 11 and 14 years? Do children really get taller by being measured? And, as many a primary teacher has sourly noted, if you spend all your time weighing pigs you don't have much time left to fatten them!

Thus, we appear to have a situation which is far from satisfactory. We have had a "reform" act (believed to be the longest and most complicated Educational Act in British experience). This act came hotfoot on the genuine improvement achieved after establishing a more flexible form of examination at sixteen years (the GCSE). It was, and still is, clear that we need a wider form of examination at 18 years. The conventional 'A' levels are probably far too narrow; and whilst they appear to provide the basis for a very efficient, but elitist and narrow, university system, they are not helpful in terms of width, general education or the varied applicability so necessary in modern advanced industrial societies.

In many respects too, our secondary system has been wasteful of talent, demotivating and certainly not very good in encouraging independent study skills. But, in my opinion, the blanket imposition of a watered-down Grammar School system, via the National Curriculum, and the preoccupation with altogether spurious notions of testing, standards and accountability at far too frequent intervals is likely to do untold harm. Nowhere is this going to be more apparent than at the level of Primary Education. This has been flexible, modestly process-oriented and genuinely non-classist in its operations since the demise (or near demise) of the eleven-plus examination. More, primary teacher-training has been thoroughly imbued with a strange admixture of Froebel, Dewey, Piaget and Plowden (to mention but a few). True, this has often been half-understood and even less well articulated. But it has been impressive in what it has produced. For the most part autonomous and moderately independent learning can be detected in the average British Primary School; even less likely to be observed at university! Change was necessary at the older levels, therefore. But not the current changes and NOT at the price of slowly strangling that most precious of British institutions, the state primary school. I think we should remember the point made years ago by Ted Sizer, the sometime Dean of Graduate School at Harvard University. Elementary (primary) schools do not knock up against the dole queue and the profession. They can therefore afford to be based on less commercial and less immediate societal needs than secondary schooling. Creativity, happiness, serendipity should be able to be found there. In my opinion, overtesting, failure, deminished self-esteem should not. The latter seem extremely likely to ensue from what I see as the damaging effects of the National Curriculum. We need a new Educational Reform Act which bases its first principles on developmentally acceptable practice; on experience, not assertion, and which uncouples the overtly political 'market forces' approaches from the education of our young and aims for the preservation and extension of a culture worth having.

A dog that barked in 1976

Sir Alec Clegg, writing in October 1976, warned us about the dangers of adopting a National Curriculum, because we had been through all this before in the 1850's when a new code of regulations of the Education Department was produced following a survey undertaken by the inspectors of that time. The core curriculum was specified in the code, and teachers had to follow it so that children could be compared with children, teachers with teachers, and schools with schools on standards reached regardless of all other considerations. The inevitable effect of this was that subjects that were not in the code did not count, and children who could not manage the subjects that were in the core did not count either.

Alec Clegg pointed out that the man who was responsible for supervising all this early in the century was the Senior Chief Inspector, Edmond Holmes. When he retired he wrote a book in which he condemned, lock, stock and barrel, all that he had been doing for the last thirty years. Two or three quotations will illustrate his misgivings and perhaps those who are apparently going to follow in his footsteps might heed what he said. Here are three of his statements about the effects of his common core:

"In nine schools out of ten, on nine days out of ten, in nine lessons out of ten, the teacher is engaged in laying thin films of information on the surface of the child's mind and then after a brief interval he is skimming these off in order to satisfy himself that they have been duly laid".

"The State, in prescribing the syllabus which was to be followed in all the subjects of instruction by all the schools of the country without regard to local and personal consideration, was guilty of one capital offence. It did all the thinking for the teacher, it told him precisely what to do each year in each class, how he was to handle each subject, how far he was to go in it, and what width of ground he was to cover."

"To be in bondage to a syllabus is a misfortune for a teacher and a misfortune for the school in which he teaches. To be in bondage to a syllabus which is binding on all schools alike is a graver misfortune. To be in bondage to a bad syllabus which is binding to all schools alike is of all misfortunes the greatest."

But of course these comments were written 60 years ago and it might be said that things are totally different now. But are they? Sir Alec Clegg wrote:

"Not so long ago Derek Morrell was mainly responsible for establishing the Schools Council. I knew him well at the time and it was obvious that his intention was to bring to all schools' curricula expertise from whatever source he could find it. But after a spell of two years he made a recantation which, though not as full, was at least as powerful as that made earlier by Senior Chief Inspector Holmes. This is what Morrell wrote in an article in the Times Educational Supplement. 'When I was at the Schools Council I should have found it difficult to perceive as I now do that the curriculum, if it exists at all, is a structure erected on a basis of personal relationships. I should have found it difficult to assert as again I do that in the curriculum we are concerned with human beings who see feeling and aspirations as far more real and immediately important to them than the cognitive development which is the educator's stock in trade.'

There will be those who will assert that neither Holmes nor Morrell are significant enough in these matters. What they want is some of the good old grammar school exam pressure. But here again we must be cautious. This what Einstein said is the reason why youngsters don't regularly pursue science after they have left school. 'One had to cram all this stuff into one's mind whether one liked it or not. This coercion had such a deterring effect that after I'd gained the final examination I found the consideration of many scientific problems distasteful to me for a whole year.'

But the major problem we have to face today is whether we are going to continue to educate in the same way that the people who have produced the world as it now is, were educated. If the world is as we want it, we should carry on doing as we have done. If there are elements that appall us we should try to change things for the better.......

So is education to respond to what experienced educationists like Holmes and Morrell said, to what thinkers like Carlyle, Ruskin and Einstein have told us, or are we to teach solely what the building up of the gross national product demands, and the devil take the hindmost?

If we do the latter, the hindmost will be the children who can least cope with the common core, and we shall need a plentiful supply of plastic bullets to control them."

The new National Curriculum initiative: teaching the telephone directory

The latest White Paper from the Department of Education was quite short:

Key Stage Extra

Beginning with the commencement of the forthcoming school term, all year five pupils will be taught the local telephone directory. Each teacher, working in co-operation with his or her immediate supervisor, will devise appropriate instructional methods and procedures necessary to effect an efficient and appropriate achievement of the above stated goal.

No-one quite knew where the idea had come from. Some speculated that the Secretary of State for Education had obtained more shares in British Telecom. Others expressed the theory that he had been promised a seat on the board of British Telecom if their sagging profit fortunes could be revived.

Others thought it was part of the drive for 'high quality' in education. Yet others saw it as a piece of curriculum that lent itself to clear, straightforward pencil and paper-based testing. Some saw it as the final answer to the problem of stamping out all vestiges of 'progressive' teaching.

The new term began. Most teachers were too busy settling the classes and establishing the new term's timetables and routines to begin the new initiative at once. But on the second day the telephone directories were handed out.

"Boys and girls!" a typical teacher began, "we are going to have an exciting new module this term. As a way of studying our city, we will be going through this amazing collection of information which tells us so much about our local society."

Another was more down-to-earth: "There will be an examination of the material in this new module at the end of term so you had better settle down and start learning it."

A more sensitive soul began: "Now, I know you will not want to upset my feelings by not memorising these few names and numbers, so we will make a start."

The children dutifully took their new shining telephone directories and wrote their names on the labels. They were reminded that their new texts would be checked at the end of term to see that no disfiguration had taken place. The class then filled the parental contribution forms so that the school could recoup 75% of the cost from the parents.

Lessons on the telephone directory began all over the country. Mrs Thatcher-Major, a typical teacher, was heard to say: "Now, boys and girls, let us look at our new textbooks. You will notice that it has a logical structure. It is arranged by alphabet so that there is no need for an index or a contents. The main section has no illustrations, but when you turn to the yellow pages there are a few drawings."

Later in the lesson, the children set about their tasks with the enthusiasm that accompanied a new term. Many noted with respect that the teacher was right. Alphabetical order prevailed page after page after page. Finally, the homework, obligatory now by law, was written up on the board: Read and memorise the A's.

At the end of the day, the children set off home with their bags bulging with the new telephone directories. Later they settled down to do the homework. It was not easy, but then they had learnt by now that life was no picnic, so it was only right that school should be no picnic either. All that feeble-minded stuff about enjoyment in learning and a curriculum that sometimes touched on or referenced against the learners' interests, was now safely buried in the past. Teacher and parents were said to be of one mind. More rigour, more uniformity, more army-style discipline was the answer. It was all for their own good.

Next day Mrs Thatcher-Major began her lesson. "Who can tell me the telephone number of Miriam Andrews?" A hush fell over the room and five hands shot up.
"Yes, Diane?" the teacher said.
"357-7272" Diane proposed.
"Good, but do remember the prefix of 021 because when we go outside the city boundary, other prefixes are found. Next question, who lives at number 15 Lord Joseph Boulevard?"
Most hands went up because the teacher had thrown in an easy one. It was the address of Dr. Acton, the head teacher. A good teaching point, she felt, to give everyone an early feeling of success and she selected the slowest class member to answer and he got it right. Everyone felt good about the lesson.

Not all the parents appreciated the new initiative at first and some telephone calls were received and letters arrived asking for reassurance. The head teacher and senior members of staff - the management team - together with a few trusted governors, worked on the official answers to be given out:

To the question,
"Why teach the telephone directory?"
an official answer was agreed as follows:
"It develops good study habits, trains the child to concentrate and develops a sound memory for facts. These are the qualities they will need as adults, for disciplined adults are what we need."

Question: **"Surely, the information will be forgotten soon after the tests?"**
Official answer: **"The lower ability children may forget most of it at first, but we intend to have regular reviews and revision in later classes to increase the level of retention."**

Question: **"Why memorise the directories when they are readily available for reference when you actually need a number or address?"**
Official answer: **" This could be said about almost anything we teach in schools. If we wanted our people just to look up information when they actually needed it, why teach anything? Furthermore, life is hard and difficult, and the sooner our children learn this thoroughly the better off they will be."**

In the classrooms the work proceeded systematically letter by letter. Flagging motivation was countered by the news that the test on A through to M was to be held next month. The cram sessions began in earnest, organised by anxious mothers and fathers. Some promised toys, computer games and other rewards for good results whilst others threatened to suspend pocket money and other privileges. Standards of memorising telephone numbers, addresses and names reached heights never known before.

Some children did very little revision. The only numbers they seemed to care about were the ones they used regularly themselves. But then there are slow learners in every community. They would be identified in due course and given special classes which would work mainly on the yellow pages where the illustrations and greater interest value would help them.

The day of the test came and went. The papers were marked, the grades decided and the results put on to the record cards and made known to homes via reports. The idea of telling the world via league tables of comparative school results was suggested.

Work on the N to Z section of the telephone directory began. Mrs Thatcher-Major was restless and rather bored with the lessons herself. She tried to liven things up with a visit to the telephone exchange and a visiting speaker from British Telecom. But the final examination came nearer until she had to allocate thirty days for the final revision sessions.

The thirty days passed grimly. The tests were endured and marked. The results were declared. The league tables were published. The telephone directories were collected and stored for another year. Parents were sent bills for any disfigured ones. Mrs Thatcher-Major felt more drained than she had ever felt before at the end of the year and strangely uneasy and uncomfortable.

The notice board sported a new notice:

"The success of the telephone directory curriculum has earned the respect of the teachers, parents and the popular newspapers. The rigour of the exercise has been impressive in place of the previous softness of the primary school curriculum.

The next stage of the project will be to learn the directories of other parts of the country. European directories will follow and then those of the USA."

Mrs Thatcher-Major felt a strange sensation in her stomach. She realised what it was. It was nausea.

(Adapted from "The year the schools began teaching the telephone directory" by Merrill Harmin and Sidney B. Simon in the *Harvard Educational Review,* Vol. 35, Summer 1965)

Attitudes towards the National Curriculum - a survey

Colleagues are invited to tick the statement below which most closely represents, in their view, the truth about the British National Curriculum.

1. The Berlin Wall of Education
    (source: Professor Frank Smith)
2. One Medicine For All Diseases
3. The Set-Menu Curriculum
4. Regressive Education Rides Again
5. The Cloning Curriculum
6. The Package Deal With No Options Approach
7. The Grand National Theory of Education
8. An Education That Creates Huge Gaps
    but Removes All Skills That Might Equip Learners To Fill Them
9. The One Dimensional Curriculum
10. The Dog-Training Approach To Education
11. The Trivial Pursuits Curriculum
12. The Subject Junkie's Approach to Curriculum
13. Learning How To Be Taught But Not How To Learn
14. The Hitler Memorial Curriculum
15. The Stalin Memorial Curriculum
16. The Marshall Tito Memorial Curriculum
17. The Committed Rapist Approach To Learning - Learning By Force
    (source: Peter Jones)
18. Knowledge In Pursuit Of The Child
    - Not The Child In Pursuit Of Knowledge
    (source: George Bernard Shaw)
19. The 'Life Is No Picnic, So School Should Be No Picnic' Curriculum
    (source: John Holt)
20. Mad Curriculum Disease
    (source: Professor Ted Wragg)
21. For Academic Excellence Curriculum and Educational Selection
    (or FAECES Curriculum)

22. A Simply Wonderful Idea
    (source: Conservative Party)
23. A Simply Wonderful Idea That We Thought Of First
    (source: Liberal Democratic Party)
24. Such A Wonderful Idea It Should be Extended To Private Schools,
    Home-educators, Dogs, Cats, Parrots and Stick Insects
    (source: Labour Party)
25. The Entitlement To Become As Uncritical, Passive and Supine As Most Adults
    Curriculum
26. Education That Is Mediocre, Generally Exhausting, And Virtually Worthless.
    (source: Mikell Billoki, USA)
27. A Charter For Adult Chauvinism
    (source: Patrick Pringle)
28. The Micro-fascism Curriculum
    (source: Chris Shute)
29. The Entitlement To Mindless Conformity Curriculum
30. The Cuckoo That Heaves All The Other Educational Eggs
    Out Of The Nest Curriculum
    (source: Royal Society for the Protection of Birds)

Please return your selection to Professor Roland Meighan at the University of
Nottingham.

(Complaints, insults, and suggestions as to what Professor Meighan can do with his
critical faculties can be sent to the same address.)

Interim Results:

The market leader, to coin a phrase, is number 10, followed closely by number 11,
and number 7.
Other responses obtaining high scores are numbers 2, 8, 12, 13, and 17.
There are also regular returns in favour of numbers 1, 18, 19, 25, 26, and 29.
'Most disturbing ideas' reported to date are numbers 13, 17, 18, 19, 25, 26, and 29.

Class teaching for stultification?

Although current arguments about the curriculum might seem at times to point towards more choice and variety, even a more independent style of learning, they quickly run into the barrier of class teaching, which was evolved to suit wholly different beliefs. With due guidance, thirty university students or thirty primary-school children working the 'integrated day' may, at any one time and in their own time, be learning thirty different things. Thirty children, while being taught in class, learn one thing - and someone has to prescribe exactly what that one thing shall be. Worse, our method of class teaching requires that we fill out the syllabus outline with close detail, particularising minutely, compulsory item upon compulsory item, period by period. It forces us to make a succession of prescriptive decisions and then to impose them upon children, 'each for all and all for each'.

The importance of offering a greater choice of subjects and activities is often put forward as an argument for having large schools. But the range of activities going on simultaneously in a primary school provides evidence that it is not small size alone but rather small size combined with class teaching that is the bar to flexibility. So long as we teach in classes, trying to extend choice puts us in an economic dilemma. If we have a small school and want to offer numerous options, all fully taught, then we shall be forced to subdivide our classes into groups of an uneconomic size. In a large school we may indeed be able to offer numerous options and still find each commands a class of economic size.

In sum, when we believe the content of a subject to be directly useful to everyone, it makes sense to collect classes of children and to teach them. If we shift ground and encourage personal involvement and 'discovery', a more individual and fluid style of working becomes appropriate. Similarly, by emphasising induction into modes of thinking, arts and habits, all of the widest value and significance - often thought to be embodied in particular subjects but actually to be found and practised in many other ways - we open the way to increased personal selection of subject matter. If children are put into classes and taught, however, then we are bound to select among matters of indifference a single 'right' course for all to follow, to teach one set of particulars as though they were essentials. If children are in classes and taught, then personal exploration and 'discovery' between bells, by subjects, is unrealistic. If children are in classes and have to be taught, then we simply cannot afford to offer them much individual choice. Thus class teaching obstructs attempts to make sense of the curriculum. There is a strong case for examining any reasonable alternative.

The effect of our teaching method on the school curriculum is important but obscure; other constraints imposed by class teaching are more obvious and we can deal with them briefly. First, **class teaching tends to be passive.** Teachers may try hard to prevent this but the weight of numbers undermines the best efforts. What size should a class be? For no particular reason we have picked thirty as the usual size in secondary schools. The Russians think forty perfectly all right. For active scouting, Baden-Powell established patrols of eight. For sixth-form learning, where an easy exchange of views in discussion is sometimes thought to be important, sixteen is reckoned to be all that a teacher can handle. For those familiar with the Christian legends, Jesus fixed on twelve, and one of those went astray. The size we select is a function both of what we can afford and of what sort of learning we intend. With the customary ratio of one teacher for thirty learners, we plainly have a sedentary, a passive process in mind.

But beyond mere passiveness, **classroom teaching requires actual docility.** Mark Hopkins described education in the terms of a man or a woman, and a boy or a girl, answering each other's questions on a log. We have to translate that into a teacher and thirty pupils in desks lined up, in Dickens' phrase, 'like figures in a sum'. If pupils are to hear what the teacher says, then they must be quiet. Alas, the qualities that make for an inspiring teacher may conflict with those needed as a disciplinarian. Rules war with relationships. An aside in the back row of a classroom is as disturbing as an aside in the gallery of a theatre; a pupil unwrapping an illicit toffee as distracting as a theatre-goer fumbling for the favourite chocolate among the crinkly papers. The teacher cannot simply rise above the intrusion, but has to ensure attention from every single pupil, even at the risk of breaking the concentration of thirty others. A small child learning from a 'toy' or a student from a book, works a bit, dreams a bit, fidgets, stands up and stretches - not so the pupil in the class. We impose on adolescents in their most active years a relative stillness few of us as adults could sustain and we have to enforce it with an apparatus of entreaties and commands.

Because all thirty children in the class are getting their information from a single source - the teacher - they must all, as we have seen, **follow the same curriculum.** Some meals are more pleasant than others, some presented more attractively than others; in general, though, we cannot expect children to approach what is compulsorily set before them with the sort of zest they might display in choosing from a larder.

Again, a teacher can teach only at one speed. To some children in a class the message may be as clear as day, but they must stifle their yawns while the teacher lights pound upon pound of candles until even the blindest can see. A private tutor can vary the style, the depth, the speed of his instruction to suit the child; the teacher has to set a pace estimated to be right for a fictional average of the whole class. The same content, the same speed for all thirty children in it - the Americans call this **the 'lock-step' of the class.** It matters greatly, of course, whom you are lock-stepped with and by. A single source of instruction is most effective when matched to a single known receiver. Since we cannot economically reduce all teaching to tutoring, we do our best to make our audience as homogeneous, as close to a single known average as we can. We 'stream' and 'set' children, grouping them by their ability. A child in a bright, keen class is well away, but the reverse can be a disaster.

Classes made up of those who find academic work rewarding, sometimes - and other classes often - develop a 'tail'. Some reluctant children may just sit and dream in the back row, or play the fool with questions, sallies and antics that delight but disrupt the class; but the stronger ones may protect their self-esteem by a bullying assertion that work is 'sissy'. All such can establish an unseen picket line between the teacher and those who would like to work hard.

Scarcely less important to children than their companions are the teachers they draw in the lucky dip of the timetable. When the Royal Society quizzed its members about the influences that led them to become scientists, much the most important was a bright science teacher. Heads you win; but tails, alas, you lose. We do not know how many were deterred by a dim teacher. Indeed, the problem is more complex. The brilliant Maths teacher may delight Smith but stupefy Jones; the new English teacher, however, may make Jones's spirits soar but completely puzzle Smith. Those who manage schools tend to shrug off these frustrating hours of incomprehension. It's life. You can't always work with people who suit you. But the stakes for a young child can be unduly high. Tastes and skills are yet unformed. Further, normally, you have to stay with each teacher for a year. It may be a critical time in a child's development; it is certainly a long time for children bewildered or stifled by a teacher they cannot understand. Moreover, schools tend to put their better teachers, however defined, into the classes made up of the more willing and capable pupils. Often, then, a pupil shackled to bad company finds any difficulties compounded by having an incompetent overseer. Schools illustrate the sad paradox: "Unto every one that hath shall be given and he shall have abundance: but from him that hath not shall be taken away even that which he hath".

Lack of sympathy between a particular teacher and a particular pupil, of course, is a common topic in teachers' meetings. Sometimes it is explicit. 'I can't get Jones to understand logarithms,' says the maths teacher. More often it is concealed within another theme: 'Jones is a fool and lazy too!' And the teacher who taught maths to Jones last year wonders if this can be the same pupil they knew and found so willing. At home parents worry about their child's unexpected lapse. Should they see the head teacher? And if they do, can the head teacher do more than console them with hopes for the best?

Because we have to group pupils in classes of roughly equal size and assign teachers to them, we are forced at present into constructing a timetable in which everyone changes classes at defined moments. The bell rules. It demands that we learn in episodes of rigid, equal length. It cuts short our brightest and our dimmest moments indifferently. The timetable becomes a sort of solemn Mad Hatter's tea-party. No matter what, how, where, when the bell goes we must all move round and face, in any old order, one dish or another on the table before us. It may be necessary; it is certainly bizarre. Which of us would choose to study this way? For the constant disruptions make it painfully slow. A pupil can, for example, learn the equivalent of all the school hours of French to an examination level during a month's immersion in Paris and a sales representative too, gets further in a fortnight's intensive course in a language laboratory. Of course, motive is a key factor in the contrast. The person in Paris wants to eat, shop, find the way around; the sales representative wants to make sales and further a career. But lack of motive aside, learning in fixed instalments is calculated to nip in the bud the more delicate inducements to learning. It cuts across tentative understanding, cumulative absorption, growing excitement, half-formed invention and simple pleasure.

No doubt this brief glance at class teaching gives an inadequate picture of the best practitioners of the art (as of the worst), but it may serve to display the method's main tendencies. Do our present circumstances suggest that some other method of learning may be more appropriate?

(adapted from *Resources for Learning* by L.C. Taylor , Penguin Books, 1971)

Children learn what they experience

If children live with criticism they learn to condemn...
If children live with hostility they learn to fight...
If children live with fear they learn to be apprehensive...
If children live with pity they learn to feel sorry for themselves...
If children live with ridicule they learn to be shy...
If children live with jealousy they learn what envy is...
If children live with shame they learn to feel guilty...
Alternatively, if children live with encouragement they learn to be confident...
If children live with tolerance they learn to be patient...
If children live with praise they learn to be appreciative...
If children live with acceptance they learn to love...
If children live with approval they learn to like themselves...
If children live with recognition they learn that it is good to have a goal...
If children live with sharing they learn about generosity...
If children live with honesty and fairness they learn what truth and justice are...
If children live with security they learn to have faith in themselves and others...
If children live with friendliness they learn that the world can be a nice place...
If you live with serenity your children will live with peace of mind...

*   *   *   *   *   *

If children inherit a racist culture, they are likely to become racist...
If children are born into a class-ridden society, they tend to become classist...
If children experience a male chauvinist society, they often become sexist...
If children go to single sex schools, they are likely to have their sexism reinforced...
If they are encouraged to be competitive, they learn to become greedy for success,
        or selfish, or just greedy...
If they are required to spend 15,000 hours in the company of their peers, they may
        learn the tyranny of the peer group and become ageist in their outlook...
If they are compelled to learn religion, they may become dogmatists...
Alternatively, if children live with tolerance, they may learn to resist racism...
If they experience fairness and justice, they may want a less class-ridden society...
If they encounter gender-equality, they may learn to get rid of their sexism...
If they experience co-operation, they can learn to share...
If their social life is broad, they may learn to resist the tyranny of the peer group...
If they are allowed to research alternative life-stances, they may become suspicious
        of dogmatism...
(The first 18 lines are adapted from 'Children Learn What They Live' by D.L.Nolte)

The problem of adult chauvinism

In regressive education theory, children are seen as unfit to make any decisions about their learning. Decisions have to made by the wise, experienced and competent adults, especially those called leaders.

One of the 'unfit' children in the USA points to a little weakness in this adult chauvinist position. The track record of the adult body is that of ruining the world rather than running it to any standards of excellence. The sorry state of the world is the creation of the adults not the children.

SORRY TO THE NEXT TO ARRIVE

Sorry to the next to arrive.

Sorry, we have contaminated the land
with plastic bags and soda cans.

Sorry, about the laboratories
that unrightfully slaughter innocent animals
just to put mascara on convenience store shelves.

Sorry, about the wars that have killed so many people.

Sorry, about the ozone layer that we have nearly destroyed.

Sorry, we have left you such a dreadful world.

We cannot say how sorry we are.

(by Emily Cook, aged 12, Farm School, USA.)

The hijack of young children's learning

by Janet Meighan
University of Derby

It is with concern, then frustration, then helplessness, that parents and educators of young children have noted that their curiosity, confidence and enthusiasm for learning evaporate. In addition, the key element of personal management of their activities, so frequently changes to one of passive dependence as they grow older and pass through our educational system. Learning how to learn gives way to learning how to be taught. The lost opportunities for learning and personal development are only too apparent as we witness the large numbers of teenagers and adults who resist the idea of continuing education yet appear to be failing in achieving personal satisfaction in their lives.

As the demand grows for an adult population able to contribute to the challenges of a developing modern society, and at the same time achieve greater personal fulfilment, it is essential that individuals are equipped for this challenge. To have some stake in a constantly changing society involves some degree of personal participation, initiative, responsibility and critical appraisal. Our present educational system is sadly failing to support and extend personal development of this nature. Paradoxically, these characteristics are very evident in the confident learning behaviour of young children.

So, frequently, the processes engaged in by young children during their learning are taken for granted. When observing infants attempting to grasp a desired object which is almost out of reach, we recognise the effort, stimulated by curiosity and self-motivation, that is made. There is learning by repeated trial and error; self-reliance in solving simple problems by attempting new tactics when the first ones fail; the self-directed sequencing of movements. Only if all autonomous attempts fail do we hear the call for the help of others!

Play is children's work!

The play of young children has been widely researched and many generalisations made about its contribution to learning. But it is perhaps in the opportunities it presents for exploration and concrete, first-hand experiences that we find evidence of self-directed activity and observe situations where the child has some control.

Young children familiarising themselves with a new toy or object, prior to playing with it, engage in 'exploratory play'; a preliminary stage to playing, as first the child attempts to learn something about the toy or object - what it looks like, how it feels, what can be done with it - learning from first-hand exploration. When some degree of familiarity, mastery and confidence is achieved, the child is able to move to the stage of playing that involves working towards a self-determined goal. For example, Susan, aged four, having explored and mastered the possibilities of an assortment of wooden blocks, decided to build a garage for her new toy car. The self-directed activity involved her in some simple planning, imagining based on past experience, decision-making and problem-solving in the positioning of the blocks, plus dealing with frustration when the roof caved in.

John Holt's close observations of young children, as reported in books such as *Learning All the Time*, yield the same conclusion about the quality of their learning. He proposes that children are "...acting like scientists all the time, which is to say looking, noticing, wondering, theorising, testing their theories, and changing them as often as they have to."

When young children's imaginative play involves the adoption of roles, as in the creation of a cafe situation, we may see imitative play resulting from observation of and reflection on adult models. We may also witness fantasy play as new experiences are developed, providing opportunities for the organisation of ideas and the development of complex, abstract, divergent thinking. This example of play may be a solitary activity, as is frequently the case with very young children, or co-operative. Working with others, whether they are peer group or adults, presents other challenges for the self-governing learner. "Do I accept the ideas, the help, the advice they offer?" "If so, how will they affect my ideas, my plans?" Language, increasingly, becomes an important element in communication and in the reasoning necessary for personal management of experiences.

Adults as learning 'coaches' or learning 'hijackers'?

The contribution of adults to the young child's skills in the management of their learning is increasingly debated. The need for the support and encouragement of sympathetic adults in the confidence-building process is evident, but John Holt gives two warnings about too much interference and uninvited teaching:
  "...interfering very much in the play and learning of children often stops it altogether."

"Not only is it the case that uninvited teaching does not make learning, but -- and this was even harder for me to learn -- for the most part such teaching prevents learning."

Steve, aged three, investigating an old, but still working typewriter, which had been given to him, made full use of his parents by asking "What's that?" and "Why?" in his early explorations, before moving to the stage of independent activity and learning. He asked for help only when his own problem-solving strategies failed, and even then he learnt that it was not always immediately available! Perhaps the view of the adult as 'learning coach' is an appropriate analogy.

There is much evidence of opportunities for self-directed learning in many good nursery schools and classes in this country, but the ideas developed in the Ypsilanti, Michigan, Pre-school Project at the High/Scope Foundation present a particularly useful model for the development of skills in learner-managed learning which may be modified to fit a range of settings and ages. Quite simply this can be expressed as 'Plan - Do - Review'. At the High/Scope Foundation children as young as three were encouraged to plan their activities, with the support of an adult, which involved consideration of the decisions which needed to be made. The implementation of the planning involved perseverance to see it through, as well as opportunities to develop both a range of skills and the ownership of subsequent knowledge. The process of reviewing the activity on its completion with both an adult and peers, encouraged reflection and even justification for courses of action taken. Although the plan-do-review approach as developed in Ypsilanti required a high adult:child ratio, and was structured to encourage the development of skills in decision-making and evaluation, many nursery and infant teachers in this country have incorporated the fundamental ideas into their own practice of enabling young children to develop some autonomy in their learning.

It is no surprise, therefore, that these teachers together with parents are concerned, frustrated and helpless when the young learners, who have been developing autonomy, appear to be subjected to a hijack in the dubious cause of substituting dependence in the form of 'learning how to be taught' for the independence of 'learning how to learn'.

Can you get an education from the National Curriculum?

There are several basic problems with the concept of a National Curriculum. Here are four to start with:

1. Long experience around the world shows that the idea does not work.
2. Putting the various National Curriculum offerings side by side exposes them as a mish-mash of adult hang-ups, country to country.
3. A National Curriculum prevents children from undertaking more important types of learning.
4. Fourthly, the concept of a National Curriculum is immoral.

There are other objections, such as the celebration of nationalism rather than internationalism, but I will leave these aside.

The idea of a National Curriculum has been tried many times throughout the world. Hitler was very keen on the idea and it formed the backbone of the Nazi schooling system. Stalin was another enthusiast and adopted it for the USSR as well as the occupied countries such as Poland. Tito adopted a National Curriculum for the former Yugoslavia. The UK tried it in the 1800's and abandoned it as a failure.

The reasons for adopting the idea of a National Curriculum are instructive. Stalin thought it would do two things. It would bind the former nation states of the USSR together and create patriotic identity with the new state. Next, it would raise the standards of education and establish economic growth so that the USSR would become the super-power. Hitler thought it would do two things. It would raise the standards of education and establish economic growth so that Germany would become the super-power and that it would forge strong patriotic identity with the new German state. Tito saw a National Curriculum as the means of replacing the former nation states of Yugoslavia with a new patriotism and binding the various religious groups together in a national identity. It would also raise standards of education and ensure economic growth. Recent events could hardly have provided more spectacular evidence that the theory was wrong, and the consequences of over thirty years of National Curriculum in some cases, had failed in all respects.

The Government of the UK introduced a National Curriculum in 1988 for two main reasons. Firstly it was claimed that it would raise educational standards and promote economic growth. Secondly it was claimed that it would ensure a growth in patriotism, which was thought to be on the wane, particularly in the former nation states of Scotland and Wales. It would appear that the only thing we learn from history, is that we don't learn from history!

What does the National Curriculum look like country to country? When you put them side by side, they show marked variations. Sweden devotes about 30% of the time to the Social Sciences. The UK version devotes none and is so worried by the social sciences it even leaves economics to feature in a low status 'cross-curricular theme'.

The USSR had no space for religion except as part of historical studies. The UK version has compulsory Christianity. Other countries have compulsory Islam, or whatever religion geographical accident has determined as the local belief system. I have just come back from Poland where over forty years experience of a National Curriculum has convinced most of the people I met that it is a moribund idea. The dictatorship of the Reds requiring Marxism as a compulsory study, is now replaced there by the dictatorship of the Blacks (i.e. the clergy) requiring Catholicism instead.

Each country puts its own national geography and history first and world studies a poor second, if it features at all. Sweden is, perhaps, exceptional in giving attention to international studies. In literature, the UK requires the study of several plays, featuring dated ideas in elegant but ancient language. There is no mistaking the nature of these National Curriculum contents. Music, art and science show the same patterns. They contain major elements of a mish-mash of adult hang-ups selected according to various national prejudices.

There is always an opportunity cost. Whilst children are being compelled to learn this material, they lose out on learning other things. As George Bernard Shaw observed:

"My schooling not only failed to teach me what it professed to be teaching, but prevented me from being educated to an extent which infuriates me when I think of all I might have learned at home by myself."
There is more to it than this. John Taylor Gatto in his book *Dumbing Us Down: The Hidden Curriculum of Compulsory Schooling* concludes that schooling in the USA is a twelve year jail sentence where bad habits are the only curriculum truly learned and that school 'schools' very well, but hardly educates at all. Gatto's compatriot, John Holt, concluded that the outcome of schools with an adult-imposed curriculum was that people learned how to be taught, but not how to learn.

Like Gatto, Chris Shute is a teacher with over twenty years' experience, but from the UK. In his book *Compulsory Schooling Disease,* he too writes of the bad habits learned by gradually absorbing fascist tendencies from the unwritten curriculum of a National Curriculum. Both writers note that children are taught to avoid thought and to become dependent on the authority of other minds than their own. Not surprisingly then, Adolf Hitler observed that it was good fortune for the rulers that the people do not think.

Finally, in what ways can a National Curriculum be said to be immoral? A member of a home-based educating family, Peter Jones, expresses it thus:

"We can no more ordain learning by order, coercion and commandment than we can promote love by rape or threat."

A National Curriculum can thus be seen as mind-rape. The victim is compelled into a place chosen by the adults. They are then subjected to the learning will of the adults and their agents by being forced to learn, whether they want to or nor, what the adults prescribe. The methods are dictated by the adults. The adults proclaim that the children need it and like it really. The children become passive and resigned after 15,000 hours of this treatment, though some become angry and resentful. John Holt put it slightly differently and perhaps a little less starkly:

"School is the Army for kids. Adults make them go there, and when they get there, adults tell them what to do, bribe and threaten them into doing it, and punish when they don't."

Whether it is more like mind-rape, or army, or as George Bernard Shaw maintained, "worse than a prison because at least in prison you do not have to read the boring books written by the prison officers...", or as Charles Handy concluded, like a concentration camp, is a detail. What is moral about this kind of oppression, however you describe it? The more a National Curriculum is adopted the more severe the oppression. Compelling children to attend school, but then treating them humanely with some participation in decision-making might be defended to a limited extent, though not by me, but add a National Curriculum, and the mind-rape becomes total.

Is it time for us to devise some principles of educational reconstruction?

The language of regressive education

This is a confidential briefing to all members of the
No Turning Back to Genuine Education Group
NO leaks please

Regressive education requires that we go back to choice only for the favoured few, with the rest given the illusion of choice. It means going back to diversity for the minority only and imposing uniformity for the majority. It allows freedom for the elite, but conformity for the rest. Since this is not likely to be a generally acceptable agenda, we shall need to disguise it by the careful use of language. The key advice is given by Humpty Dumpty:
"When I use a word, it means just what I choose it to mean - neither more nor less."

CHOICE

In regressive education, this actually means choosing between school A, authoritarian in style, operating the National Curriculum as decided by us, limited by a centrally imposed testing system, and shortly to have even its methods of teaching limited by law, and school B, which is the same.   The only distinction between the two will be that one has, temporarily, stolen a march on the others in the centrally imposed league tables.   Although this means that, because a 'top' school is currently in the Scilly Isles, large numbers of parents should move there at once, it would not be helpful if this happened, so avoid mentioning it.

It is, of course, the Henry Ford theory of 'choice': you can have your car in any colour you wish provided that it is black.   It is pseudo-choice.   Your task is to present this pseudo-choice as if it were real choice.

PARENTAL CHOICE

This really means giving privileged parents the right to maintain inequality by choosing comfortable schools rather than run down ones, or to opt out into the Independent sector, leaving the unprivileged even more deprived of resources.

As regards choice, we know that most parents would choose a small school in preference to a large one, and so would most pupils and most teachers.   Only those with enough money can actually have their choice. All others must continue to have largeness thrust upon them, whether they like it or not, but then they have become quite habituated to it.

EDUCATION

Although education is quite different from schooling, and also from training, pretend that this is not the case. It is rather inconvenient that Winston Churchill, perhaps in an unguarded moment, pointed this out in a letter to R.A. Butler in 1944 and spilt the beans by pointing out that schools have not necessarily much to do with education, being mainly institutions of control where certain basic habits must be inculcated in the young. Our opponents, however, are not usually well briefed, but if they are, just bully them in a loud, assertive but 'cultured' voice until they give up.

Special warning: The success rates of home-based education are so stunning that you must avoid debate about them at all costs. Dismiss them gently as an eccentric but quite likeable minority.

OPTING OUT OF LOCAL AUTHORITY CONTROL

This is really about dismantling the power of the local authorities and reinforcing the movement towards centralised control and dramatically increasing the dictatorial power of our Secretary of State for Education. But it must be presented as if it were increased freedom.

DISCIPLINE

This really means increasing the existing authoritarian relationship in severity between teachers and learners so that it continues to instil the attitudes needed to run a divided society - i.e. an unthinking respect for authority, obedience and servility. Most people have not the faintest idea that there are better alternatives so you will not encounter much trouble here.

The democratic form of discipline where students and teachers work together co-operatively in a power-sharing manner so that they can both become more critically aware of their rights and responsibilities within communities, must remain an official secret.

STANDARDS

This is the fun one: it is our means of attacking public education, and forcing the opposition onto the defensive. It's important to appreciate that the 'falling standards' catch-phrase is not founded on any factual evidence, so do not try to quote any.

(For confirmation of this see the recent DES. statistics; McPherson and Willans' evidence on Scottish Comprehensives in Sociology, November 1987; and *Bending the Rules* - Brian Simon, Lawrence and Wishart (1988), where it notes that the percentage of the age cohort gaining five or more GCE O levels at grades A to C has increased by over 45% in the fourteen years between 1970-71 and 1984-85. Burn copies of these documents if you get the chance.)

Just assert, always in a loud but 'cultured' voice, that we should recognise that raising standards for all school students comes from an increased emphasis on drills, exercises and tests within a competitive, imposed school curriculum. This encourages obedience and submissiveness.

BASIC SKILLS

Of course, schools have never really been doing anything else **but** stress the skills of reading, writing and arithmetic, but pretend that this is not so. If we can reduce 'skills' to technical competencies, to be mechanically ticked off in a check-list of boxes, they are transformed into a central part of social discipline.

BENCHMARK TESTING AT 7, 11, 14, AND 16

This really means an intimidatory way of arranging pupils, schools and local authorities into a competitive league table of results. This is not for the benefit of the children but to promote the forces of selection and privatisation in the country at large. But pretend that it is something to do with 'standards'.

A RELATIONSHIP BETWEEN SCHOOLS AND INDUSTRY

For the regressive educator, this really means finding covert ways of socialising disaffected youth into the habits of deference and docility. The main strand in this is the pretence of training for increasingly non-existent work as our 'anorexic' economic policies continue.

THE NATIONAL CURRICULUM

It is, of course, **our** National Curriculum, fellow regressive educators, which is why all social sciences were ruthlessly removed and compulsory Christianity installed. Few of our group actually believe in Christianity, but it is a useful control device, as dear Karl Marx used to point out.

Another gain is the grabbing of power away from the local authorities to reinforce the move towards greater, centralised control.

It also means perpetuating elitist, tiered schooling by reinforcing the narrow, traditional subject-base of the foundation curricular structure. This emphasis is geared to the interests of the privileged few at the expense of the majority of academically average and below average children. The National Curriculum is also about social regulation in that it is an attempt by central government to control what children and people should or should not know, and what counts as valid knowledge. It is also an effective way of disciplining dissenting teachers.

OTHER POLITICAL PARTIES

They are daft enough to believe most of what we say, so no trouble there! It is the few better-read educationalists you have to watch out for, but since most of these long for official recognition by being put on our committees, or lie low to try to protect their careers, they can soon be turned into collaborators or appeasers.

Remember our watchwords:

Do not let the facts confuse the issues involved!

If the facts do not support our belief, so much the worse for the facts!

(adapted in part from D. Jackson and G. Jenkins, "A Primer of Educational Thatcherism" in *Libertarian Education,* Summer 1989)

Remembering Pastor Niemoller

First they came for the Social Science teachers, but I was not a Social Science
teacher, so I did not protest.

Then they came for the Peace Studies teachers and since I had never met one, and
thought there could only be five in the whole country, I did not protest.

Then they came for the 'progressive educators' and since I did not regard myself as
one, nor really knew what they were on about, I did not worry.

Then they came for the Real Books enthusiasts, but since I used mixed methods in
my work as did everyone I knew, I ignored it.

Then they came for the teacher trainers, but I was one, so I did not protest.

Then they came for the Local Authority advisors, but I was not one of them, so I
carried on regardless.

Then they came for the small schools, but since I worked in a large school for
reasons of salary, I did not protest.

Then they came for the playing fields and sports teachers, but this was not my
curriculum area, so I pretended not to notice.

Then they came for the group work enthusiasts, but nobody I knew used this
method exclusively, so I did not protest.

Then they came to cleanse governing bodies of pupil governors; I ignored it.

Then they came with the mind-rape approach of a compulsory National
Curriculum, but I was so used to doing what I was told that I went along
with it. After all, even The Guardian seemed to think it was all right to do
this to children.

Then they came with an obsessive compulsory testing scheme, but I used tests quite
a lot in my everyday work, so I carried on regardless.

Then they came for me! I was astonished. Hadn't I always accepted everything and
followed orders because of the mortgage? I looked around for help, but,
alas ..... there was nobody left to speak up for me.

I had learnt a lesson:

Those of the fascist tendency in education keep coming back for more.

(Based on the Pastor Niemoller piece on how the Nazis came to power.)

The question of technical excellence

Regressive schooling often stresses a celebration of 'technical excellence'. It is asserted that 'The Economy' requires from the school system a highly trained workforce as the top priority. The following letter is from an observer who thinks there may be considerable doubt on this point: the price may be too high.

"Dear Teacher,

I am a survivor of a concentration camp. My eyes saw what no man should witness:

Gas chambers built by learned engineers
Children poisoned by educated physicians
Infants killed by trained nurses
Women and babies shot and burned by high school and college graduates.

So I am suspicious of education.

My request is: Help your students become human. Your efforts must never produce learned monsters, skilled psychopaths, educated Eichmans.

Reading, writing and arithmetic are important only if they serve to make our children more human."

(Quoted from: *A Sociology of Educating*, R. Meighan, Cassell, 2nd edition, 1986, page 383.)

The new Ten Commandments for non-regressive teachers

Bertrand Russell, writing in 1951, proposed a Ten Commandments that, as a teacher, he would wish to promulgate. I have taken the liberty of putting them in a different order and adding some minor adaptations.

1. Never try to discourage thinking, for you are sure to succeed.

2. Do not fear to be eccentric in opinion, for every opinion now accepted as obvious was once eccentric.

3. Do not feel envious of the happiness of those who live in a fool's paradise, for only a fool will think that it is happiness.

4. When you meet with opposition, even if it should be from your spouse or children, endeavour to overcome it by argument and not by authority, for a victory dependent upon authority is unreal and illusory.

5. Find more pleasure in intelligent dissent than in passive agreement, for, if you value intelligence as you should, the former implies a deeper agreement than the latter.

6. Be scrupulously truthful, even if the truth is inconvenient, for it is more inconvenient when you try to conceal it and almost inevitably fail.

7. Do not think it worthwhile to proceed by concealing evidence, for the evidence is sure to come to light.

8. Do not use power to suppress opinions you think pernicious, for if you do the opinions will suppress you.

9. Have no respect for the mere authority of others, for there are always contrary authorities to be found.

10. Do not feel certain of absolutely anything.
    (Addendum: except, perhaps, death?)

Regressive education requires the compulsory teaching of religion in general and, in the UK, the teaching of Christianity in particular. The view that religion is a 'good thing' is shared by fewer and fewer people as the opinion polls demonstrate. This piece, from a BBC Radio broadcast in 1976, represents the dissenting voices.

Why I don't like religion

by Sir Hermann Bondi

Our society has a very peculiar attitude to religion. It recognises that different people have different beliefs, it occasionally even allows for the existence of people without belief; but it takes it as read that religion - any religion - is, by its nature, a good thing. People regret it if they have not much faith, and try quite often to see to it that their children have more.

Now my attitude is quite different. I do not think religion is a good thing. I recognise, of course, that religion is a very widespread property of humans, but that is no argument for it - after all, greed is a very widespread property of humans, and we don't therefore all agree that greed should be fostered. What worries me particularly about religion is its divisiveness. After all, we do know that there are many religions in the world, that quite a few of them - though not all - are very firm that they alone are right and that the others are wrong. The moment one takes this attitude, one adopts a level of arrogance that I find immensely repulsive. The idea that one should say, "I know, and you poor lot don't," is something that I find quite detestable.

If, on the other hand, one takes a more detached attitude, I think one falls into a similar intellectually repulsive attitude. To say there are lots of religions, and you can follow any one of them and they've got a great deal in common and at least the stuff they have in common must be right in some sense, strikes me as equally insupportable. After all, religions do have very particular statements, very particular injuctions about whether you can have one wife or more, whether you may drink alcohol or not, whether you may or may not eat pig meat, and the like. And to say that any of these, which the faith itself regards as integral, are somehow less important than the rest, doesn't appeal to me at all. To say that there's some common element is a little like police investigating an accident at a cross-roads where there was a hit-and-run accident and the first witness says it was a blue car going north and the second one it was a grey car going east and the third one it was a yellow car going south, and the policeman says: "Well, we are sure of at least one thing; it was a car and not a motorbike!" Surely, what the policeman would say is, "This is a lot of very unreliable witnesses, and I don't believe a word of what any of them say." And this is, I think, an attitude that one must take here; that there are contradictions between religions, that at most one of them can be right, and that it is therefore a human tendency which we must recognise in ourselves - that religious issues are matters on which people of the greatest intelligence, integrity and sincerity differ and cannot be brought together.

Once we have recognised this, we must surely recognise that a society is something that must contain - that must be able to contain - people with different views on these matters, that such a society can live and flourish only if people in it are sufficiently tolerant, if they are sufficiently used to living and co-operating with those whose persuasion differs from their own. This is often called a pluralist society, and I'm all in favour of it - though I would prefer to call it an open society.

In such a society, the important thing is to stress those matters on which people agree, and not those on which they disagree - to bring them together, and not to separate them. If we look at our own society, the glaring absurdity that we have is the existence of - indeed the strong support we give to - religious separation in schools. To have denominational schooling, to my mind, runs counter to a principal aim of education: to make people live together and work together in a society in which people differ in their beliefs. What we should surely aim for is to get people together.

What people now share is a general philosophy of life that I think one can call humanistic. Non-believers like myself are often told that we live on the spiritual capital of religion. I think this is utterly wrong - it is not a true statement of the situation. On the contrary, religion now attains its respectability by living on the spiritual capital of humanism. It is, after all, a fact that those features that were thought to be very important features of religious observance, like burning certain people who were called witches, is not something that has dropped out because of a better analysis and translation of the Old Testament - it has dropped out because of a humanistic philosophy. If the schisms that have led to such bloody wars between different Christian denominations, and that even nowadays lead to terrible troubles between people of different religions in various parts of the world, are not approved of now, it is not because theology has improved - but because the general humanistic philosophy that it is wrong to kill people for their faith has become an accepted background of our lives. The idea that to go and live a hermit's life in a desert is something laudable because it is good for your immortal soul has died out, and the idea of service to the community has come in, not because of a change in theology - but because of the acceptance of humanistic values. It is not difficult to find in any religion many repellent things that are not stressed today because they belong to a pre-humanistic age, and it is to humanism that we owe the fact that we can generally live together reasonably well.

Of course, there are many things on which I, and the likes of me, feel much sympathy with sophisticated and thinking religious people, not least in the dislike of religion for convention's sake. The only argument for any religion can be that it is true, and the kind of thing I detest - and I think many religious people detest - is the sort of thought that says, "Let's give religion to the young; it protects them from delinquency." This is a degree of dishonesty that is thoroughly bad. Religion is to my mind a perfectly acceptable private matter in which we make our private choices, as we do when we marry. We don't then try to foist our choice on others, nor may we permit this in an open society to happen in any of the religions of which it is made up. And so the way I always like to put it is that I have no quarrel with private religion, it is its public pretensions that I find so objectionable - whether it is the difficulty of importing contraceptives into Malta, or eating ham in Israel, or getting a drink in a Muslim country. In each of these, it is a case where a group, because it happens to have power, through majority rule or otherwise, foists its private beliefs and dislikes on others. And it is this pretension of a right of public imposition of what is essentially a private matter that leads to these, to my mind, very regrettable consequences.

Not all questions are simple. Most social questions are difficult and require long debate, and differing views may honestly be held. But to foist a particular view on others because of religious sanction, is to my mind, wholly repulsive. If I may give a particular example here from our present society. I recognise very well that different people may for very good reasons have differing views on abortion. What I think is not a good thing is that, if some people have their views formed by religious presuppositions which they do not share with others, they should try to force these views on others. And I would regard this again as a typical example of a public pretension of private religion.

Recognising that we all have different views on these matters, we must actively attempt to live together. And I think, broadly, we are doing this not too unsuccessfully. But the strains of intolerance are always there. And if I am intolerant of anything, it is intolerance.

The triple tyranny and regressive schooling

Our chief educational problem is deschooling school, rather than deschooling society. Or as John Holt put it, to make schools less like schools. Schools, as currently organised on an adult imposed day-prison model, set up for children a triple tyranny. Regressive schooling serves to accentuate all three.

The first tyranny is that of the **National Curriculum**, a massive exercise in adult chauvinism that Professor Frank Smith has described as The Berlin Wall of Education. A Polish visitor, Professor Eugenia Potulicka, a member of the Solidarity Education Commission and a Professor in Comparative Education, said she would be reporting back to Poland that it was totalitarian. She saw it as from the same stable as the National Curriculum of Stalin, or Hitler, or Tito. Poland has experience of two of these in living memory so she should be able to recognise the signs.

The second tyranny is the **unwritten curriculum,** also known as the hidden curriculum. The unwritten curriculum carries the long-term, permanent messages, many of them identified by Postman and Weingartner in their writings, including:

> Passive acceptance is preferable to active criticism,
> Discovering knowledge is not a task for pupils,
> Recall and regurgitation are the highest forms of intellectual achievement
>   suitable for pupils,
> The voice of authority is to be automatically obeyed,
> The feelings of pupils are irrelevant,
> Education consists of memorising the provided Right Answers,
> Competition is more important than co-operation,
> Helping others always gives way to getting on oneself,
> Writing and reading are more important than talking and thinking,
> Men are more important than women,
> Dogma is more desirable than doubt.

No teacher I know sets out to teach these by design, except perhaps some teachers of religion in the case of the last one. The messages are conveyed gradually and persistently by the apparatus of an institution that is based on compulsion. These messages are even more severe under the principles of regressive schooling.

The third tyranny is that of the **peer group.** Children are compelled to spent 15,000 hours minimum in the forced company of their peers. There is an opportunity cost. They lose the chance to mix with adults out and about in society, and gradually become enrolled and imprisoned in the youth culture instead. The price to be paid varies from an ageist outlook addiction, to clothes-fashion addiction, to pop-music addiction, to smoking addiction, to drug addiction, to minor and sometimes major crime. Families who decide to opt out for home-based education frequently refer to the 'tyranny of the peer group' as one of the key reasons for their decision.

All three tyrannies operated under the 'progressive' era in the UK of the 1960's and 1970's. The National Curriculum was sub-contracted through examination boards rather than being centrally imposed, and the unwritten curriculum was softened a little by some sporadic child-referencing, i.e. taking some account of what adults thought were the needs of the child. Under the regressive era of the 1980's the three tyrannies are simply imposed with more central control, increased institutional aggression and general severity. Thus police patrols are used to round up any pupils who truant, and clocking-in systems using plastic cards inserted into attendance recording systems are introduced without any qualms. One former teacher revolted by all this has written his verdict under the title of *Compulsory Schooling Disease or How Children Absorb Fascist Values.*

John Holt once contemplated writing a book entitled *How To Make Schools Worse.* It could have been the blueprint for the changes in UK schooling since the mid-1980's. It is, perhaps, time to consider some intelligent principles of educational reconstruction?

BOOKS BY EDUCATION NOW

Learning All the Time by John Holt £6-50
...quintessential Holt; readable, accessible, kindly, immensely observant...
Professor Philip Gammage

Flexischooling by Roland Meighan £6-00
*...a great pearl in his writings.....*Professor Aleksander Nalaskowski

Never Too Late by John Holt £10-00
*I applaud this book heartily....*Sir Yehudi Menuhin

Anatomy of Choice in Education by Roland Meighan and Philip Toogood £10-00
...precisely what is needed to clear up present confusion and set coherent, purposeful, productive patterns for the future... Dr.James Hemming

Learner-managed Learning edited by Paul Ginnis £5-00
..learners really start to explore and exercise their potential only as they take charge of their lives..

Democratic Learning and Learning Democracy by Clive Harber £5-00
Democracy is the worst system of organisation - except for all the others!
Winston Churchill

Learning From Home-based Education edited by Roland Meighan £5-00
...the rich diversity of the home-based phenomenon is demonstrated..

Issues in Green Education by Damian Randle £5-00
*..it certainly succeeds in provoking thought...*Chris Hartnett

Sharing Power in Schools: Raising Standards by Bernard Trafford £5-00
...our students are becoming more effective, self-confident and imaginative learners and workers. examination results are improving...

Education Now is a non-profit research, writing and publishing group devoted to developing more flexible forms of education within the range of human-scale contexts including home-based education, small schooling, mini-schooling, and flexischooling.
Education Now, 113 Arundel Drive, Bramcote Hills, Nottingham NG9 3FQ

EARLY CHILDHOOD EDUCATION: TAKING STOCK

After the 1944 Education Act, early childhood education in the U.K. gradually earned itself a high reputation both within the country and internationally. Its philosophy and practice was firmly based in research and experience. Improvements were possible, of course, and many Local Education Authorities showed considerable commitment to extending provision and to steadily improving the quality of educational opportunities for young children.

Recent government policies, however, including the introduction of a National Curriculum, are bringing about highly questionable changes and are not building on previous strengths. In addition, current suggestions that the training of teachers for young children should be shorter, less academic, and increasingly at a non-graduate level, is a down-grading which is going to be a disaster.

In this report, the writers try to take stock of the situation lest the myths about early childhood education adopted by officialdom destroy years of patient work and force us steadily backwards into the dark ages of schooling. The themes include the dubious developments affecting the education of four year olds in infant schools, and how recent government legislation has muted and marginalised early years professionals. There is a review of the provision in other countries; the comparative evidence shows the gains to be made from high quality teacher training as well as the pay-off for investment in early childhood education. This evidence points to the fact that the policies currently being adopted in the U.K. are in the wrong direction; a heavy social and economic price will be paid for them in the future. The conflict between a utilitarian, social control model of early years schooling and a developmental model of early years learning is central to the work.

This is essential reading for all involved in the education of young children.

The following distinguished scholars are contributors to the report:
Professor Philip Gammage, University of Nottingham,
Jenefer Joseph, Early Years Consultant,
Iram Siraj-Blatchford, University of Warwick,
Ros Swann, Cheltenham and Gloucester College of H.E
Marian Whitehead, Goldsmiths' College, University of London,

ISBN 1 871526 13 2   Price £5-00

From: Education Now, 113 Arundel Drive, Bramcote Hills, Nottingham NG9 3FQ

COMPULSORY SCHOOLING DISEASE

How Children Absorb Fascist Values

by CHRIS SHUTE

I agreed to write this book because, after twenty-five years of school-teaching I became convinced that I was engaged in a form of microcosmic fascism. It seemed to me that schools, whatever they claimed to be doing, were training most young people to be habitually subservient. I recognised that there were many seductive arguments for keeping children under strict control. It made them easier to handle and it pleased their parents, whilst society in general felt comfortable for it appeared to make the whole task of taking responsibility for their upbringing safer and more predictable. However, when they grew up I noticed that many school students became morose, unsociable, and philistine. The process looked satisfactory but the results were often deplorable.

In this book, I have tried to set out why I think that compulsory schooling and its apparatus of imposed discipline and control are dangerous to the mental and social development of children. This is not a book written by an expert to influence the thinking of other experts. It is based not on systematic research but accumulated experience. It records how I have come to believe that compulsory schooling is the cause of many social problems which it claims to cure, and why I am no longer prepared to defend it.

Home-based education or home-schooling is not discussed. This is not because I do not take it seriously as a method of educating children. In fact, I believe it is currently the best way to educate most children. But I hope that one day soon it will be possible for children to use schools as they should be used, as places where any person who happens to need help with their studies can go and receive it. Until that time, I must confine myself to commenting on schools as they are now, and challenging us to consider whether their regime contributes to enslaving the minds of children rather than setting them free.

Price £6-00   ISBN 0 9518022 2 4

Educational Heretics Press,
113 Arundel Drive, Bramcote Hills, Nottingham NG9 3FQ